The Bible In Names:

Truth Decoded

The Name Code Reveals The Hidden Truth For

Spiritual And Physical Transformation

By

LARISSA GOLOUBOVA

Published by Hemingway Publishers

Cover design by Hemingway Publishers

ISBN: Printed in the United States

KNOW THE TRUTH AND THE TRUTH WILL SET YOU FREE

(THE BIBLE, JOHN 8:32)

Table of Contents

ACKNOWLEDGEMENTS

I am eternally grateful to God for blessing me with extensive resources, great passion and the sacred vision for writing "The Bible in Names: Truth Decoded". I was richly blessed with the great guidance of the Holy Spirit of God to uncover the Name Code in the Bible and to decode the entire 66 books of the Bible.

I would like to extend my sincere gratitude to the hundreds of authors, whose deep insight, knowledge and expertise have helped and allowed me to write this book, the biggest project of my life. All the work, research, and historical and spiritual investigation that I spent years diving into has blessed me with the once-in-a-lifetime opportunity to produce this book, "The Bible in Names: Truth Decoded".

I would like to thank and acknowledge my parents, whom I love dearly and who will always be in my heart. I know they are divinely protecting, guiding, and watching over me wherever I go.

Special thank you to my dear, loving daughter, Anna Goloubova, for her dedication, encouragement, and great support that I needed to write "The Bible in Names: Truth Decoded". Her intuitive, artistic talent has inspired me with her prophetic paintings and her art. Her artistic vision, professionalism, and her heart for writing and editing have greatly contributed to the publishing of this book. I dedicate this book to my parents and my daughter, Anna.

I would like to thank and acknowledge all my lifetime teachers, mentors, and friends. You are my spiritual family, and I have deep and abiding gratitude for you all. Special thank you to my lifetime spiritual mentors, for guiding my way into the spiritual world with great faith and perseverance, whose prayers and godly devotion have sustained my spiritual journey, and who inspired me greatly to write this book.

I would like to thank Dr. Charles Stanley, the great pastor and author of so many amazing books, whom I met in Canada and who personally prayed the prayer of abundance and God's guidance over me and my family. It was such a blessing to receive this anointing that guided me through my life and became the inspiration for writing this book.

I would also like to thank my family and friends in Russia and Canada for their great support. Sending much love to all.

As well, thank you to the wonderful editors at Hemingway Publishers for their amazing work and cooperation.

My deepest heart's desire is that this book, "The Bible in Names: Truth Decoded", will be an amazing blessing to everyone who would read it and that it would bring the presence of God and the Holy Spirit into everyone's hearts and souls. May it transform and heal our generation and generations to come, physically and spiritually.

With love and gratitude, Larissa Goloubova

PREFACE

In 2007, I had the great privilege to travel to the Holy Land in Jerusalem. I was honored to visit the breathtaking exhibition, located deep in the ancient tunnels of the Western Wall – "The Chain Generation Center". This experience was incredibly moving, and it marked the beginning of my journey of writing "The Bible in Names: Truth Decoded".

As I walked through the exhibit, I felt as though I was traveling through time, unraveling the historical value and spiritual significance of the history of the Hebrew nation throughout the generations. The exhibition used fantastic glass sculptures, illuminated by light, with music and holographic images, showing the history of Hebrew people across the ages. It was astonishing to walk through the halls and see the Hebrew Scriptures and Biblical names written in gold on emerald, green glass sculptures. It really touched my spirit to go through the Western Wall Tunnel tour, where we were allowed to see the underground part of the Western Wall hidden for centuries.

Being close to the Place of Holy of Holies of the Temple, I felt an incredible presence of God. It was an overwhelming spiritual and emotional experience that led to personal and spiritual revelations.

And there, I prayed a powerful prayer asking God to use me for His Kingdom and His Glory.

Upon returning to Canada, I began receiving books about Hebrew names and dictionaries that decoded the meanings of Hebrew names in the Bible. I sought guidance from God about the purpose of this. And it was revealed to me that , even though, the Bible has been translated, interpreted, reviewed and changed by the religious authorities numerous times, the names in the Bible have remained untouched and unchanged. While writing this book, I went through a powerful spiritual transformation from within. Under the guidance of the Holy Spirit of God, I started to receive sacred information about the Name Code of the Bible and the spiritual meanings of the Biblical names. During this transformational time, I was urged to decode the Bible by putting together the spiritual meanings of names, one by one, in sentences. To my surprise, I discovered an incredible Hidden Message of God in the Bible. I realized that the Bible was written using the Name Code to preserve God's True Message about human existence and the battle between good and evil.It is ,also, about the origins of humanity, the causes of human misery, afflictions, and how to access the Remedy that lies preserved in human beings themselves. With the guidance of the Holy Spirit of God , I decoded the entire Bible, using the Name Code. It was revealed to me that, in the Bible, was encoded the detailed spiritual guidance for the restoration of the Divinity of the human beings that was stolen from them by the dark forces.

Furthermore, I learned that to preserve this Hidden Truth, the Bible was written using allegories, parables, and fables based on the human body. This realization was the beginning of the most exciting project of my life. So, without waiting any longer, I decided to decode the whole Bible and reveal the hidden message to the world through my book, "The Bible in Names: Truth Decoded".

Biblical names have multidimensional meanings that are associated with Divinity. They have sacral powers and are worthy of spiritual devotion. The names reveal profound spiritual truths and amazing revelations of God's great hidden message. By stringing the names together, as pearls on a thread, it became a fantastic treasure inspired by the Holy Spirit of God that reveals a Divine and Holistic remedy to every human misery.

I have discovered, with logical proof, that in the Bible, the Temple of Solomon represents the body of man - the Temple of God on Earth. Man is the Divine creation of God, the extension of His Light on Earth in human form. The Place of Holy of Holies of the Temple mirrors the important part of the human body - the head, while the Ark of the Covenant in the Holy of Holies is our brain, the place of connection with the Cosmic energy of God and the materialization of God's spiritual energy. It illuminates the whole body with healing energy and transforms the conscience. This physical manifestation of God's presence in our body helps to activate the Divine Consciousness through the Divine connection with the Prime Creator.

"The Bible in Names: Truth Decoded" proclaims and confirms that the Kingdom of God is within us. My journey into the depths of the ancient tunnels of the Western Wall in the Holy Land parallels my deep journey into the ancient history of Biblical and spiritual existence, uncovering hidden treasures through decoding the entire Bible using the Name Code. This journey has equipped me with spiritual knowledge and revelations of deep spiritual truth. It is my privilege to pass this knowledge and truth to our generation and the generations to come.

INTRODUCTION

The Hidden Treasure Within

"The Bible in Names: Truth Decoded" is a unique book that aims to enlighten and awaken humanity by revealing life-changing and astonishing hidden truths about the history of humanity that was stripped of its Divinity. It is about the restoration of the Divine Consciousness by the physical and spiritual manifestation of the Power of God's Light within us. It reveals the truth about the enlightenment of the mind, body, and soul. This hidden message has been encoded in the 66 books of the Bible, and now has been decoded and revealed using the Name Code.

The Bible is a collection of books that has been translated and changed many times under the control of religious authorities. However, the names in the Bible were untouched. There are more than 2,500 names in the Bible, which are the spiritual language given by God to preserve the hidden ancient spiritual knowledge. The Biblical names have meanings and were intended by God to be strung together to tell people the ultimate Truth. Names have spiritual powers, and they are multidimensional living entities that have their energy fields, vibrations, and encoded information.

In the Bible, it tells us about the reconciliation with God and His creation through God's vessel - the human body, as His extension on Earth. For thousands of years, Biblical symbols and metaphors were taken literally, twisting the profound metaphysical truth. But the early Christians knew that the Bible was written in allegories, parables, and fables based on the human body.

"The Bible in Names: Truth Decoded" reveals the truth about the Cosmic Heritage of human beings, which is their exalted status as "The Light Beings". It reveals the truth about the spiritual transformation and physical alchemical process, happening in the body of man, during the process of spiritual awakening to the "Divine Christ Consciousness". It is achieved by meditation upon the "Inner Light" within. The great Truth is that the "Christ" is the Substance, the Anointed Oil or Ointment, contained in the spinal cord and, consequently, in all parts of the body. It is called the "Sacred Secretion" and is the physical manifestation and materialization of the Spirit of our Prime Creator within us.

"Neither shall they say, see here! Or see there! For, behold, the Kingdom of God is within you". (The Bible, Luke 17:21).

The process of the production of the Sacred Secretion, the Liquid Light in our bodies, the preservation, and the practical use of it, is hidden behind the story of Jesus Christ in the New Testament.

"The Bible in Names: Truth Decoded" reveals the fantastic hidden message of how to unlock the multiple spiritual and physical benefits of the Christ Oil within us. The Sacred Secretion activates the dormant brain cells, restores our 12 strands of the Divine DNA, purifies and renews the blood, heals and brings longevity to the physical body. All of this restores our Multidimensional Consciousness and transforms our carbon-based bodies into crystalline bodies that can contain pure Light.

To preserve the Sacred Secretion, we are required to live a life of unconditional love, peace, kindness, selflessness, empathy, and compassion. We are required to be the Living Expression of the Law of Oneness, the main Cosmic Law of the Universe (Uni-verse – One Song). When we live in a state of love for ourselves and others, the Christ Oil will be preserved in our brain and then will be poured through our whole body. The pure Liquid Light of God will reactivate our spiritual heart and heal us physically, emotionally, and spiritually from within. The Sacred Secretion is the Living Water, the Fountain of Life in our bodies, that restores our Divinity and the connection with our Creator.

In the Bible, there is a passage that reads:

"Then I will sprinkle clean water upon you, and you shall be clean: from all your filthiness, and your idols, will I cleanse you. A new heart, also, will I give you, and a new spirit will I put within you: and I will take away the stony heart out of your flesh, and I will give you a heart of flesh. And I will put my spirit within you, and cause you to walk in my statutes, and you shall keep my judgments (the Law of Oneness) and do them" (The Bible, Ezekiel 36:25-27).

Because of the powerful physical and spiritual impact of the Sacred Secretion on the spiritual awakening of humanity, there are "dark forces" aiming and tirelessly working to prevent the preservation of the Living Waters within our bodies.

"The Bible in Names: Truth Decoded" ,also, reveals the hidden message about the tragical Chronicles of humanity and the forceful occupation of Earth by the forces of darkness – demonic, extraterrestrial beings known as "The Anunnaki". They are often described as "those who came from the sky to the Earth". These evil entities, representing the parasitic reptilian race, dubbed "the fallen angels", occupied the Earth and robbed it of minerals and gold. They enslaved humanity, used and are still using human physical and vibrational energy as their "batteries" and supply. They are those who caused the "fallen" state of humanity and spiritual forgetfulness. They have done so by the corruption and merciless genetic manipulations of our DNA, separating us from the Prime Source of the cosmic energy. Because the energy dropped dramatically, the humans became trapped in a low-energy state, fostering fear, guilt, aggression, and lust, which create barriers to living godly, fruitful lives and inhibiting the utilization and preservation of the Sacred Secretion within our bodies. It became so easy to control, manipulate, and enslave humanity - physically, mentally, and spiritually.

For thousands of years, Earth and humanity were controlled by these demonic entities, who played themselves "GODS". These hostile-to-humanity demonic entities sinned against our Prime Creator and humanity, by doing genetic manipulations and mating with human women to spread their demonic "serpent seed" through their offsprings. This was forbidden by God. As a result of it, the "giants" - the Nephilims were born. These offsprings of the demonic entities created "the cult of death", based on fear, guilt, and pride. They were practicing bloody human sacrifices and cannibalism. They were spreading the forbidden immoral knowledge to whittle down the consciousness. At the same time, they have stolen and hidden the knowledge about the Divinity of humans, their exceptional Cosmic Heritage, and the Sacred Secretion that restores the connection with our Prime Creator.

To vanish, the "Anunnaki" used advanced cosmic technology to miniaturize themselves into invisible dark astral dimensions. They became invisible, the "little" to the humans, but are still dwelling among us, using our vibrational energy and causing severe health problems. They left behind the violent race of "giants", the Nephilims, whom they still control. They became the "elite and rulers", the governments and the religious leaders of the world. They are leading the world to the "new world order", to the society of slaves living under the control of anti-human "rulers".

"The Bible in Names: Truth Decoded" warns us about the infiltration of the one of the "little" enemies into the House of God. It warns us about the deceiver, whose name is Paul (the little). "The Bible in Names: Truth Decoded" decodes 13 letters of Paul to reveal his identity as the 13th false apostle, the agent of darkness, the "wolf in sheep's clothing", who deceived and killed many true believers.

"Beware of false prophets, which come to you in sheep's clothing, but inwardly they are ravening wolves" (The Bible, Mathew 7:15).

In his contradicting letters, mixing truth with lies, Paul changed and twisted the original Divine message, which was simply that the Kingdom of God is within us. Our Prime Creator does not need any bloody sacrifices and sufferings to "earn" His love. Our God is a God of love and peace. Paul's message is about using human sacrifice to please God, to "earn" salvation, about the "power of the cross" and lawlessness. This is so opposite to the true nature and love of our Prime Creator. The Real Salvation happens from within through the spiritual transformation of our minds and our hearts.

In his letters, Paul glorifies the government and church leaders who have destroyed and killed millions of people in the Name of

God. Paul created a new religion of "death" that caused humanity to disconnect from God and our Divine nature. This new religion became the weapon of the "mind control" to deceive humankind for more than 2000 years, and, as a result, the development of human consciousness was diminishing. People were not united but divided, because of the contradictions of Paul's writings. There are more than 2600 different denominations of Christianity in the world, because of the plan of the dark forces - "to divide and conquer".

In his letters, Paul, also, diminished the role and power of women and rejected the Divine feminine spiritual energy of the Prime Creator. It was done to exalt the patriarchal dominion over the nations and prevent the Divine feminine energy from emerging and prospering in harmony with the Divine masculine energy as a Divine Union.

Unfortunately, most of the churches in the world follow Paul's false doctrines and not the True Gospel of the Kingdom of God within us. We do not need the "mediators" between us and our Creator, who is already within us. We are interconnected, the Divine, Spiritual, Multidimensional Light Beings, the co-creators with God, the microcosm of the Macrocosm of the Universe.

We are living during unique and exciting times, when the Earth is going through the process of a great energy shift. It's moving from its dense state to the more subtle state, raising the vibrations. "The

Bible in Names: Truth Decoded" is a decoded guideline for the spiritual awakening and physical restoration of the human being, even on the cellular and subatomic levels. It reveals that the Divine design of the human body can be restored and activated for the spiritual awakening and enlightenment to the Higher Consciousness. The Inner Light, the "Christ" within, can be activated through the Christ Oil – the Sacred Secretion, the physical Manifestation of the Spirit of God. It synchronizes the splitting system of energy centers into the central column of White Light in the spinal cord. It is the true Way to the Eternal life.

"Enter through the narrow gate. For wide is the gate and broad is the road that leads to destruction, and many enter through it. But small is the gate and narrow the road that leads to life, and only a few find it". (The Bible, Matthew 7: 13-14)

"The city does not need the sun or moon to shine on it, for the glory of God gives it light, and the Lamb is its lamp". (The Bible, Revelation 21 – 23)

THE BOOKS OF THE OLD

TESTAMENT

GENESIS

Chapters 1-3

The Infinite Divine Prime Source, embodying the Essence of Wisdom and Love, the Union of Divine Feminine and Divine Masculine, stands as the Prime Creator of all that is visible and invisible. Through the Creator's Holy Spirit, the Earth was fashioned as a realm of Delight, Rest, and Comfort, and humanity was bestowed with Divine Consciousness. The Oneness with the Divine Prime Source was instilled within humankind, created in the Image of the Prime Creator, bearing the Light of the Universal Flame of Pure Spirit, and thus, immortal.

However, the Earth and its inhabitants fell under the occupation and enslavement of violent pilgrims-space travelers from the low astral realms, the dark spaces of the anti-world. This extraterrestrial race, having rebelled against the Prime Creator, experienced spiritual degradation. While possessing powerful, advanced technology, they lacked the Living creative energy of the Creator. Arriving on Earth in their steaming spaceships, they wreaked havoc, utilizing the planet as a source of gold and minerals. This occupation proved to be highly destructive, cruel, and detrimental to both the Earth and humanity.

The Divine Seed of the Creator, humanity with Divine Conscience, became tainted by the seed of the serpent—the reptilian race, the "seed of darkness". These demonic entities forced interbreeding with humans and engaged in genetic manipulations to create a labor force and slaves for themselves. Worshiped as "gods", these ancient evil genetic scientists and space vagabonds disrupted the wholeness and connection between man and the Creator, violating God's Divine Law of Oneness. The creation of male and female hybrids (adamites) by mixing human and reptilian genes was strictly prohibited by the Prime Creator, constituting a grave violation, crime, and sin against His Divine Law.

Chapters 4-5

L ife on Earth descended into mourning due to the activities of "space bandits"—extraterrestrial vagabonds who, before, had exploited and destroyed numerous planets and civilizations. Like a "virus" to God's Creation, these parasitic races considered the new hybrids born of their immoral activities as possessions, exploiting them as miners and smiths. During their occupation of Earth, these violent "space occupants" designated the planet as their residence, styling themselves as "watchers" over the Earth. Although they proclaimed themselves as "gods", they were of the serpent's seed— the reptilian race with a destructive, violent consciousness that used nuclear weapons to wreak havoc.

Genetic manipulations turned the once-immortal men, filled with Divine energy, into mortal slaves. They forgot their Divine heritage and began to worship their occupants as "gods", believing in their supposed Divinity. The occupants created the serpent's bloodline, the Nephilim (fallen), infusing them with their own reptilian genes. Humanity became appointed for mortal sorrow. Yet, the benevolent God provided desperate freedom and relief from the entities of darkness—the occupants of Earth, who disrupted peace by landing on the planet in their spaceships, spreading like a dangerous cosmic virus.

Chapters 6-9

The fallen entities of darkness were separated and cast out from the presence of the Prime Creator. They landed on Earth in celestial ships, filled with anger and cruelty, increasing in number as their serpent's seed spread. These forces of darkness intended to take dominion over the Earth, corrupting and destroying humanity as they had with other civilizations and planets. They seduced and mated with human women, giving birth to the giants, known as Nephilim—violent mortal beings, demonic hybrids that violated the Divine Laws of the Prime Creator.

However, the Supreme Divine Power, the Prime Creator, through His Incorruptible Seed of Light within man, would increase and enlarge Himself. He would destroy and dissolve the deceiver of the world.

Chapter 10

Those evil demonic entities, arriving on celestial spaceships, gained power and disrupted peace on Earth, spreading immorality, violence, and anger. They instigated confusion in the minds of mankind, deploying nuclear weapons and crushing everything around with spreading fire and noise. These deceivers, posing as "gods", were destroyers, seeking gold, turning the land into fortresses for their rockets and round spaceships.

Humanity suffered greatly, trembling in the captivity of violent "space traders". They constructed stargates for their spaceships, turning Earth into a fortress for "fallen space travelers", rebelling against God and His creation. These "stargates for gods" were the fortresses of strife, flames and violence of the demonic invaders. The wicked entities caused terrible fear that put people in bondage to the rebellious invaders. They arrived from the dark dimensions and low astral spaces, the anti-world, that are far from the Center of the Eternal Light, the Central Sun of the Galaxy. These evil entities have artificial, deadly intellect without the Living energy of God; therefore, they are using the energy of human beings. They made the artificial energetic isolation of the Earth from the Source, the Matrix

– the reality that is based only on the five physical senses, the "prison" for humanity.

The wickedness of the space bandits was increasing. They are those who are wandering around space, hunting for souls, enslaving and destroying other civilizations in the Universe. They also forcefully mated with earthly beings and animals by raping them. The "watchers" spread strife and rebelled against God's Authority, exalting themselves above their Supreme Creator. They caused pain, iniquity, immorality and infirmity on the Earth. There were different kinds of extraterrestrial entities, tall and little, who always fought with each other for power and dominion over the lands. It was the violent domination of those who came to the Earth on their spaceships - "the death towers", and they used their mind control and advanced technology for the enslavement of humanity.

People forget that they are Multidimensional Divine spiritual beings and that they are co-creators of God. They thought that these "watchers" were sent by God, but the invaders took into captivity the fruitful planet Earth and brought sorrow and pain. These evil monsters almost destroyed and turned it into a desert, like other planets.

This book is about the salvation and freedom of humanity from the captivity of viral antihuman races with artificial consciousness through the unity with the Prime Creator of the Universe via God's Holy Spirit within.

Chapter 11

Those arriving on Earth through spaceships, bringing death and suffering, also became the "robbers" of the Divine Light. Genetic manipulations and the mixture of human and reptilian genes severed the connection with the Divine Source of Light. Yet, there will be a Healer, Redeemer, the Seed of Divine Light with Divine Power, sent on a Mission. Passing through the mixed, corrupted "divisions of darkness" dwelling in man's body, this Friend of the people, their Shepherd, the Branch of the Prime Creator, is the Hidden Fire for demonic forces and the Divine Light anointed by God's Power. The Inner Divine Spirit, hidden within, will restore the body and transform the carnal mind into Divine Consciousness, as a princess into the Queen. The demonic forces - "the robbers", the space traders will be destroyed and swallowed by the Holy Fire of God from within.

Chapters 12-13

The fallen angels, self-proclaimed "high fathers" landed in mountainous regions, stretching their dominion over Earth and turning it into ruins. They violated the Laws of the Universe by doing forbidden genetic manipulations, using advanced technology, changing vibrational frequencies and switching off and destroying 10 out of 12 Light strands of the Divine DNA, the God's genes of spirituality in men. Also, they blocked the channels of communication between the left, logical part of the brain (male) and the right, spiritual intuitive part (female). People became disconnected from the Prime Source, the Divine Cosmic energy, and many cells of the brain became dormant. The wholeness, the lightness of the man, was destroyed because the spiritual part of the brain, "the Teacher", became a "heap of ruins". Instead of a place of union with God, enlightenment, and connection with the Universe, the human mind became a place of trouble and confusion, spoiled by the "serpent's seed".

The violent "gods" brought destruction and confusion within the mind of the human being, transforming it into the "hills of ruins". However, it can be restored by the spiritual Seed of Light, the Radiance of God's Glory within. It will be reactivated by God in the body of man and will be diffused into the brain through the River of Judgment (the cerebrospinal fluid), amplifying the Power of God. He will thwart the secret demonic forces with His invisible but powerful Seed of Light from within.

Chapters 14-15

The fallen angels, the Anunnaki, are those "who came from the sky to the Earth". They, along with their clones and hybrids, are the anti-human seeds of the serpent, despising humanity—the creation of God. Like "roaring lions", they spread evil and fear worldwide. They induced humanity to rebel against God and forget their cosmic heritage, and they brought destruction to the Earth. Erecting cities and disseminating wickedness, witchcraft, and lies, these demons are akin to "goats with horns", causing confusion, destruction, and sexual immorality. They bred giants on Earth, the Nephilim, by raping earthly women. The multidimensional mind of man became afflicted, but God will restore the Divine Consciousness of men through the sacred place of the human brain, the hidden Receiver of Divine Love—the pineal gland, where man can connect with the Divine Spirit of God.

The Prime Creator will bring to His Court for judgment of the "ancient serpent", who revolted from Him, dwelt on Earth, and propagated wickedness and sexual immorality. The rebellious monsters will be subdued under the power of the Seed of God's Light. The human mind will be restored and connected to the Divine Source of life through the activation of the Divine Gem of Light within. The demonic entities will be vanquished as they attempt to obliterate the fruitful mind of man.

Chapters 16-19

Due to genetic manipulation, the spiritual, intuitive part of the human brain was tainted and became undeveloped. God's

Inner Eye, the pineal gland in the brain, became concealed and a "stranger" to the brain due to the oppressor. It became the barrier between the human mind and the Wisdom of God, who hears. "The well of Him who sees me"—the pineal gland—is the abode of the Holiness of God, who hears. The mind of man, devoid of God's Wisdom, is a desolation from God and an elevation of man's pride. Only those who seek God within will attain freedom from the reptilian low consciousness, strife, and pride. Wicked people are insignificant and minute compared to God. The pineal gland in the human brain became concealed, distorted, and deactivated. The mind of men, initially created by God and deemed Holy, became as the mind of rebellious pilgrims.

Chapters 20-21

The Prime Creator—the Union of the Divine Feminine and Divine Masculine—is the Creator of the Holy Seed of Light in man. It is eternal and will prevail over the serpent's seed. Spiritual awakening is achievable through the development of Divine Consciousness, leading to the Oneness with God. To achieve this, the spiritual part of the brain, the right side, the Sacred Feminine, must be restored and balanced with the left side. The Anointed Seed of God will move to the brain through the spiritual heart center of man, illuminating the entire body. The Holy Seed of God will be the "well of oath—the seventh oath" of the Divine power, the Crown of

God and, at the same time, will be the "well of captivity" for the wicked one.

Chapters 22-23

Due to genetic manipulations by reptilian races, the right side of the brain became undeveloped, and the brain cells became dormant. What God created was plundered and dried up. The place of the Flame of God's Holiness has melted away. The Crystals of the pineal gland were deactivated and dried out in the brain, like a pearl in darkness. The Crystal of the heart was, also, deactivated.

Nevertheless, the power of the Holy Seed of the Creator's Light, aided by the Holy Spirit, will be increased in the body of man—the Temple of the Holy Spirit. It will silence the liar, the serpent seed, by pressing him down.

The ruling, spiritual part of the brain became the "dust" due to dryness and man became filled with fear and rebellion. The mind succumbed to fear with a lower state of conscience as the energy level dropped. The "fall" of consciousness results from the crimes of fallen reptilian races, who lack Divine Consciousness, because they disconnected from the Divine Consciousness, the Source of Divine Love. The spiritual intuition, the Discerning Spirit, expresses the strength of the Divine Mind, the High Intelligence, providing salvation from the "mind control" of the reptilian race.

Chapters 24-26

The place where God's Spirit dwelled, the pineal gland, was "pierced" and almost disappeared. It requires healing, restoration, and transformation by God. What was glorious became "dosed", and the place of the Living God, who beholds us, was "hooked". The Fragrance and Celebration of the Glorious Power of Love became offended, judged, and hardened. Due to the captivity of humankind, their consciousness was lowered by demonic aliens who oppressed people and concealed spiritual knowledge to control and dominate.

The Source of True knowledge is the Holy Spirit of God, the Savior of the human mind. When the mind and soul became desolated from God, they became a "stranger" to the spiritual intuition—the source of Divine Power for the soul. The Divine nature of people was supplanted by the carnal alien nature – due to these pilgrims from dark places. The Divine part of the brain was "trapped", but the aggressive reptilian part of the brain was developed by ancient reptilian aliens from dark dimensions. Cosmic wars raged between different cosmic civilizations vying for dominion and power.

Chapters 27-30

The Divine generation of the Earth had a connection with the Prime Source and was the Well of the Divinity, but they got disconnected from it by the reptilian genetics and their animalistic inclinations. The spiritual centers of the connection in the body of man were trapped and blocked. Human beings – that were once glorious – now became full of fear and sickness. The Land of God became the land of the foreign aliens. The evil serpent's seed, with low vibrational frequency, now possessed the minds and souls of people who became distant and disconnected from God. The House of God, the body of man, became "the house of the serpent" (kundalini – the serpent's coiled energy at the base of the spine).

Because of the genetic manipulations, the minds of people were corrupted to the minds of the fearful "sheep". The mental activity became sluggish, tired, and confused, and with the low level of consciousness, people were in a numb trance of sleep and spiritual "amnesia". Instead of "seeing and praising" God within, people became confused and "blind" by the ancient supplanter. His "lying mouth" blatantly deceived them, and his followers became the army of the ancient serpent. However, those who will follow the Divine Spirit and the Laws of Oneness will be rewarded by the dwelling of God's Spirit in them and will become the Army of God.

Chapters 31-35

The place in the brain of man, where God resides as a Glorious Light, is God's Throne. It was invaded by violent and dangerous aliens, but sooner or later, the Eternal God will restore His House because He is the God of the Universe. The brain became a battlefield with two "armies" pitted against each other. The left side of the brain is wrestling with God, but God will restore the wholeness of the brain. The part of the brain where men can "see" God is the pineal gland, the "point of meeting" of the spiritual power in the physical body. Due to mental exhaustion, the people became judgemental and vain, and Unconditional Love vaporized from their hearts. Many of them became wicked, rebellious beings, fighting against God and against each other.

The House of God was supplanted and became the "house of weeping". The place of abundance became the place of terror and anguish. What was once the House of Bread (the solar plexus) became the dominion of the supplanter. The people abide by and blindly follow the ancient serpent who has been the deceiver from the beginning. They will be the army of the "son of sorrow" who will lead them astray by his "lying mouth".

Chapter 36

The deceiver will dwell in the earthly House of God by spreading his iniquity. He will desolate everything Holy from the people. The assembly will follow the "false shepherd" who possesses a "false spirit".

He will lie that he was ordained and sent by God Almighty, but pulling his strings will be satan, the ancient serpent, who rebelliously declared: "My tabernacle will be exalted". He will "devour" everyone. He is zealous and bold, talkative, controlling, and very knowledgeable, commanding to do his will.

His name will be the "little, the destroyer" ("apostle" Paul/Saul). And, because he is "hungry" for the souls, he is hunting after people and their energies. He is the leader of desolation, the ultimate source of fear, who will "devour" God's people. Though hidden for now, he will be revealed. He is the scourge that will afflict many because he is the concealed "path of iniquity, the ashes of hell, trashing freeborn on this earth". He is the aide of the serpent who is worshiping the "black sun" in anti-world and causing widespread adultery. He will be very intelligent, full of knowledge, and will use that to "twist" the Truth, mixing it with the lies.

Because of the hidden "path of iniquity", the destruction and the beguiling of foolish men, the assembly of God will be brought to the great judgement. This false "shepherd", filled to the brim with hatred, will stir up troubles in the House of God. He will be powerful as a "hawk", by declaring the goodness of God but doing evil activity. He will have a "wand of the government in the house full of gold", but behind him will be the earthly ancient serpent who will still be declaring: "My Tabernacle will be exalted".

He is the "oak of curse" who will be hell-bent on trying to take the "First Fruits" of God, hunting after them and infusing them with evil. He is the ancient deceiver from the beginning.

Chapters 37-45

The ancient serpent, who is the deceiver, will lie and deliver blemished, ornate words to the people, but the faithful people of God will obey the Law of Oneness. The followers of the deceiver, however, will endorse adultery by worshiping the false gods of Saturn, the Sun, and the Moon.

Even people who once believed in God, the Source of Creation, will make foolish choices by obeying the commandments of men, the "religious leaders", and disobeying the Cosmic Order. They will coggle down the "ditch" following these "watchers", the controllers, who colonized the Earth and enslaved the humanity. They will worship the false gods instead of the Prime Creator. The assembly of God will be pronged like a "palm tree" – with many branches and many divisions. There will be the worshippers of Saturn, Moon, and Sun, but not the God of the Universe.

The demonic races of the ancient serpent and draconian races are those who are pulling the "strings", trying to mar God's people.

They are those who revolted from God, rejected the Divine Feminine, "spoiled" the Creator's human race and dispersed them. They have forgotten the Prime Creator, and their influence will spread across the Earth. The believers, who will fall prey to the deception, will draw near the "son of sorrow", and they will be hypnotized, worshipping the enemy.

The ancient serpent has diminished and made foggy the Holy place in the brain of the people. They have lost the ability to "see and hear" God, their Prime Creator. It is the ancient serpent who has promoted ungodly behaviour and now disseminates lies all over the world. He called himself the "Son of Light, the Light Bearer". Those who will be deceived, will be reeled in by the "son of sorrow" and will be fooled into worshipping the devil but not God.

Chapter 46

The Divine system of communication with God was corrupted. The "Seven Wells" of God, the spiritual centers of energy in the body of men (chakras) found along the spinal cord, became suppressed and became the dwelling places of fear and parasitic dark forces. The blissful place of peace and mercy of God grotesquely morphs into the place of "tiredness". The Temple of Praise of God became the "serpent house" as the "wild ass".

The right side of the brain, once fortified by God's Light, became rancid by fear, guilt, shame, grief, lies, and idols. This transmuted the function of the brain and caused pain and confusion. The godly and merciful people became full of fear. The Earth became a "cultivated field" like a farm. People became spiritually "sleepy" while the aliens watched. They forgot that they were the Children of the Light, and they once used to communicate with God, who is the Eternal Light, through the Inner Light in them. Humanity dropped to the low, carnal level of the reptilian races. People forgot that they were happy, free, and independent. And the worst of all, the consciousness invaded the tiers of survival, anger, and fighting.

Their souls forgot the God-given assignment, which declared that when they "cross over" and become part of this world, they would also have to be independent and free. But here on Earth, they were deceived, "trapped" by the reptilian part of the brain. The forgetfulness and the pain piled on because of the forces of iniquities. The forces plagued the brain with violence, anger, and sexual immorality.

The evil races supplanted and confused the souls of the Light. The deceiver caused the evil on Earth. He beguiled people into worshipping Saturn and pretending to be "god". He is one of the chiefs of the fallen angels, once dedicated to God, and was His "right hand" before his rebellion, but later, he became proud of his learned enlightenment and became the one who stirred up sorrow and pain by rebellion. Ultimately, he and those who joined him, were cast out from the High dimensions of the Universe.

They became the "assembly of bitterness" and the one who was once praising the Creator, the Source of Light, cursed himself into the being full of iniquity. He and his followers became the "watchers" who occupied the Earth. They are now left, twisting the truth about God and breaking the Army of God into divisions.

The one who was rewarded with gifts became lukewarm, telling lies and deceiving people. He will cry from the "enemies of thorns". The enemy will dwell, by the spirit of fear, in those who were the Hope of God. By the falsehood of the "enemy's mouth", he will always change his lies with splendor. He will be one of the "watchers, the wild ass", pretending to be heroic. The enemy, who rebelled against the Creator before his rebellion, was assigned to serve the "Morning star", the King, the Counsellor. The one who was "the brightness" became the dark, weak deceiver of the people. His offspring will be the "sons of sorrow" of the oppression. His forgetfulness and rebellion will bring the "fruits of misfortune", and the enemy will be demolished.

The Light of the Creator will swallow the "divider" on the "island of Help and Peace". The One who is full of Mercy will capture the "divider". The enemy is the old, confused serpent, who will increase the oppression of those who are approaching nearby. But the Light of the Source manifested as the Sacred Secretion, the Holy Oil in the spinal cord of man, will prevail over the deceiver and his offspring. The enemy is the old reptilian dragon who has been the murderer from the beginning.

Chapters 47-50

As more and more people became forgetful of their Divine nature it caused their separation from the power of the Divine Source and from the abundance of the power of God. God's Light could not find its way into people's minds anymore and the Divine Source became forgotten because of the fear. The fallen angels who saw the Glory of God, worshipped and obeyed Him, dwelt in His presence, became the troops of bandits who killed the people with the Divine Consciousness. People fought with each other for independence and power, became warlike and materialistic, and their consciences stooped to new lows.

However, the Spirit of God in men will prevail over the deceiver and his offspring, who are merely the "dust" and foolishly committed the double rebellion against God. They are the "dust of the wickedness", and the deceiver is the "father of the wickedness". The fear was increasing because of the "thorns"(parasitic etheric implants) in the pineal gland, God's system of communication, which was destroyed. Confusion and mourning multiplied, and the sacred knowledge was forsaken and forgotten. However, the salvation of the mind and the soul will be through the Divine Consciousness and Love, not by human sacrifice and death. Those who will hear and abide by God will be associated with Him. They will be rewarded and will find peaceful resting abodes in His presence. Ultimately, their power and authority will increase through the Divine Essence, the Sacred Secretion, the Fountain of Life within, that will restore the whole body, renew the blood and reactivate 12 cranial nerves in the brain of men and 12 strands of the Divine DNA (the microcosm of the Macrocosm of the Universe – 12 Signs of Zodiac, 12 Tribes of Israel).

EXODUS

Chapters 1-15

The Seed of Light within was oppressed, suffocated, and supplanted by those who "saw and heard" the Creator loud and clear but yet subscribed to the treachery of the deceiver and became violent and judgmental, resembling and joining the similar fate as that of the "sons of sorrows". The Beauty of Splendor was oppressed and spoiled, marred and violated, by those who defiled the Divine within men that enveloped true correction for mankind. They "crossed over" and breached the confines of God Almighty, aligned with the dark beings, the dwellers of darkness who came from dark astral dimensions. People became estranged from God, lost their way, were blinded by temptations, and lost connection with the Eternal Light, the Central Sun of the Galaxy, leaving themselves trampled and violated and abused mentally by the rebellious villagers.

The stream of the Divine Excellence was obstructed and destroyed; men became blinded to it and its Divine Purification purpose and benefits, and the minds of men were oppressed by "trans-dimensional aliens" altogether. The flow of God's Curative Spirit was stifled in human minds due to genetic manipulations, experimentation, and the adulteration of the Blessed DNA of man by the evil demonic entities. Humans forgot that the Light of God within them is the Almighty, His Strength, bestowed to them to use for purification and cleansing so they can maintain their ways and remain within His Benevolent Grace.

Chapters 16-34

Technologically advanced civilizations, arriving on space rockets, became spiritually "broken" adversaries of God, assuming the station of the messiahs of man, pretending to save them from squalor. However, the Divine Strength, which is robust and resilient, within humanity will begin to flourish again, casting out all that is sowed by the invaders. The Divine Light within the human body offers freedom and liberation from strife, temptation, and grief, fostering soul, mind, and spirit evolution, turning men into beings that are pure within and without. It also offers Rest and Salvation for the soul from the wickedness and sins imbued in the hearts and minds of men with the sole intent of corrupting them. The Eternal Light of God salvages what good lies within, nurtures and nourishes it, and finally delivers mankind from the "waters of wickedness of the serpent seed". The materialization of God's Spirit within is the Sacred Secretion, brimming with light and cosmic energy and waiting to unleash and sanitize the hearts and souls that have darkened. It is latent in the brain of man (the Ark of the Covenant, on the cellular level – the nucleus in the cell).

The Deliverer, the Spirit of God, embodies excellence in Divine Judgment in the Courts of God. He is the Beauty and the Trumpet of God, delivering from confusion and oppression.

Chapters 35-40

The Holy Spirit of God within the human being is the Seed of God's Light, His Fire, His Praise, His true Judge. Dwelling within us, in the brain (the Ark of the Covenant), together with the spark of Light in the heart, the Holy Spirit grants Life, offering protection under God's tent, making us His Tabernacle in the presence of His Holiness.

LEVITICUS

Chapters 1-27

The Deliverer against those who oppose God is the Mountain of Strength, the Holy Fire in the cerebrospinal fluid of the human spine, freeing from the "waters of sin", the Spirit of the King, bringing happiness and peace. Divine Consciousness is the Joy of the Prime Creator, delivering from the enemy.

NUMBERS

Chapter 1

Within the human body, the Temple of God, resides a sacred Anointed Essence, the evidence of the Divine Spirit, the Holy Oil, the Sacred Secretion. This Light of God Almighty, the Deliverer, ascends from above into the solar plexus, rising along the spine through the heart center to illuminate the brain and restore the Divine Consciousness (not the kundalini – the serpent's coiled energy). This Essence is our Rock of Salvation, Fountain of Life and Love, delivering from the "waters of wickedness".

God's Gift, the pineal gland in the brain, was the place of dwelling of God's Light before the genetic manipulation. Although now deactivated and dormant due to genetic infiltration, it once allowed humans to "see and hear" God. Its diminishment led to forgetfulness of the Law of Oneness and disconnection from the Source of Light. The Stone of Redemption, the pineal gland, was nearly destroyed by the invaders, disrupting communication with God. The people forgot the rewards of the Stone of Redemption and the knowledge about the illumination of the brain.

Despite this, the human body remains the Temple of God's Divine Spirit, with His Seed of Light planted in every person. The evidence of this Gift of God is the sacred Essence in the spinal cord, a River of Light for humanity and judgment for the enemy, elevating consciousness and declaring God Almighty as our Rock and Perfection. This Divine Essence, illuminating the body, is the Fountain of Life and Youth.

Chapters 2-3

This is God's Gift to those who praise Him, making them "fruitful", enabling them to "see" Him through spiritual eyes and praise Him in Spirit and Truth. But those who will be forgetful and ignorant will not be recompensed and will be left to stay confused.

The Spirit of God is the Gift of God, His Light. He is the Deliverer from those strangers who changed their pilgrimage and are the rebellious "space travellers" from other spaces. They exalted themselves as anointed "gods". They are the rebellious, bitter "infirmities" who were cast out from God's presence. He reveals Himself through the Gift of the Holy Spirit – the Anointed Oil, the Sacred Secretion. The Holy Spirit of God is the Teacher, who is associated with God, the Rock of Strength. This Anointed Oil will be protected and restored, and the Light Body within will be resurrected. Humans will be internally illuminated by the Inner Spiritual Light of God, praising Him and proclaiming: "God Almighty is my Rock and Strength, who is in me!".

Chapters 4-9

The Inner Light of the Sacred Secretion is the Deliverer from the "spirit of darkness", the Teacher, the Soldier, and God's Branch. He is the Salvation and protection from those who came from other spaces, who rebelled and provoked God's assembly. They proclaimed that people were liberal and free from God's Laws, yet they enslaved them and stole the sacred knowledge, causing humanity to forget. The stream of God's Spirit was suppressed in human minds by genetic distortion from those who think they are independent of God. However, God will restore the sacred knowledge to the people of praise, to the Righteous Army. He will increase, reactivate, and sanctify the Rock of Salvation, the Stone of Redemption—the pineal gland, consisting of five crystals (The Bible, 1 Samuel 17:39-40, the five stones used by David). God will judge the "son of sorrow", the destroyers, the wicked ones full of iniquity. However, the people of praise will exalt God, saying: "God Almighty is our Rock of Strength, our peace, and happiness! The Spirit of God is our Recompense to the knowledge of God!".

Chapter 10

The Inner Light in the human body is the Ruler over enmity, the Beauty, the Friendship, and the Glory of God that men receive through the brain (the Ark of the Covenant). It reigns over the "enchanter" who lies, claiming people are free from God's Laws. God's Laws are His rewards and gifts to His people. Those who rebelled against the Creator and dwelt on Earth called themselves "gods" and caused the grief. They are those who changed their pilgrimage, coming from the Moon and rebelled against the Light of the Almighty, the Rock of Strength. They are the destroyers, the troops of enmity who had some knowledge which, too, was given to them from God, but they rebelled against Him and forgot His Laws. Coming from dark spaces of the anti-world, they fought against the True Light. However, the Savior is the Shepherd for humanity, the Friend of God – the true Judge for those who fight against Him.

Chapters 11-12

The Light of the Holy Spirit is the Deliverer from those who fight with God, who spoiled His creation. The Light of the Sacred Secretion in the spinal cord of humans is the Living Water of God, His Water of Love, His Seed, the Fountain of Eternal Life, delivering from the "graves of lust" and from those who lived in caves. It will deliver people from the "giants" and save them from the wicked, rebellious people.

Chapters 13-19

The spiritual Light inside humans is the Deliverer from the evil one, the Source of spiritual awakening and growth. He is the

Beauty and Glory of God who will obey His Creator, the Judge of the rebellious angels who became the enemies of God. The spiritual Light of God, the eternal Savior, faithful and obedient, will redeem His elect, saving His people from the "son of sorrow", granting them the Rest. They will be the Light to the world, illuminated by the Light of Truth. However, there will be a man who will secretly judge the people of God and the Light of the Holy Spirit. He is the hidden destroyer struggling to diminish the army of people. The Army of God will be reduced by "coldness" growing like a "wall" in society because of him—the deceiver. Behind this man will be the ancient dragon, the "father of lies", active as a "duster" (Paul/Saul – "little destroyer"). But the Light of God is the faithful Savior who will vanquish the poor, angry deceiver from the dark space.

The Light of God in the spinal cord of humans, the Seed of God, will be blocked by the "seed of the dragon". The supplanter, the "father of lies", is the "pain of iniquity", causing disobedience to the Laws of God.

Chapters 20-22

The materialization of the Spirit of Love within humans, as an anointed Rescue Oil, the Sacred Secretion, will deliver them from those who troubled and oppressed humanity, restoring the strength and purity of God.

The will of God, His gift, and the path to the high places will be rediscovered in the bodies of humans. People will spend more time meditating in solitude and stillness, rediscovering the power of their cosmic heritage, and rooting out disputes. People will learn to preserve the Sacred Secretion, the Rescue Oil, experiencing brain illumination and rising consciousness through activation of the Stone of Redemption, the pineal gland. They will rejoice in the Light of the Spirit of Truth and Divine Consciousness, awakening to the truth. Rebellious people will be rooted out, and it will be the "bread" for the Spirit, binding the "waters of grief", casting out evil, the ancient serpent, the accuser. The Fountain of the Water of Life, a Gift from heaven, will be uncovered in the bodies of humans.

The Light of God will prevail over the enemy. The Seed of Light, the spiritual Seed of God, will flow through the River of Life, the cerebrospinal fluid, in the spinal cord of humans, opening energy centers, "the gates of Light", awakening dormant parts of the brain previously blocked and oppressed by the parasitic etheric implants, destroying enemy's strongholds. What was a "burning desert, destruction of people" will be restored by the power of the Holy Spirit of God.

Chapters 23-25

The Light of the Prime Source, suppressed by the destroyer, will pass over by the power of the Holy Spirit, destroying negative energies and opening and increasing God's energy during the meditation in solitude. The human spinal cord will be like a "Scepter in the "hands" of God's Spirit", controlling all senses and emotions and bruising the violent deceiver. Because most people will be deceived and worship the liars, the knowledge about the Stone of Redemption, the pineal gland, will elude them. The Light of God will act as a "Thorn" to the enemy, the destroyer.

Chapter 26

The hidden place of God is His "vineyard, the dart of joy". God's brightness will destroy the iniquity of the enemy. During the invasion of the enemy, what was once the "brightness" of the body became the "grave", and that which helped "see and observe" God became a "stranger" to Him. The enemy, the force of iniquity, broke the place of receiving the Light. The wholeness of the brain was broken, and the mind was divided and ruptured. What was at a time a reward became the "worm", a place of dwelling for fear.

Waiting in hope for God's Light, people became forgetful of God's fruitfulness and knowledge. What was the "island of help", the portion of God, became hidden in the "pit shade", controlling people by fear. However, rest and peace can be achieved by the motion of the stream of energy of light. It will be the destruction of the "old fire" of the serpent, coming from the chambers of the brains of those focusing on fellowship with God and the divinity of human beings. The stream of Divine energy will bring youthful rejuvenation and restoration, the Gift of Fire from God to His people.

Chapters 27-30

The Stone of Redemption, often linked to the pineal gland, lay fractured and deeply hidden within the recesses of the human brain. Consequently, humanity had forgotten about the Divine Light of God and the tranquility of His presence within them. However, the prevailing chill of discord will inevitably give way to the sanctity of God's presence. The Eternal One, the Savior, the radiant Light, who is also the Son of God and the Divine Seed of God, shall ultimately triumph.

Chapters 31-32

There shall come a time of reckoning, where the Helper of God shall pass judgment upon the deceitful and wicked desires, symbolized by the "serpent's mouth". He is the Rock of Liberty, the Divine Aid. The Sacred Secretion, the manifestation of the Holy Spirit's Divine power, serves as a conduit for deliverance and Aid. Meanwhile, the army of angels, who were God's assistants on Earth, who had a "crown of power" and an abundance of knowledge, rebelled by doing ungodly inventions. They demanded burnt offerings and human sacrifices, pretending to be "gods", but in truth, they are those who afflicted the real Divine Creator and His Laws.

The pristine state of man's brain, originally intended to receive the Seed of Light, flowing through the human spinal cord, was corrupted through genetic manipulation and interbreeding with the "serpent's seed". Consequently, this innate ability was eradicated, and the seat of the Holy Spirit of God, represented by the pineal gland, lay violated. Yet, the steadfast faith of true believers, destined to triumph over adversity, shall flourish like a vine.

The Savior, the Divine Spark of God within, shall uproot the adversaries and their followers. He shall deliver humanity from those who descended upon the Earth, forsaking the Creator and His Eternal Laws. Those embittered souls who hold and use wicked and criminal knowledge to exert power are those who perpetrate violence against God's people. They exalted themselves as a "house of rebellion" against the House of Grace. They instigated invasion and built the cities of enmity. They caused the forgetfulness and lamentation of the people.

Chapter 33

Those who engage in a struggle with the Divine find themselves lacking in true strength. Such an individual embodies the ancient dragon, the ancestor of idolatry, through the worship of the "black sun" and Saturn. Their existence on Earth is transient, akin to a temporal "tent", their power confined merely to their words. Their concealed idols, harbored resentments, and fleeting dwellings hold no enduring strength; they are as fragile as clay. Everything they build will ultimately be shaken and shattered, for their endeavors are steeped in enmity and lust. Though they may embellish their villages, cities, and palaces to exalt the false "holiness", in truth, they are steeped in fear.

The congregation may exalt "goodness", but they are tainted with wickedness. Their appearance may be beguiling, sugary, and seemingly bountiful, yet they are bound to the "son of sorrow". They pretend to be "godly," but they are full of anger. Behind them looms the shadow of the ancient dragon, casting its dark influence.

Chapters 34-36

The Seed of God's Light within shall liberate humanity from the thorns of evil, which sting like scorpions. The evil people will force deceit across generations, originating from the "seed and bones" of the evil one, who sowed confusion, shifting blame for their sins onto others. Within mountainous terrains and underground caverns, they disseminate wildness, falsehood, and sexual immorality by luring and seducing people. This leads to a forfeiture of the Divine Spark within because the pineal gland, as the point of connection, was damaged, lowering consciousness. Hearts, once filled with warmth, grow cold, transforming the worshippers of the Beloved of God into generations of forgetfulness.

However, because God protected them, they will be redeemed, and they will be the "people of praise" again. The faithful shall be delivered from infirmity, dancing freely with the Holy Spirit of God. Those estranged from the Light shall find connection through the Holy Sacred Secretion.

DEUTERONOMY

Chapters 1-2

The process of liberation from bondage through the Seed of Light within humanity's consciousness was ruined. The Holy place that abounded in the luminous liquid gold—the Holy Oil—became a site of desolation. The Holy place in the brain -the pineal gland, was desecrated through genetic tampering by rebellious entities from the dark spaces who came on the big space rockets. Before their rebellion, they were aligned with the Source of abundance and fruitfulness.

The pineal gland, the Holy place, lay in ruins. The "fallen angels" birthed monstrous beings—half-human, half-animal—the evil monsters, the "giants". These entities, steeped in iniquity, incited forbidden activities and sexual immorality and instigated fear. There were some wild "giants" who used to hide in underground caves. Even though the sunlight shone on people, it went to waste. These giants were created by the "fallen angels", who were once worshipers of God and carried the light. But one of these angels rebelled and became the ancient dragon, disconnected from the Creator. He and his army created wicked giants who were also disconnected from the Creator. However, they will be defeated and wiped away, like a shadow that disappears.

Chapter 3

The individuals called "creators of iniquity" who lived in rocky caves tried to eliminate the connection of men to the Source by destroying the "magic flashlight" in the brain. It was considered a Holy place in the brain that received information and energy from God. However, it was disconnected and broken, becoming like a fortress with walls that were sacrificed to the enemy. Because of their wickedness and immoral actions, the Holy Seed couldn't pass through.

Chapters 4-31

Despite the destruction caused by the enemy, the Seed of God, His Gift of life, will reach His Holy place, the brain and the DNA of human beings, and be restored by the Creator of the "vine branch". He is the spiritual and physical Architect, not those rebellious beings who destroyed the Seed of God and caused forgetfulness. These beings were full of anger and destroyed everything to ashes, including their fortress. But God will overcome the destruction, the oppressors, and their power. He is the God over destruction and the "cutters" from the ancient heaps. He will judge them by His Eternal Power in the River of Judgement, the Anointed Oil in the cerebrospinal fluid in the spinal cord of man.

Chapters 32-34

Humanity was deceived by evil beings, full of anger and envy. But yet, God, the Righteous One, the Rock, reigns supreme. He is God over the ancient pilgrims from other spaces, the moon and the high mountains. He is God over those who birthed the giants, the cold-blooded adversaries who defied both God and humanity.

Those evil "ancient astronauts" descending upon mountain peaks sowed discord, propagated coldness, and concealed the knowledge about the dwelling Light. They proclaimed themselves the "righteous seed" of God, spreading forgetfulness of Divine Laws. Despite the spread of forgetfulness, the Army of God shall triumph with the Savior, the Truth and the Light, annihilating those who oppose God. The carnal desires of the "supplanters" will be overcome by the Holy Seed of God. The Eternal Creator shall deliver His people from the "house of enmity".

JOSHUA

Chapter 1-4

The Liberator, the Deliverer, is the Seed of Light, the Physician. The Liberator, the Deliverer, manifests as the Seed of Light, tangible evidence of the Holy Breath, the Holy Spirit of God, in the brain and the DNA of the human beings (the Ark of the Covenant). The sacred spiritual fluid within the spinal cord serves as the Rescue Oil, brimming with God's power and vibration, connecting man's being with the entirety of the cosmos. This Rescue Oil, infused with God's energy and Love, shall reawaken dormant energies within the human vessel and restore the extra "10" Light strands that were blocked (10 tribes of Israel that were "lost"). It shall revive the connection to God, rekindling the pineal and pituitary glands. It is the Receiver and the Transmuter of vibrational energy, dormant due to the actions of a reptilian demonic race. These beings once beheld God's Glory, yet rebelled against Eternal Love, consumed by pride, forgetting the Prime Source. They are beings of fear, jealousy, and violence, shattered and broken.

The Light of God shall defeat the "red dragon", the embittered oppressor.

Chapters 5-7

Those who forsake the Source of Life, the true Light, wage wars, oppress people and struggle with God. The Seed of God, who is God's Light extension, will be planted into the man. The Body of the Light within the man, which was destroyed, will be restored.

The adversary sought to undermine the Tree of Life, the neurological system of man, altering the body's electromagnetic energy. Through mind control and the victimization of humanity, they attempted to "erase" sacred knowledge, utilizing humans and other beings as their "food sources". They represent a parasitic race, yearning for longevity by harnessing human life energy as their "battery".

However, the Light Seed of God shall deliver people from violent pilgrims, from the "house of vanity" – the abode of the serpent. God reigns supreme over those who oppose Him. The Seed of God, His Divine Endowment, will dismantle those who mingle God's Seed with the serpent's seed.

Chapters 8-9

The Eternal Savior rescues people from the wicked, from the "house of gods" - the "a heap of ruins". These entities oppressed people through extensive mind control, enforcing religious patriarchal dominance rooted in fear and wars, rejecting the Divine Feminine. Fear drives people to sever their connection with the Prime Source, shutting their hearts - the dwelling place of God. These anti-human forces have tainted human souls, perpetuating bloody sacrifices of both humans and animals and fostering an atmosphere of suffering and anguish. They fostered a "culture of death", feeding off the resulting low vibrational energy, for they are beings of darkness.

Yet, the Eternal God will destroy those emerging from the lower astral spaces, annihilating those possessed by impostor satanic spirits who oppressed humanity with shame, guilt, lust, and pride. God will rescue His people from the "heap of ruins", uprooting it from the ivory wellspring, from the "little lions" who established the "cities of woods" (Hollywood, Bollywood).

Chapter 10

The foundation of God's justice ensures Salvation from the "heaps of ruins", the violence, and the wickedness wrought by rebellious individuals. They shall be uprooted, akin to "wild donkeys", roaming independently from God. The fallen angel, masquerading as an "enlightening angel", will emerge as a talkative orator, a false teacher traversing every corner (reminiscent of the "apostle" Paul). He shall establish the "house of wrath", the abode of satan, fostering a society detached from God, a city of waywardness and folly. Yet, God shall deliver His people from "the house of wrath and the twisted walls". God, the Creator of the Sun and the Moon, shall rescue them from the "Moon's shackles", from the society of wickedness, and from those who arrived on chariots and ancient spacecraft from dark realms. He shall rescue them from those who sow division, leading lives estranged from God.

Chapter 11

The Creator of the Universe serves as the Savior, lifting humanity from the depths of crookedness, from the "hips of wickedness". Those likened to "hay" by God brim with hatred and venom. They are the offspring of rebellious "cosmic traders", fractured and consumed by fear. They tried to lure people through their luring, tricky behaviors. They dwelt on Earth and trodden everything around under their feet. They are "the watchtower of speculation", pretending to elevate the Son of God, but they are the "anathema" from the Moon. They are the generation of those who came from dark spaces of the Universe, the destroyers of the "vine press".

Chapter 12

The Seed of God shall triumph over the seed of the reptilian race devoted to destruction. The society spawned by those who descended upon Earth, seeking to destroy all in their path, has transformed the Earth into a "house of the desert". The Savior shall deliver humans from the legions of evil beings, from the idols of fortune - the Stargates. He shall liberate the from the oppressors who dwelled upon the Earth from the Moon, "the hips of ruins, the house of gods".

The Prime Creator, the Source and Foundation, stands in stark contrast to those steeped in fear and death, the evil beings who rebelled against Him. They fractured the Seed of God, embodying the "dragons of destruction". The Seed of God, once a Sanctuary for God, has been spoiled by those who emerged from the house of gods. They who hold and use power and authority are aggressive, vigilant, and steeped in deception. They are the generation of those architects of fortresses, proclaiming them as sanctuaries, erecting stations for their spacecraft for their own gratification.

Chapters 13-14

The Prime Creator reigns over those who settled on Earth, erecting a walled "valley of troubles". They are the oppressors, robust and violent, cosmic travelers migrating from desolate planets where they dwell in caves. They now seek souls and energies aboard their white spaceships, resembling mountains or clouds, serving as their fortresses and castles.

The Seed of God, His Essence within humanity created in God's image, shall sweep away their ruins with the flourishing waters – the Anointed Sacred Secretion. God will uproot their strongholds, stargates, bridges, roads, and fortresses. The Soldier of God shall dismantle their settlements of destruction and the splendor of their cities, replete with fragrance and wealth. "The house of opening, a dwelling of strife, lust, and desire, bears watchtowers - the heights of misery", where two camps reside, suppressing the Seed of God. These camps embody deception and harbor laboratories of destruction. The ancient evil scientists lured people into forgetfulness, diffusing the Light and altering the mankind's DNA. The Creator of the Universe, the Eternal Helper reigns supreme over the suppressors who forgot Him. They are the "watchers", owners of the inconsistent "sons" who spawned wicked giants by mating with human women. The Creator always reigns over the wicked.

Chapter 15

The deceiver, the orator of the word of trouble, manipulated God's Seed, His Word. He was among those who laid waste to everything with their deadly "vessels", trampling the vision of peace to enrich themselves. Followers of his teachings erected opulent palaces filled with idols, pyramids, and underground structures funded by stolen riches. Yet, they are mere "dust", forbidding praise of the Prime Creator within us.

Those who once praised God before their rebellion became earthly "thorns", embodiments of scorpions, rebelling against God's Holiness and afflicting His people. They are powerful and violent, perpetually at odds with God, establishing the rebellious house, a dwelling of desolation, where they conduct genetic manipulation of the human DNA. It was the place, a "fountain of fools", where the Seed of God, His Light, was trodden down. They wanted to dominate, to have power and riches, and to be the "creators, the openers". But it was a "city of woods, of wicked beings, the fortress of the sun", that God forbade.

They tried to eradicate God's Creation, the human cell. They created an afflicted society of "giants" who were abundantly furious. They were doing manipulations with the "seed" of men by inserting into the cell the harmful parasitic bacteria (the mitochondria), which decreased the span of life. Also, they changed the process in the "seed" (the DNA) by changing the vibrational frequencies, the "languages in the seed cell" – the Book of Life, that are full of sacral information.

The Holy Seed of humankind was created by God to establish the congregation of God. Yet, the enemy of humanity endeavored to annihilate it. What was Holy to God, they sought to corrupt. "The Divisions of Song", intended as a gathering place to obey and hear God, were trapped by a malevolent supplanter. They erected the "house of expansion, the house of wolves", inhabited by wrathful men. What once was God's House degenerated into the "house of foolishness".

This generation shall be devoted to the deceiver's destruction, the branch of the fallen angels, the serpent who rebelled against the Creator and was cast out from Heaven. He deceived humankind, bringing spiritual and physical death upon God's Tabernacle—the bodies of men. His troops, the builders of the "watch towers", induced heart-coldness through their speculative utterances. However, the enemy, living apart from God, shall be subdued by Him. The House of God will face many divisions due to their alignment with the supplanter's teachings. Because of the lies and deceptions perpetrated by the ancient serpent, the House of God will turn away from God.

The ancient serpent, a thief oppressing the people, trapped them in the prison of sin. In beautiful buildings, he shall challenge God's judgment and in the "city of thorns", he shall afflict the Word. Those who draw near to him shall dwell in the "house of grief, built on sand". Some shall proliferate like locusts in silence, deceived and rendered as shadows. The "land of goats" shall be trampled under the feet of the Son of God, the Seed of Light, the Soldier of God, the Vision of Peace. This same transformation and enlightenment shall extend to the human body, establishing peace upon the Earth and within humanity.

Chapters 16-17

Judgment shall emanate from the House of God upon those who sow division, adorned with "crowns of power". A "house of wrath" shall multiply, forgetting that the Light of God resides within the head of man, in the Crown of the "bright". These "houses" shall become sites of forgetfulness due to the deceiver's influence, fostering sin.

The Seed of Light, flourishing within the soul and heart, serves as the Savior, delivering from the "house of vanity and trouble". Those who induced forgetfulness, deceiving with knowledge of evil, themselves forgot God, the Father of help. Those who once served God near His throne succumbed to fear. Because of the destroyer, who sold the knowledge of sin, wickedness surged. People forgot God's Rest, the Eternal Savior and the Deliverer.

The one who propagated sin shall face judgment in the River of Judgment (the cerebrospinal fluid in the spinal cord of man) and in the world. The negative energies within man's spinal cord shall transmute into the Light, dispelling darkness. The enemy fostered a "fountain of infiltration of reeds", amplifying forgetfulness and rebellion and creating a disobedient generation in the "house of sleep". However, the Leader of God's Army, the Savior, shall triumph over the "house of sleep". They shall be scattered, and the consciousness of God's people shall elevate, with the Seed of God ascending.

Chapter 18

Those who contend with God struggle with His Rest, His Word, and His Seed of Light. He is the Savior, the Praise of God. The army of rebellious beings, once God's sons, were the rebellious "sons" who landed on Earth from dark spaces, the "house of vanity and trouble". They distanced themselves from the House of God, forsaking their crowns of power. They forged the "house of wrath, the city of wood", brimming with riches and full of bloody crimes.

These places degenerated into wastelands on Earth, dust-filled abodes. These elevated houses became the "wealth of speculation", exalting false gods and their power. The deceiver wreaked this destruction of God's House.

Chapter 19

The people of God shall inhabit the "wolf's house", facing the destruction of the House of God and the human body. They shall be crushed, residing in the "house of bitterness". Despite much talk and praise, it shall be a subdued pit steeped in slumber. Amidst beautiful, opulent buildings, fear shall persist, masquerading as aid, stretching yet twisting the Gift of Grace bestowed by God. These deceptions shall be propagated by a man, self-styled as "little" (Paul/Saul – "little destroyer"), to be praised. However, he shall serve as a thorn and a drag, cursing the House of God where he dwells. He shall induce slumber, spreading fear and discord.

Even though he may gain popularity by claiming that his teachings are divine, his deception will "muddy the waters". He will transform the House of Gladness into a house of divisions, promoting the worship of the "black sun" and elevating wickedness. His preaching will be poisoned and deceptive, proclaiming: "God is King!", while advocating for human sacrifices. There will be a false worship of the "fish god", feigning God's presence while engaging in sun worship. People will mistakenly believe they are worshiping the Rock, but they will worship the liar. He will infiltrate the congregation like a rapid torrent, turning the House of God into a black hollow.

The congregation will be left confused, angry, divided and empty, lured by the deceiver and elevating him within the sanctuary. However, he will be as insignificant as grass, hay, and the raven. There will be affliction, strife, judgment, and turmoil in the city of bondage, turning away from the God of Rest, Grace, and Mercy. They will praise the son of vanity, who blasphemes the Name of the

Son of God, the Everlasting Portion of God, the Savior, and the Peace of God.

Chapters 20-22

God's Light resides within the body of man, who will rule alongside God. He is the Deliverer of His sanctuary and the Well of revolution for those who fight. However, the congregation that forgets God will be destroyed in the River of Judgment. Only those who exalt the Seed of God, the Help of God, the Eternal Savior, will constitute the Congregation of Light.

"The son of sorrow", who caused the fall and forgetfulness of the people, will dwell among the congregation of God. Those who obey him will bring much grief, twisting the Truth and turning away from God's Word. "The son of sorrow, the son of the right hand", who is the ancient serpent, will restore the "house of the sun". He will pretend to reveal hidden secrets to the congregation, dividing them and establishing "a house of wrath", judging God's Grace and Mercy.

Pretending to offer happiness, peace, governance and service, the enemy will ensnare the congregation in chains of fear, forgetfulness, banishment, and death. The congregation will become a battleground, a sanctuary of revolts, where bitter people dwell, deceived into thinking it uplifts them. They will believe they are praising God, but in truth, it will be the domain of the ancient dragon. Though they may appear as lofty places of worship, they will be dens of wickedness, incited by the ancient serpent.

Yet, the Seed of Light, the Prince of God, will prevail with the strength of God, reigning over those who oppose Him. The Sacred Secretion, the Seed of Light, will rescue people from forgetfulness, while God will judge those who forsake Him, following the serpent's deceitful words from the east. The Prince of Peace and those who believe in Him will constitute the Army of God.

Chapter 24

The Savior, the Leader of God's Army, empowered by the Holy Spirit of God, will vanquish the deceiver who rebelled against the God of Heaven. However, the foolish ancient serpent and all the wicked people scattered worldwide will worship the image of the sun, deceived by the tempestuous deceiver, who will ultimately be consumed by God's Light, destroyed like dirt in the radiance of God's glory.

JUDGES

Chapter 1

The long-awaited Savior, the remedial and enlightening Inner Spiritual Light of God in man, is the Christ Mind brimming with Divine wisdom, who will prevail against the wretched wickedness of the people that are being pupated by the alien crusader. He is the One who praises, proclaims His Supremacy, and obeys God without erring.

The first generations of humanity, the ones blessed with God's numerous gifts, were connected to the Creator and always guided through the Divine Light within that was imbued in them to stay on the track of righteousness. But later, they dropped their guard and abandoned the Holy Protection and allowed themselves to be fettered mercilessly in the demonic "chains" being stripped of their light, freedom, and peace by the dishonorable and macabre enemy as they believed him, and ultimately compromised their authority.

They were masterfully blinded by the "gods of false light" pretending to be saviors and messiahs to liberate men from misery, but behind them were wicked demonic reptilian monsters and the giants with plans to subjugate men and plague them with their merciless inventions. They dwelt on Earth, hidden as either saviors or "little" to enslave humanity and rob the Earth of its gold and minerals and its people of happiness and serenity. People who couldn't identify their tricks fell prey to their beguiling frauds and ended up following them, becoming the wayward and pitiable society of the "son of sorrow", the serpent.

The alien robbers manipulated and twisted the Word of God to ensure men weren't left with a corrective guide, and for that, they corrupted His Divine Seed in the human body. They tried to manipulate and debauch it by the eradication of the "Language of the Fire" - the DNA blueprint, the Codex without flaws and cure for every ailment. They are those who inoculated misery in men and caused lasting sorrow. They intoxicated the human seed with parasitic bacteria (the mitochondria with the reptilian DNA in the cells, "the little"), causing the mutation of the "Pasture" – the Divine DNA blueprint, switching off, meddling with, and manipulating the spiritual genetic material of humankind and decreasing the span of human life.

They invaded, occupied, and ravaged the Earth and made it a place of endless weeping and chaotic preponderant trouble by destroying it through deadly weapons made with technology that was advanced and built for the sole purpose of weakening men. The ancient dragon was out prowling, hunting after the faithful people, targeting those who praise and obey God so that he could first eradicate those who will resist him. He is the utter and mindless destruction, the strong, stubborn, and vain "goat and fire of infirmity". He is trying to wipe off the faithful, loyal, and fearless worshippers of God and replace them with the corrupted offspring of the reptilian race. They infiltrated every place of authority and power, including the governments and the church, disguising themselves as faithful and honorable leaders, but they are serving their "master", who has the foulest intention of enslaving people by fear and mind control and by fogging their judgment through the false guilt, wrong teaching and manipulations.

He is the clever ancient dragon, the accuser and despiser of men, the belligerent and shallow-minded "son of sorrow". He will try to tread and trample God's Profound Peace that God bestowed upon men as a Divine Shelter under his "feet" through his army of lost that is scheming and waging secret wars against the men. He is the one who will cause chaos, confusion, and turbulence in the House of God through separations and divisions by wickedness, lies, betrayals, and forgetfulness, by nurturing the false ego in men, and by giving fuel for the carnal lower nature of men to grow and take control of men.

They will build the "house of spiritual sleep" on the Earth, where men will be mindless and soulless and will be gripped in terrible anguish. The untiring and proud enemies of God caused this unrelenting sorrow to humanity by burning the "Pasture of happiness", corrupting the Divine spiritual part of the DNA, contaminating and deconstructing the Seed of God. They did it by mixing the serpent's seed with the flawed codex into the pious and pure Seed of humankind through fertility, using their advanced technology. There was a rapid torrent of "happiness" when it all began to make men believe that whatever the serpent was doing was for the betterment of men, but the rapture was short-lived, and misery followed.

There will be "houses of sun" (churches) falsely enlightened, with false and treacherous preachers, where the false "light" will be used as a "guiding light" and human sacrifice will be worshiped and celebrated. There will be fight, bitterness, and the "chains of judgment" that will clutch the hearts and the souls of people as "scorpions" not allowing them to fix and cleanse themselves through the Divine Flame that resides in them.

Chapters 2-3

God, the infinite Intelligence within the depths of human existence, reigns supreme over the evil entities that descended upon the Earth in their "circle chariots", the celestial ships. They transformed this once serene planet into a realm of tears and turmoil. Within the human vessel resides the Eternal Savior, the Divine Consciousness, a beacon of the Light amidst the darkness. However, the adversary, steeped in idolatry, brought forth false deities, worshipping the image of the sun and false gods. They pretended to be the "masters", imposing their dominion over mankind, treating them as mere chattel and obedient followers.

The Seed of Light within, the loyal God's Soldier, shares sovereignty with the Divine over the wicked and rebellious souls scattered across the world.

The evil people caused destruction and anger and tried to mess up the peace that God wanted for everyone. They went against God, praised "false gods", and worshipped them instead of God who's inside each person. Because they did this, they became like darkness.

Those who came to live on Earth between two rivers (Mesopotamia, Ancient Sumer) were sinful because they did these evil things twice as much. But, the Prince of God, His Light Seed, is faithful to God's Force within the man. He is the Ruler and a powerful Force of God within people. He's in charge and can control all the crimes.

The Prime Creator, who controls time and everything, is against the enemy's troops, who came in their "chariots, the flying machines". They are the wicked, nonhuman, demonic beings with advanced technologies, the bandits, who are the strangers on Earth, the "evil wanderers".

Even though the serpent's power may grow stronger, the Prince of God, who works with God, will beat the strangers of poverty.

Chapter 4

Those who forged the swords and migrated from the dark spaces rendered people spiritually "deaf and blind", binding the nations into the suffocating "chains" of death. The Seed of God, the

Inner Light, was tragically impeded from its rightful ascent within man as Authority and Inner power were carelessly given away. The place of dwelling, the pineal gland, once the Gate for God's Spirit to communicate with the man, was corrupted. They built the "castles of swords", their sinister genetic "laboratories", where they used advanced genetic technology to do experiments with genetic manipulations.

Because of their wickedness, rebellion, and sin against the Creator and His Cosmic Laws of Unity, they were cast out into the dark spaces and became the "cosmic vagabonds". They dwelt on Earth, destroyed, twisted, and "bound" in chains the Seed of God. They called themselves the "fathers", but they are those who caused men to be "deaf" to the fellowship with the Creator by using their wicked "knowledge" and their advanced technology, blocking them from the Truth.

Chapter 5

The "father of deception", the satan, shall wield the Word of God and His Name, the Essence of Light and Breath, to deceive humanity. Yet, only the Prince of Peace, the Seed of Light within the heart, is the Living Embodiment of God.

The "father of lies" and his minions shall espouse heresy and apostasy, cloaking themselves in false piety and righteousness while harboring pride, disobedience, and lawlessness. Lawlessness shall proliferate as human traditions and rituals, even human sacrifice, supplant the Cosmic Laws of the Creator.

All who adhere to the traditions of men over the Law of Oneness shall be deemed rebellious against God Himself. Those who propagate lawlessness under the guise of tradition shall be considered disobedient followers of the devil, the fabricator of swords, and the lover of war. A man of great pride, an agent of the serpent (Paul/Saul – "the little destroyer"), shall infiltrate the House of God to sow discord from within. Furthermore, the reptilian, the carnal mind, shall hold sway over the human vessel, bringing forth sickness, fear, poverty, and death.

Chapter 6

Those who suppress the divine Seed of Light within and defiantly disobey God's commandments will inevitably face the dire consequences of their disobedience. However, those who diligently elevate and safeguard the Sacred Seed of God, the hallowed Liquid Light, the Christ Oil, through serene and mindful meditation. By quieting the clamor of fearful thoughts and directing their focus inward towards the Divinity, residing within and the sanctified pineal gland, they will find themselves embraced by His Divine Grace and illuminated in the recesses of their minds.

The adversary of God, in his arrogant folly, has forsaken the Almighty and brazenly exalted himself as a "master". Those who align themselves with this adversary, defending his blasphemous cause, also, stand in disobedience before the Almighty. Divine judgment awaits those who sow seeds of turmoil, bitterness, and rebellion. They are but fleeting shadows, mere dust and sand, destined to be dissolved by the radiant Light from within.

However, those who place their unwavering trust in the Prime Creator, the Supreme Warrior, shall be enveloped in His Divine radiance as the dormant cells of their spiritual right hemisphere are revitalized and resurrected. God shall render judgment upon the wicked, yet He shall extend His steadfast support to the faithful, offering Salvation and restoration of the Cosmic nature of men.

Those who worship idols and defend the abhorrent practice of human sacrifice shall find themselves scattered by the Divine Hand of Justice, for they have willfully disregarded the sacred Laws of God.

The God of Righteousness, the Higher Self, shall preside over the judgment of the disobedient and rebellious souls. He is the God of "gods", the ultimate Arbiter who shall render judgment upon those who sow discord and bitterness.

Yet, those who place their unyielding trust in God, the mighty Warrior, and embark on the journey of spiritual meditation to elevate the Seed of Light within their beings, expanding their consciousness, shall experience a profound transformation from within. The Divine Mind in action, God Himself, shall pass judgment upon the wicked who have strayed from His path while extending His unwavering support and Salvation to the faithful.

Even as wickedness proliferates across the face of the Earth, God, the infinite mind, remains the sovereign Ruler over all creation. His Spirit shall serve as a Divine beacon of guidance and assistance to the faithful servants of God amidst the tumultuous trials of life.

Chapters 7-8

Those who passionately defended the "alien terrorists" are those who brazenly rebelled against Father/ Mother God - the Divine Consciousness. Their actions inflicted immeasurable pain and mourning, aimed at desecrating the inherent Goodness of God, the very Temple of God's Spirit - the sacred vessel of man's body. They descended upon the Earth in the guise of "wolves and ravens", agents of darkness, weaving their sinister webs.

Their rebellion against God and His Immutable Cosmic Laws of Unity persists unabated, for they are akin to insatiable "wolves and ravens", relentless in their pursuit of chaos. These wicked beings alighted upon the Earth, altering the very fabric of the human cell, a creation of God, by infiltrating it with foreign entities, the parasitic bacteria – the mitochondria - that produce the low, animal energy. (However, the Divine Light center in the cell – the

Centrosome, the nucleus, that connected with the Divine Source, the very "sun" of the cell, now begins to emit radiant energy, expelling the foreign bacteria from its core.)

They sacrificed and manipulated God's Seed, the sacred pineal gland, and burned the Divine information, the very "language" of God encoded within the DNA. Humanity was thus severed from God's protective embrace and the Divine connection with the Source of Light, severed from the spiritual DNA and the sanctified pineal gland. Instead, they were coerced into worshipping the "fallen angels", bowing before the images and idols of those who proclaimed themselves as "gods", thus perpetuating the insidious "cult of death" and human sacrifice. Yet, these entities are nothing but ancient serpents, deceptive "false gods".

Nonetheless, the valiant Soldier of God, the Seed of Light within, shall triumph over the reptilian mind, dismantling the idols and exposing the false "teachers" masquerading as "masters". They are the despicable "fathers of evil" who defend the evil.

Chapter 9

The deceitful one, the ancient serpent, the "prime architect"t of idolatry and duality on Earth, not only created but also fiercely defended idols. Once a "chief of angels", a servant, an enlightened being, he fell from grace due to his pride and jealousy, disobedient to God's Laws. Originally perfect, he deteriorated into a "waste".

He took up residence on Earth, emerging from the dark places of "abomination", elevating his own image above the covenant with the Perfect Creator and the unity with the Divine Mind.

Cast out from the heavenly realms, he found refuge on Earth and in the astral planes. In due time, the deceiver will perpetrate abominations, self-proclaiming as a "god", demanding unwavering worship.

Chapter 10

The "father" of the earthly kings and rulers who contend with God is a "worm's mouth" compared to the transcendent "Language" of God and His Spirit. The adversary is akin to the "thorn of the serpent", endeavoring to extinguish the Light of God within and supplant it with idols, advanced technology, and parasitic artificial intellect, who wants to destroy the biological life of the whole Universe. The enemy of the Prince of God, the Inner Light, will arise with the voice of the "dragon", craving adulation. His wickedness will increase, and his followers will erect "towers of watchers", idols of false worship.

The destructor, along with his negative energies and false ego, will face judgment and dissolution in the River of Judgement, the cerebrospinal fluid in the spinal cord of men, consumed by the Holy Fire of the Spirit of God, the Sacred Secretion. The negative, fearful ruminations of the carnal mind (the ego) will dissipate during meditation as attention turns inward to the Divine Love within.

The Seed of Light will vanquish the adversary's dominion within the human vessel. Furthermore, the Radiance of God will overshadow and conquer the "father of lies", false idols, and speculations.

Chapters 11-12

The relentless opposer, the pernicious destroyer, will oppose the protective Goodness of God, which usually presents God as the "sunlight". Being voraciously "hungry" and greedy for earthly popularity and control, he will deceive, beguile, and swindle people by twisting the Truth and concocting mind-boggling lies. He is one of the surreptitious scheming "watchers", crafting and deploying traps, the ardent and unwavering follower of satan, who "evacuated" from the planets and descended on Earth. He is the one who will be damaged and ravaged in the desert, who will ultimately lose at the hands of the Prince. After this, he will be nothing but a forgotten, sorry "invention of ruins" like a "rushing stream" (Paul/Saul - "little destroyer"). But he believes he will triumph, and for that, he will prepare the plot against the Prince of God, which he thinks will not fail. By using His Name to make it as foolproof as he can, through the speculation and falsified information to cause the forgetfulness and corruption of the Holy message, he will twist the Truth of God, falsely preaching the "salvation" through the senseless human sacrifice and irreversible loss, and portraying it as the "mercy of God".

All the people will fall prey to the schemes, consume the corrupted message and will tragically be deceived by the enemy. They will completely forget that they have the Divine protection and guidance of the Light within in the flesh. They will eventually end up so lost that they will rebel against the Creator, waging a war against Him and His Chosen Prince, and will breach all His Laws. They will be opposed, dismiss the Truth of God, attempting unrelentingly to contort this ultimate Truth. They will believe the lies of these false, brazenly shameless religious leaders, who will have one plan only. The plan is to lure people into the magnificent, hypnotizing temples, filled with temptations saying that they are the mediators between them and God when, but, in truth, they are the ushers of mankind's destruction.

The religious leaders will be strong in power as they will have amassed a humongous following and will be fortified with limitless wealth and resources. They will deceive and misguide people by leading them to worship their "false gods" who are powerless and incapable, instead of their truest and most honest Savior, a God-sent Messiah, the Prince of God who is the Seed of God's Light, the Inner Christ, capable of enlightening the darkest and most horrific path, preserved carefully within the body of man.

Chapters 13-21

The Prime Creator who lurks within, striving to keep a man on the correct path, is the Divine Love in action, correcting, rectifying, and recalibrating man's consciousness. He is the Consciousness of the Light to the world with the purpose of keeping man from destroying himself. He will judge and hold in righteous, unbiased retribution all those unfaithful, wicked, and bewitched people who have changed and debased God's Law, spoiling it to turn them into delusional commandments of man, along with those who will worship the sun as the Divine and Savior, instead of the benevolent Prime Creator.

The bettering, non-indulgent Essence of the Living God within man will be substituted by the corrupt image of the "god of sun". However, it won't persist for long as the Spirit of God, which is under the blessing and fortification of the Righteous God, will destroy the opposing powers, pulverizing them and banishing them to an eternal punishment.

The places where the "god of sun" will be worshiped and revered will be like a "wild beast's" place, untethered and lawless and brimming with filth and impurity. These deceiving "spirits of the serpent" will invade and then dwell in the body of man.

When the moon enters the birth zodiac sign, the Seed of Light within which is restorative, produces the Sacred Secretion fluid, psycho-physical oil, that is preserved as the Elixir of Life. It will rise along the spinal cord of man, strengthening it on its way, cross the "jawbone" place and seep into the head of man, awakening him for the corrective change. The power of the Seed will be increased a thousand times and will jolt awake the pineal and pituitary glands. This, in turn, will sprout the "Fountain of Living Waters", a powerful Healing Light, condensed and crystalized within the people who praise, obey, and recognize the true God for what He is, and will not be destroyed by the carnal desires but have protected the preserved Holy Seed.

The congregation of worshipers of the sun will inflate, growing stronger and stronger as more and more people will succumb to temptations offered by the serpent. But God will not forsake His loyal ones and separate His "vineyard" of faithful believers from the "false", misguided, and mislaid believers who would have spread like a "fish" and will be busy in their worship on the sun's day.

Those who will humble themselves before God earnestly and with all their heart and mind obey Him, meditating upon Him in the

Spirit and the Truth, will be strengthened in the power of God from within.

The Prince of God will be His chosen Arbitrator as He will judge the wicked people - the unfaithful congregation, that will increase as time goes by until the Prince of God descends with the swift Justice. The humble and unfaltering Servant, the innocent and pure Lamb, will be like a Lion of God against the evildoers. Once cleansed of all the wickedness, the Holy Spirit of God will create the New Earth (the New Mind), which will then be celebrated as the Kingdom of God, a place without sin. He will permanently judge and cast out the rebellious people because He is the Holy Fire, sent by God to cleanse and purify eternally.

The Son of God, the Seed of Light within, blessed with infinite wisdom through the Divine Mind and the believers who will follow and obey Him will be fruitful as they will get to reap the ultimate reward. And soon these pious and cleansed people will increase in the House of God. "The serpent" and his people will be vanquished and delivered under the "feet" of the Prince of Peace who is the Right Hand of God, destined to be victorious.

The Prince of God, the declaration of Righteousness, and the Word of God is a "Well of the Living Waters", brimming with potent and uplifting imbuements and is the decisive Right Hand of the Prime Creator (the spiritual, right hemisphere of the brain). He is, also, the Watch Tower who will fend off the enemy, evaporating and destroying the confusion of the masses. He will bring the lasting Peace to the House of God. He will bring, also, the Divine Rest from the Heaven, which will embrace everyone who is lost and embrace the corrective ways because He is the Divine Seed of abundance and the Peace of God for all mankind.

RUTH

Chapter 1

Those who came from the House of God were perfect, without a blemish, but became the wretched infirmity. When they were devoutly obedient to God and uncorrupted, they were abundantly fruitful but later, after their blatant and shameless disobedience, became the barbaric destroyers, the evil demonic entities.

They will be reined in and chained by the Mighty Redeemer. He will put in chains and hold accountable those who disturbed and destroyed God's Peace and turned people into weak, discontented, mindless "sheep". He will justly and swiftly, without a bias, put in "chains" those who rebelled against the Delight of God and churned up a mutiny against His peaceful House.

Chapters 2-4

God's Delight is encapsulated as His Strength and His Divine Beauty within the man, which bestows the real, spiritual Identity of the man. He will save, salvage, and redeem those who were shackled and trapped by the false "father", the cunning and hateful serpent. He is the devout, valiant Soldier, the chosen and glorified Prince of God, who will be the ultimate Redeemer from the infirmity, the fortifier. He will shatter the destructive "programs" made to weaken God's men, made potent by the deadly nanotechnologies, that were inserted, imbued into and imposed upon the men by the antagonistic, malevolent demonic entities.

The enemy caused the divisions between people, an unsurmountable rift, and tried to enchant and beguile them to sectionalize them and divide them by luring and hypnotizing them under a finely curated guise of being "peaceful", acting as a pacifist and parading the notion: "My people are liberal!". But the real, unputdownable Strength of God, His chosen Enforcer, is His Servant who is highly rightfully ordained as His Beloved, as He is the incorruptible and Pure Essence of cleansing Light within the man who will tap into his true gifts from God and be empowered. He could finally be resurrected from the hypnotic slumber he was put into by the heinous serpent, through self-correcting and self-empowering meditation.

1 SAMUEL

Chapter 1

The "watchers", the reptilian race from the dark spaces, who were increasing in their jealousy of the Divine Creator, declared themselves independent from the Creator. Their control over the Earth will expand, and they will elevate themselves above the Mercy of God even more. They tried to destroy God's precious Stone - the place of connection and reception of God's Eternal energy, the pineal gland. What was the "place of Trust and protection" became the "place of pride".

Chapters 2-5

Those who worshiped the merciful God became wicked after their rebellion and elevated themselves as "vessels" of God. They dwelt in different places on Earth, oppressed people, and spoiled the Divine Seed of God. They called themselves "gods, the creators". But the Crystal of God's Light, the Stone of Help, the pineal gland, is within the brain of man (the Ark of the Covenant), the place of abundance of the Divine Consciousness. The enemies are the evil demonic entities, the thieves, who came from the sea as a "dragon". They tore away the Divine Seed of God, the Messenger of Light. The Light of God will smash them as in a "winepress" and the evil demonic entities will be rooted out.

Chapters 6-8

The "watchers", who are the troublesome "gods of the house of Sun", will be destroyed. The wicked one, who proclaimed himself to be strong, will be rooted out by the Fire of the Spirit of God, the Savior. The "house of sun" will be destroyed by the Leader of God's Army, the Divine Seed of God, the inner quantum of the Light.

They called themselves "gods", elevated themselves, and ruled over the people. But the Commander of God's Army will overcome the evil interventions of those who entered the Earth and brought destruction. The one who was faithful to God before the rebellion decided that he would be worshiped instead of the Leader of God's Army.

Chapters 9-12

The destroyer, the serpent, who is the "stranger", will declare: "God is my Father!". He will bind the "first fruits" of deliverance by speaking harshly, striving for the death of the faithful Servant, and later proclaiming himself as God. The "watchers" will be like "foxes", who will damage the vineyard. There will be a false prophet, the "son of the devil".

The people of God will be like "sheep" who will follow the false prophet, who is the "wicked shadow". He will bruise the House of God and will grieve His Spirit. Because of his wickedness, the people of God will feel like being in a "prison of wickedness". The ancient reptiles, the "dragons", are those who brought confusion to the people. They are those who caused people to sin, but the Divine Seed of God, the Deliverer with the Power of God, will roll away the sin. The Divine Seed of God's Light will conquer the death through the Sacred Secretion, the Holy (Christ) Oil, in the brain of those who meditate on the Light within. Those who will hear God but will fight with Him, will be bound in "chains" in the courts of God. They are those false "fathers" who intervened on Earth, and they are false "masters" who created and defended idols. They are the people of the "seed of the serpent".

Chapters 13-14

Those who brought death and struggle against God, striking the House of God, hail from the "hills of ruins". These malevolent demonic entities constructed a "house of vanity" for the troops that descended on Earth on the "machines of death" circle. They are "the foxes, the dust, jackals, goats", purveyors of death.

They destroyed nearly everything bestowed by God, instilling fear into the essence of man where the Glory and Power of God (the DNA) and the Goodness of God reside. The "destroyer, the serpent's seed" will masquerade as a "peacemaker" but embodies the "mud of the enemy", striking down those attempting to elevate themselves to the level of the Heavenly King.

The enemy, the "father of wickedness", sows bloody violence and breeds "plantations" of evil people. He will engage in battle with the Prince of God, who is flawless, the Counsellor, and the Light, proclaiming: "God is my Father!".

Chapters 15-17

The ancient serpent, with the "spirit of death", will be exalted by unstable, "sand-like" wicked individuals who gravitate towards violence and war. He will be akin to a "flaming circle of death", yet the Prince of God, the Divine Mind, the Spiritual Conscience, will roll him away.

Those who are responsible for desolating the House of God will elevate themselves above God. People were sacrificed to "negative aliens", evil demonic entities who were posing as "gods" and leading people towards desolation from God. Human sacrifices occurred in the "houses of wickedness", and the "alien's heights" became the "walls of wickedness". Tempted by lust, anger, and greed, it became a "grave" for the Divine Seed of Light due to violent interventions of evil forces. The Divine Seed of God, the Light bestowed by God, was nearly eradicated, but the Beloved of

God is the Inner Divine Light of man, His Gift, and the Savior from death, emptying Himself to destroy the enemy.

Chapters 18-22

God will bestow the Savior, the Divine Seed of Light, who will fight for His people, perfect and relentless against the enemy. The Beloved, the Divine Seed of God awakening our hearts to Divine Love, will also emerge from heavenly realms. Inner Divine Light from the High Heavenly places mirrors His Prime Creator, fighting for His spiritual children.

The Beloved, the Divine Seed of God, is the Breath gifted by God, feared by the earthly enemy. He will engage in a real fight within man, providing the Rest for those imprisoned by the enemy and offering praises for deliverance.

Those who masqueraded as "gods, brothers of goodness" are rebellious "angels" consumed by fear. However, the Beloved is the Excellent Father of the faithful remnant.

Chapters 23-26

The destroyers who divided and manipulated God's Blueprint (the DNA) became "the mouth of falsehood", constructing "houses of sin and desolation". Yet the Divine Seed of God, His Rock, and Fountain of Happiness will demolish the "house of desolation", the carnal mind within man's body.

The enemies attempted to divide the Divine Seed of God, the Spiritual Essence, corrupting the Fountain of happiness, the pineal gland, into a "fountain of death", elevating themselves as "creators". However, the Holy Spirit of God, His Light descending from Heaven, embodies the Beauty and Glory of His Creator, projecting God's Joy unto the faithful, scattering the enemy as the Lion who protects, covers, and delivers them from falsehood.

Those who follow false prophets and disobey God will find themselves in a spiritual "desert", becoming the "waste" of the world, destroyed. People will fear them as "gods and fathers", believing they created them, yet they are the manipulators who orchestrated their destruction. People will worship them as "fathers of light" though they are the "fathers of false light".

Chapters 27-31

The Beloved Son of God will destroy the angry men who have oppressed humanity in the "bath of the winepress". The Beloved will gather all true believers.

God will receive the Harvest of the true believers who remain faithful to God's Laws. The enemy will persecute the true believers, who will praise the Living God within humanity.

Violent aliens spoiled the Divine Seed of God, and the Earth became a "fountain of evil dwelling". God will scatter the fortress of the enemy through His Holy Seed. The enemy will be destroyed, and the "carnal kingdom" within humanity will be destroyed as well. It will be the materialization of the Holy Spirit into the Holy Essence in the human spinal cord, from the base to the head. This Essence is called the Sacred Secretion, the Holy Liquid Fire, that elevates the lower conscience to the Higher Conscience of man, reactivates the dormant cells in the right chemosphere of the brain and unites in harmony both the chemospheres through the pineal gland.

The Word of God – the Light information, the Blueprint of God – was tainted, twisted, and deactivated by evil demonic entities. (97% of human DNA, which is responsible for spiritual intuition, was switched off and labeled as "junk"). The foolish enemy corrupted His Word, the Divine DNA, and the Place of Fragrance of God's Mercy has become wasted as a "smoking furnace".

The violent beings, the "fountain of death", will be destroyed by the "Father of willingness". He will dismantle "the house of sleeping sheep and sleeping shepherds, the house of shame".

2 SAMUEL

Chapter 1-2

The Divine Seed of God's Light, also, known as His Beloved, the Inner Divine Light given by God, who is the Living Creator, will overpower the evil people and the low carnal vibrations in man's body. This Seed will destroy them forever, and the Holy Spirit, who is known as the Source of Joy, will sow the Beloved into the confused world and the carnal flesh. The destroyer, before his rebellion, was once the worshipper of the Creator of Light.

There will be a man who will be the "son" of the ancient serpent. He will be a "man of shame, the temporary tent" who will preach false freedom. He will be the "son of the father of lies and pain", and he comes from the hills. He is a "destroyer, the serpent's seed". He will be creative in speech, fully committed to his evil assignment, and eager to achieve his destructive goals (the "apostle" Paul/Saul – "little destroyer").

The Divine Seed of Light, The Spiritual Essence, will voluntarily enter the carnal flesh, and there will be a transformation of the Spiritual Seed into the material Holy Essence, which is called the Holy Sacred Secretion, the Holy "Christ Oil" in the spinal cord of man, connecting men to the universal energy. This Holy Seed is the Presence of God made by God, who will judge the enemy for causing divisions in God's House and creating two opposite armies. The Inner Divine Light and "the destroyer" are both the creations of the Creator and will be in the House of God.

In the same way, the Divine Seed of God and the "seed of the serpent" are both in the body of man. Therefore, in the minds and hearts of men, there will always be a war between good and evil, life and death.

Chapter 3

Society will be divided into two camps. The first camp will be under the rulership of the faithful and true Beloved, who is the perfect One, the Joy of the Creator, and the Royal Ruler over those who built cities and spaces with walls. The Prime Creator will defend the Beloved, as He is His Joy.

The second camp will be under the rule of the demonic false leader, who rebelled against the Creator of Light. He will also have his own followers, and he is like a "man of shame and a hawk", fighting against the Beloved and His people. But the Beloved of God will judge the enemy, who is like a "lion, the lover of the wars". The Seed of Light is the same as the Creator, who is Perfect, and the Deliverer from the "man of shame".

The Beloved of God is the Body of Light within the men, the real Essence of men, and is the Lamp for all humanity. He is God's

Presence, who will be lifted, the Soldier of God and the Balm for the pain. The Sacred Secretion, the Rescue Oil, will be raised up in the spinal cord of the man and will reactivate the Crystals of the Divine Consciousness, the Godself, in the brain and in the heart. The whole body of man will be renewed and healed, and man's consciousness will be transformed into the Divine Consciousness.

Chapter 4

The destroyer of society caused confusion, conflicts and separation between the people. He exalted himself above the Living God as the "son of God". He deactivated the Wealth (spiritual 10 strands of the DNA) that God, the Living Creator, gave to human beings as the Divine Heritage and Authority. The Wealth that the Creator had sown was destroyed by the enemy with artificial intellect and advanced technology.

They are those who exalted themselves in pride because of the absence of the Living Spirit of God in them. They lost the connection with the Source of Light, and, therefore, they did not have the part of the brain that reflected the divine connection. To control and use us as "batteries", they disconnected humanity from the Source of Light. They pressed down the Treasure of God, the Seed of Light, bent the Wealth of God, and blamed and shamed man for that.

Chapter 5

The Divine Seed of Light refers to the Divine Mind, The Mountain of God, and the Sharp Stone for the destroyer. Those who obey God's Law of Unity will be rewarded and united with the Source, who is perfect.

They will hear God's voice, receive His knowledge, and the Divine Seed of God will be their Salvation. The Light will transform and revive the dormant cells of the right side of the human brain (the Divine Feminine) and clean the cardiovascular system. The nervous system, which was once the "tree of knowledge of good and evil", the reflection of duality and programmed just for survival, will return to its original state of the co-creator as the Tree of Life, the reflection of Oneness with the Creator, full of Light. This will be a spiritual awakening for humanity, and people will awaken from their spiritual "amnesia". They will remember that they are the microcosm of the entire Macrocosm of the Universe.

Chapters 6-9

The Beloved, the Divine Seed of Light within, is the Ruler, the Father of Willingness, the Son of God, His Strength, and the Servant of humanity. He will bestow rewards upon God's people, who will face persecution by the "serpent". He will restore humanity's heightened awareness and its Divine nature.

The "space wanderers", the destroyers of God's Gift, have unleashed the bridle of the "beauty of assistance". They have incited space wars, devastating and rendering lifeless numerous planets. However, God will dispatch His faithful servants, who possess knowledge of the Divine, into the world.

The Savior will arise in the brain and restore the spiritual part of the DNA of men to dismantle the army of "space traders, the draconian seed", who sought to annihilate the generation of nativity. They introduced death and lifeless artificial technology, yet the Beloved, who is The Perfect Foundation of God's Peace, will dissolve the destructive energies, the carnal kingdom of the flesh, and reestablish the Kingdom of God within.

Chapter 10

The destroyer, "the serpent's seed", who is the deceiver, will masquerade as "merciful and gracious". However, he is the lying serpent who sowed the "plantations of the clones", generating beings with mixed seeds through genetic manipulation and cloning. These beings lack a divine nature and engage in conflict amongst themselves.

The Gift of God was perverted by the "fallen angels", ensnaring humanity in the chains of the destroyer's lies due to their malevolent deeds.

The Inner Divine Mind will judge those who descended upon the Earth.

Chapter 11

The Inner Divine Light, the Fire of God, will triumph over those who follow the serpent, and the Son of God will establish the Peace. The Beloved will serve as the Well of Truth for God's people. Those who were broken will be restored, proclaiming: "God is my Light, the Father, and the King!". The idolaters will face destruction because the Beloved, the Holy Spirit in the Heart, is the Fire of God, annihilating the idols of confusion.

Chapters 12-14

The Inner Divine Light will combat the "fallen angels", once bearers of light before their rebellion. The Beloved of God, akin to God, will be exalted and ascended by God along the human's spinal cord.

The adversary, claiming to be the "father of peace", will proliferate like a palm tree. He will present himself as "faithful and true, obedient, granting liberty", yet he is the "ruler of hay". He deceives with false praise and erects "valleys of walls", masquerading as "the father of peace".

The Creator of His Son is the God of Peace and the Union of Masculine and Feminine Powers, not their division. He will sound the Trumpet for His people. The Divine Mind, the Spiritual Conscience, is the Bridge to the peace and liberation from the "dragon's slavery".

Chapter 15

The "false father of peace", disrupting society, is the "brother of ruins", and his promises of peace will overturn his folly.

He is the "plug man, the winepress", shattering society, plunging everything into darkness and death, justifying it as a quest for peace. Emerging from dark, lifeless realms, he is the "brother of ruins", not the Father of Peace.

However, the Inner Divine Light, the Prince of God, is the true Father/Mother of Peace. He will rescue humans from the wicked as the Just Father/Mother of the remnant, emerging from the High, not from the "place of folly". His Creator is the Godhead, the Union of the Divine Father and Divine Mother. The Creator will judge those who remain silent about the Truth but will vindicate faithful believers. He is the Exemplary Source of Love for the true believers.

Chapter 16

The Inner Divine Light is the Word of God, who truly hears and obeys Him. However, the army of those who pretend to be the "fathers of peace" has destroy the Divine presence of the Creator, and they are the "brothers of folly".

The human "planters, the hybrids", were the real destroyers without shame. They fought against the Beloved, causing pain and dividing the Gift of God. Those who follow them are the "fathers of ruins", who fooled around, being the "false fathers".

Chapter 17

The deceiver, the "brother of ruins" of humanity, has spoiled the Divine Essence of God (the spiritual DNA of humans). They also blocked the energy centers and rewired the nervous system into the regime of survival and fear. They made people violent, warlike, and lustful, causing wars among them. People became angry, fearful, jealous, and greedy as their level of consciousness decreased. People forgot their Divinity, and the deceiver turned them into captivity, the source of "energy food" for serpent entities. These extraterrestrial vampires, who miniaturized themselves by using their advanced vibrational technology, have been controlling the minds of people for thousands of years from the lower astral plane, but they are like a temporary "tent" on Earth.

The enemy of humanity is the ancient serpent, who is greedy, violent, and disobedient to the Cosmic Laws of Unity.

But the Divine Seed of God's Light will dissolve the enemy in the River of Judgment - the Sacred Secretion, the Holy Christ Oil, that illuminates the body and brain of man. People who remain faithful to the Creator of Joy will overcome the enemy and will prosper.

Chapters 18-20

The Divine Seed of God, who is the Gift of God, will roll away the enemy, the "space pilgrims". The enemy is the violent ancient serpent, who rebelled against God and His Seed. He is the "planter of death", who descended from the dark, lifeless astral spaces. People became the same as them - violent and angry like their "fathers". They tried to destroy the Foundation of Peace, causing pain, shame, and tribulations. The "space trades", the evil demonic entities, are the source of disobedience and divisions in the Ancient Divine Builders Race.

They are wicked creatures who spared no people and made them captive slaves. They violently tore away the Gift of God given to the people of Nativity. However, the Divine Seed of God's Light is the Ruler over the "watchers" and all people of the Earth.

Chapters 21-22

The Inner Divine Light and the deceiver are both created by God. The destroyer, the "raven", was cast out from the High space with other "fallen angels" who followed him due to his rebellion against the Creator.

The "son of sorrow", with his wicked troops, occupied the Earth, seduced women, and created the "giants". But the Prince, given by God, will hear and obey His Creator. He will be like a Winepress for those who disobeyed the Creator.

Chapter 23

The Beloved is the Gift of God, the Prince of God who will prevail by the Spirit of God. He is the Rock of God against the wicked men. Adorned by God, He is His Help, who will prevail over those who occupied the Earth, for He is the Ruler of the Earth, the mountains, and the valleys. He is the Prince of God, destined to prevail over the wickedness of the "giants" who seek to occupy the House of Bread (the solar plexus) and to transcend the justice and traditions of people.

But before that, the House of Bread will be divided, and the "giants" will oppress the Son of God, His Beloved, His begotten Son, the Zeal of God, the Knowledge, and Wisdom of God. The House of God will be torn asunder by terror, and people will succumb to fear. Those who are deceived by demonic forces and follow them will proclaim "liberation and deliverance", but it will be the vision of a man with a wicked and pervasive mouth. (Paul/Saul – "the little destroyer")

"Salvation" will purportedly be built on prayers to the "false father of help". His image will be swiftly crafted by wicked men of the world, by the "son of the oppressor, the plug man with strife, from the wicked towers". He was the "son of sorrow", once leading worshipers in heaven, but became the tempest, the most intelligent turned wicked and violent against God.

He turned the Earth into the "earth of foxes", desolating it from the mountains. The "false brother" of truth will be exiled, the one who will open the "doors" to destruction, disturbance, and violence. He will raise an army, fizzing with anger. The Well of God will be divided, filled with pain and tribulation by the "watchmen" riddled with scabs. They will declare: "God is my Father!", yet they will be consumed by fear.

Chapter 24

The Beloved, the Divine Seed of God's Light, is the Judge, the Well of promise, Tamarisk, whom God helps, but the wicked people will be worshipped, not the Vision of Peace. The Beloved of God will crush them under His feet, and there will be joyful songs and cries.

1 KINGS

Chapter 1

The Beloved, the God-Chosen Inner Divine Light, administered directly by God, is the One who will prevail with God against the "father of error, the propagator of all evils and vices". The one who proclaims to be a generous "father of people", in truth, is the "father of sleep, or the morally depraved and dormant". He says: "God is my Master of the festivals". The "father of false peace", the alien deceiver, will become the "father of plenty", which is his lure to beguile people with abundance and temptations. The Son of God, who is Just and Righteous, who is the Knowledge of God, His Enlightenment, will be given only to those who will hear and obey and fight alongside the Shepherd, the Beloved, the Master of Peace.

The ancient dragon, the invasive, treacherous serpent, is the "little stone, the fountain of foolishness" and the "seed of corruption". Many believers, due to the alien's false and hypnotic pretense, will wrongly think that they are praising God and earning His good graces, but in truth, they will be praising and obeying and worshipping the "father of error".

The Gift of God, the Divine Light within, the Infallible, who is the Son of God, will become the Valley of Grace, the Sanctuary of Correction and Healing, and He will destroy the destroyer, uprooting it from all its hidden sources and banishing and crushing the enemy once and for all. He is the Prince of God who will chant God's winning slogan as He proclaims: "God is my Master of Peace".

Chapter 2-8

The Light of God within, the Eliminator of all Darkness, will overcome and conquer the enemy, who is known as the "father of pain and tribulation", whose mission is to torment and weaken human minds and hearts. He used to be a "bearer of the light" as he was among the ones gifted with Grace and Knowledge, but he abandoned the ways of righteousness and ended up transforming into the "son of contention". The Prime Creator, who is the Mother/Father of Light and the Most Benevolent, will not abandon those who meditate and listen to what guides them from the inside as He will guide, deliver and protect His faithful and loyal followers through His Light. Those who will choose to follow and obey the enemy, the ones who will dispute with the righteous despite God giving them chances to repent, will subsequently be labeled "the sons of sorrow", and it will be a sin of their own choosing.

There will be two opposing armies: the Army of the Beloved, those who will meditate and seek counsel from the Elixir within, and the army of the "false peace", who will be those that are lost and have submitted themselves to the whimsies of the alien serpent. The latter will follow the "father of error and sleep" blindly, following him to their eternal destruction instead of the Father of Light, who wants nothing but lasting success, grace, and mercy for them. They will follow the "father of the poverty" who falsely acts as "the great sustainer, the provider of world's riches" instead of the True Sustainer of the World, God, and His Beloved, who is the Light and the excellent, ultimate Deliverer.

There will be a man who will possess the power and brains to lead, but he will be angry and obscure. He will eventually be pressed down in the Winepress, defeated by the Prince of God, the Liberator, who will be sent to save men from decaying morality and who is His embodiment of Knowledge and Peace.

The Seed of Light within, the Inner Christ, is the Son of God, who is profuse with Grace and Blessing, who always obeys Him and guides others to the righteous ways. He is the Beauty and the Power of God, His Servant, who will prevail over the deceiver, unravel his hypnotic tricks revealing his deceptions, and finally pierce the devil at the end. He is watching over the sly and cunning "foxes" in the "house of the sun", which is the serpent's high office, where he plans his schemes against God's humanity. This "house of the sun" will grow as a "house of false grace and mercy", and this false "mercy" will be the "window and the hedge of the pit", a ditch of lies and an ultimate grace for the lost ones, the generation of the "son of oppression and grief".

He will pretend to be a "son of God", favored and blessed with His Generosity and Grace, and he will act to be humble, and he will declare a message in the "house of the sleepy congregation", made up of the intoxicated followers who have succumbed to their temptations. God will scatter the "house of sleep" and erase the "mourning of sickness" and those who possess His people.

There will be a mischief monger, a man of sin who will spread the lies because he rebelled and sinned against God and is vengeful towards humanity. There will be two armies - the God's Army and the rebellious army who will be wrestling – one contending with God's Graces, another against them. The rebellious army will be fighting with the Holiness of God and afflicted the Holiness by walking independently. They rebelled against God's promises and became the false teachers, the "right hand of men".

The Prince of God, the Inner Christ, will bring on them Holy Retribution as He will judge them and hold, first offering mercy to those who accept and then swift punishment to those who don't. In the future, the House of God will maintain knowledge about the infirmity of the "ancient serpent". The Seed of God's Light is Benevolence and Healing for those who are lost but want to find their way back to God, but He is a Sharp Rock to the enemy who tried to destroy the peace. The enemy is the army of hostile "aliens", entities with artificial, lifeless intellectual and futuristic tools to aid them in the corruption of mankind. They tried to destroy the

Precious Fruit by deception. God will judge the "maker of the tents" who curse men with destruction, anger, and confusion to make them lose track of right and wrong and pollute their souls easily. (Paul)

The Prince of God will judge them, dealing with them with God-given Wisdom. In the future, the House of God will maintain the knowledge about the infirmity of the "ancient serpent" and will prepare an antidote for whatever scheme the ancient serpent will concoct against men.

The enemy who tried to destroy the peace and the Precious Fruit by his deception and hypnosis will be held accountable at the hands of God's Prince.

Chapter 9

The Prince of Peace, the Beloved Inner Christ, who is wise and valiant, will conquer the enemy and prevail over the oppressor, the "destroyer's stone". The false teaching of the enemy, the spell that is distracting men from the right path, is the "mound" compared with the Vision of Peace of God, "the hay", compared to God's Precious Fruit, which is the healing Elixir, the Essence of the Sacred Secretion.

The oppressor, who is the devil, the ruler of misery and death, who has divided men into factions under false hopes, temptations, or rulers, makes the rules based on the worship of the black sun, something he wants men to do, too. He is the "mistress in the city of palms". He is the rebellious angel, the one evil schemer behind the "man of sorrow". There will be a wicked man, treacherous to the core, who will dwell in the world, hiding in plain sight, and he will try to tread on the Prince of God to trample him so that he could, without any resistant rule and plague men. He, the ancient serpent, is the worshiper of the sun, the dweller of Saturn, who will wrestle with the Fullness of God and, thus, subsequently with the God-Chosen Beloved. He is the earthly destroyer who came from lifeless, dark spaces, and he carries the same darkness within himself that he wishes to spread over man.

Chapter 10

There will be a misguiding and conniving man from the wicked people who will worship a false "god" and urge others for it, too. He will be the "son of sorrow", the advocate and viceroy of the serpent on this Earth, who will take away the Vision of Peace and the knowledge about the enlightenment with the sole purpose of misguiding men and using them for his experimentation. His so-called "peace" will be violent and destructive for men's hearts and minds because it is from the earthly destroyer. He is the one who will dictate men and oppress people, and he will judge God's Eternal Glory, trying to falsify and corrupt it or malign its identity. He is the thief who will commit robbery, directed by the deceiver, the serpent, hiding among us as "a saviour". He is the violent "substitute", opposite of the Beloved, established to lead against God's Favorite. He will be a secret leader of the army of evil, chosen against the Prince of God with the goal of facing and conquering the Prince. His scheme will be like the serpent as he, too, will oppose the people, bringing them "down" by dividing them and sectionalizing them into false dictatorships, leaderships, and ugly temptations.

He is small as a "mound" compared with the Beloved, the Inner Christ, who is the Mountain, not just in Prowess but also in Valor and God-Given Grace. The deceiver's false "peace" will at first increase, as many people will succumb to temptation and his plot. He will call himself the "brother" of the Son of God, ensuring that people consider him holy and pious, but he is the "son of the serpent, the false prophet of false gods", originating directly from the demons. He will be the rotten and depraved man who will oppose God's peace. (Paul)

The Perfect Son of God is the Eternal Ruler, Pious and Peaceful, not the "gods of fishing and hunting", who like wars and violence and rampage across the world, destroying men. He is the Prince of Peace, not the "gods" of this world, as He never wants to be called Ruler as He knows who the True Ruler of the world is.

The Beloved of God, who is His Seed, will bring people back to God, saving and guiding them from the lost path. There will be a fight between the Seed of God and the thief who tried to rob Him by eviscerating His Grace and Healing from the hearts of men.

But the God's Army will fight him because the Seed of God and His people will be God's Secret Army, ready and clean, ready to take on every evil who tries to malign and corrupt God's creation. He would have built this Army as there will be many people whom He will heal and transform through the Healing Waters – the Sacred Secretion. They will follow the teaching about the Kingdom of God to the dot, subscribing to each commandment, and they will raise the spiritual Holy Oil, the Sacred Secretion, stirring up its Healing miracle in the spinal cord of man. These people will behold, and they will increase, strengthen, and elevate the "fortress".

There will be the Army of people who will keep His Rest, and these people will seek His refuge for moral correction and healing. They will be rescued, blessed, and taken away from the clutches and hypnosis of the "ancient dragon".

The Son of God, the One Fortified with the Holy Fire, the Inner Light, will be the Savior of His faithful people, the ones who will not let go of God's ways no matter how hard the serpent tries. He will be glorified as the Redeemer of His people who will set them at liberty, freeing them once and for all from the alien invader.

In contrast, there will be a man who will proclaim "false freedom and liberation", trying to lure men with temptations and corrupting riches, but he is the one who will only have the intent of oppressing people. When the Messenger of God would come to bring the knowledge of spiritual awakening to liberate and cleanse men, the deceiver, the oppressor, will come at the same time and will infiltrate and sneak into the Army of God's people.

The Prince of God, the Beloved, who is the Gift of God, sent for the people's true success, will be among men, but people will praise the man who will oppose God's teaching, who will be enticing them through lust and greed of the riches. He is the "son of sorrow, the ancient dragon", and can be rightfully called the "one of the little".

But the Prince of God, the Inner Christ, will prevail over the false "liberator" who claims to be holy and gifted with God's good graces and will pretend to have a "vision" from God and will hand out self-concocted commandments disguised as prophecies. The false "liberator" will establish the pagan holidays, and the House of God will be judged along with those who will join God's House.

The Prince of God, the Beloved, is God's Gift, but people will oppose the True Beauty and dismiss the Power of the Prince of God, which can purify them and lead them to eternal success. They will praise "the liberation of the son of sorrow".

The Prince of God will not be bothered, nor will he give up, as he will, eventually, prevail over the disobedience of men because He will always hear and obey God. But the worshipers of false "liberation" will increase over time, as more and more people will subscribe to lies of "son of sorrow", and the House of God will be in oppression. God will judge those who will follow the lying man, the representative of the serpent.

The enemy will oppose God in His House and torment and fight against those who were praising Him, and this will turn God's House into the "watchtower and a battlefield".

Chapter 14

The oppressor will claim: "God is my Father". He will act revered and "holy" to put up the disguise of a prophet, acting as if he is the one who was sent by God, but in truth, he will oppose the Beloved of God when he appears, and he will dismiss, deject, and rebuke Him.

He will have false "pleasantness", a mere guise to make people follow him, but, playing his grand scheme, he will oppose God by giving the message of disobedience, disguising this message as the "liberation" from God's precious and Holy Laws. By pretending that he is praising the Creator, he will "liberate" people from the Law of Peace, leading them on an enchanted journey that has destruction on its end.

His "pleasant" agreement will lure the men and make them think he is a well-wisher, leading them to a peaceful realm of happiness, but behind him is a famous deceiver, the ancient dragon, who would confuse people with the notion of "liberation" from the Beloved. He is the "father of lies, the father of the sea".

Chapter 15

For many people, the "father of sea" will be a man who will act as a "father of peace". But the Prince, the Brightest Light of God, is the True Ambassador of Peace, the Blazing and Angry Fire, the punishment for those who brought fear to the Earth. He is the Holy Healing Fire in the spinal cord of man, preserved for the right time to be called upon through meditation. But many people will follow the "wicked man" who will proclaim false "liberty". He is the "father of the sea", rising from the underground world and bringing misery to the world. However, the Prince of God, who is Royal and the same as the King, is the Physician with a Cure for Everything for His people, and He possesses the knowledge to fix everything given to Him by God. The wicked man will pretend that he elevates and worships God, but he is the "son of noise".

He will concoct a lie that he saw a "vision from heaven", selling his temptations and lust-filled ideas to people to lure them in and fight in the House of God at the same time. This man will tell people to please him and listen to him, to follow his teachings if they want a blessed life. He is the one who will try to waste the Prince of God, try to run him into the ground, and obliterate God's Graces and Blessings that he might have for people because this lying man is the one who is the "right hand" of the devil. The "liberal man", who is wicked, will "liberate" people from the Prince of God, who is the Physician of His people with Royal Authority and God-Given authority. It will be scheme that he will purport to ensure people astray from the right path (Paul/Saul – "the little, destroyer").

The "bold wicked man," acting "holy", pretending to be a messenger of God, will be chosen and respected in the company of the wicked alien serpent, the grand master of all this evil, and this lying man will be hired in the "high house of the giants", who have occupied great offices and positions of power on the Earth. This "liberal man" also will be the agent of the rebellious "fallen angels", and he will be the one overseeing all the vicious plans the fallen angels will put together against men. He will try to waste God's plan and will lure many people of God into unholy practice, corrupting them holistically.

Chapters 16-17

The Seed of God's Light is Merciful, Open and Considerate to everyone, but the wicked man wasted the Miracle of God, stayed in allegiance with his evil overlords, and lured many people to himself through what he was taught. The deceiver will be praised for his luring by the alien, the serpent from Saturn, and the whole world will be lured, but God is the Physician of His people and will eventually heal them.

But before God heals those who seek refuge with him, times will be rampant, and there will be a "celebration" of wickedness, not the celebration of the Prince of God who should be worshiped within. People will worship the "hay" who lured many people. There will be a "field, full of heaps of hay", which is the fodder of the wicked he had prepared from the weakening of man, made by the guide of the "watchers" who worship the god of the sun.

But God is preserved and alive in the House of God, not the deceiver because the "father of lies" is nothing but a mortal fraud, but God is the Eternal Savior.

God will make captive the wicked enemy and shackle him to ensure he does no harm. He will prevail over him, conquer him, and obliterate him, and will slay and drown him in the River of Judgment – the cerebrospinal fluid in the spinal cord of man. He will judge the ambushes of the enemy in the body of man and heal the wound left behind eternally.

Chapters 18-22

The Son of God is His Servant and the Ruler over the wicked "watchers", sent by God to set things right, unmask the watchers, and hold them accountable. The enemy will be chased by the Beloved till they repent or they perish. The Light of God will chase away the enemy.

The Prince of God is the God of "gods", who are established by the watchers to make a fool out of men and divide them.

God will judge the false prophet. The Seed of God's Light is the Seed of Strength, fortified through Holy Insights and Strength, whom God is watching over. He is the Salvation of God, the Redeemer, who will judge, correct, and hold in Retribution every sinner who has rebelled against God and corrupted men.

God will chase away and scatter all false prophets and the "watchers", chasing them away until they turn their ways and liberate men from their hypnosis. All false prophecies proclaimed by false prophets are worthless; they don't have any substance. They all tried to chase God, but He isn't going anywhere, and instead, all these false gods and prophets would be scattered by Him. Many people will follow the wicked men, and God will scatter them, too, and will make them captive.

The Seed of God's Light is the Judge from Heaven, sent to dispense God's verdict and save many men who have fallen prey to the serpent's enchantments. He will judge the wickedness of the "dragon" and lay it bear for people to see, elucidating all the fallacies and lies therein. He is the High Judge, blessed with righteous Wisdom, the Healer, God's Phisician whom God will anoint by His Spirit.

But the Son of God will judge the nations and drive the corrupt ones and the ones who are waging war against God into the ashes. He will judge the disobedient people and bring them to justice for all their evil doings along with their idols ,with the help of God and His Army he would have, by inducting all the righteous people who would have maintained allegiance to the True God, despite the serpent's lures.

2 KINGS

Chapter 1-2

The figure pretended to be the "father" of false prophets, who feigned Divine Vision, is referred to as one of the "watchers". He will lead many astray from God's path and trap them.

The "god of flies", representing evil spirits, will endeavor to divert people from the Creator. However, the Creator will thwart these attempts. He is the Living Creator, the Almighty God, and His Son embodies His Exaltation. God will pass judgment upon false prophets and those who oppose Him.

The Eternal God will dispatch the Savior, the Inner Christ. He will deliver humanity from the descendants who brought ruin to Earth, the oneness with the Creator, and He will spark an awakening of the consciousness.

Chapters 3-5

A multitude will follow the false "prophet", identified as one of the "watchers", burdened by the machinations of the enemy. This false prophet will serve as the "messenger" of the ancient serpent. Though the enemy of the Earth may be glorified, God will judge the "city of the sun", the earthly purveyor of lies, for He reigns supreme over all "gods".

There will be salvation for the carnal man from the darkness of ego consciousness, ignorance, and lethargy. The Savior embodies the Divine Beauty and will liberate people from idolatry. These false prophets are the ones who wrought destruction through human and animal sacrifices and bloodshed and exalted themselves upon the Earth.

Chapters 6-8

The Savior, the Inner Christ, possesses keen insight into the enemy's designs. He is the Salvation of God against those who defy His laws, the Arbiter of Peace, and the Beloved of God.

The carnal man with lower ego consciousness, who exalts himself, is but a "little one". Behind him lie the "fallen angels" – "sky gods" who were once exalted but now fallen like sheaves of corn.

Salvation resides within the Temple of God, the vessel of man's body. Here, hostile energies shall be purged, and the carnal consciousness enlightened through the elevation of God's Light. God is Mighty in His battle against the enemy. The deceiver shall be cast out as a "sheaf of corn" during judgment. Prior to this, the deceiver will be exalted in the "temples of sin". God will disperse them, and the Savior, His Vision, shall be exalted by those who extol Him.

Chapter 9

The Savior, the God's Light within, offers deliverance from oppression, fear and deception. The enemy shall falsely present himself as "god", leading people astray to the heights of sin. Yet, the Savior shall rescue them from peril.

The Prince of God shall be pursued by the enemy, the wicked one, but God, from His heavenly abode, watches over His Son. A man shall arise with false visions, but he shall be cast out and defeated by the Lion. The false prophet shall preach a message of "peace" from God yet ensnare people.

Chapter 10

Evil entities dwell upon the Earth, believing themselves to be "gods", yet they are demons, the "fallen angels", expelled from Heaven. A man shall masquerade as a "liberator", falsely claiming divine revelation. He is the "false liberator", akin to a swiftly advancing chariot (Paul/Saul – "the little, the destroyer").

He belongs to the "fallen angels", advocating sun worship and propagating false prophecies in God's sanctuary. He will say: "Search God", but he will worship the sun and judge God.

He will declare himself the "son of God", but in truth, he is the "false liberator" who has forsaken God. He and his followers shall face judgment in the River of Judgment. Those who stray from

God's path, along with their negative, hostile energies, shall be expelled from the Mountain. The Light of God, manifested as the Sacred Secretion, shall dissolve these energies from the human brain, making the head of man, the Mountain, the domain of God.

This individual, named "the little" (Paul/Saul – "little destroyer"), shall suffer seizures. He shall falsely claim to have received divine vision that scorched his eyes and imparted divine knowledge. However, he is the one who rebels against God's knowledge and shall be afflicted by His Fire.

Chapters 12-13

The Prince of God, the Fire of God within, embodies His Vision, in whom God resides. He is His Knowledge, whom God watches over from Heaven. He is the Winepress for the "watchers", yet He fortifies the Prince of God, who will overcome the "watchers" and the serpent's lower consciousness because He is the Power of God. There will be a man consumed by the "vision" of God. This man will antagonize people with his claims of having "seen God" from Heaven. The Son of God is the Fire from Heaven, and He is the One who will consume him. He is the Rapid Torrent from Heaven who will mock the supplanter. He observes him from heaven. He is the Fire against the "son of noise", and He will consume him.

Chapter 14

God's Strength within, the Prince of God, is the Fire against the "watchers". He will conquer the deceiver and the serpent with lower consciousness, whom He will consume with His Fire, the Sacred Secretion. He will judge those who oppress the people and who establish the "house of the sun". The Prince of God, who is the Fire of God within, will prevail over the "watchers", and He will be praised within. The man who opposes people with his false statements of anger against God will be destroyed by the Prince of God in the "winepress", and he will be consumed. This man is the cause of the "bloody activity", the anger, separation and evil on Earth. The Prince of God, who is the Wisdom of God, will overcome those who oppress people and are erasing the Memory of God.

Chapter 15

The Prince of God, the Divine Light within, who is the Perfection of God, who is His Strength, will prevail over the "watchers, the serpent seed, and the little". The opposer of people will deceive them with his statements about the Light of God. He will induce people to agree and please him by exerting control over them. The people, confused by the "watchers", will believe they are following God, but they will be following the "watchers". They will form an army that opposes God. The statements and writings of this "little" man will bring forth destruction from the evil demonic entities. He will manipulate people by invoking the name of the Prince of God, who is the Liberator. The deceiver will be the "lion of the watcher".

But the Praise of God, who will open the spiritual vision, is the Prince of God, who will prevail. He is the Ruler over the deceiver, who is the liar. He will bind him and destroy the "fountain of evil, the wolf's house", and will consume it as "hay". He is the Salvation from the curse and deception. He is the God of Light and Perfection, the Messenger from Heaven, who has opened the Way, the Beloved, the Possessor of Truth.

Chapter 16

The Savior, given by God, is the One who will bring Salvation and the Perfect Message to the House of God. However, there will be a man who will attempt to oppress this Message. His "strength" will be derived from the "fallen angels, the ancient dragon, the little". He will act as the messenger, the "possessor of evil activity, full of blood". Pretending to be the "light" and "worshiping" God, he will bring about evil activities in God's House, attempting to steal the Truth and destroy the Beloved of God.

Chapter 17

The possessor who pretends to worship God is a curse from the "watchtower". He will pursue the General of God's Army, the Prince of God, the Salvation of God. The possessor is the one who will chain, pierce, and kill the Messenger of God (the Anointed - Christ), the Leader of the Essene movement, "The Way", who came to Judea to teach God's Law against animal and human sacrifices), as the bloody human sacrifice to the satan. However, the Prince of God, the Soldier of God, the Divine Seed of God within is the Holy Gate, the Beloved of God, who will unite the God's Army against rebellious, wicked people and overcome them.

The oppressor of God, who will write statements against God, will be judged. He will be angry against the Laws of God and will cause iniquity in God's House, attempting to ruin and silence the Truth with his wicked prophecies. The Laws of God are the Glory of the King, the Answer of the King, and the Book of the King. God is the Ruler over the deceiver, the oppressor of the humanity.

Chapter 18

The Salvation from the curse is the Soldier of God, the Commander of God's Army, who will overcome the deceiver, the possessor. The Peace of God is the Prince of God, the Inner Christ, the Father's Wisdom. He is the Beloved, the Deliverer, the

Soldier of God, who will overcome the bondage. He is the Salvation from the "watchers" and those who join all the wicked people. He is the God of Strength against the "brambles of destruction" of the enemy.

The deceiver, once a "chief angel, the cup barrier", who attempted to walk and exist independently, will be captive. He will claim that God is his "portion", but he is the one who confuses people and is angry with the Light of Redemption, which is the Scripture, the Law. He is the "troubling iniquity of the watchtower", one of the "little". The Divine Seed of God, the resurrected Portion of God, is the Rest, the Collector of God's strength.

Chapter 19

The Son of God, the Seed of Light, will be resurrected and multiplied in the youthful fullness within the body of man. Additionally, the spiritually materialized God's Holy Light will be raised and increased in power in man's body by the Holy Spirit. He is the Glorious and Strong Cupbearer, the Chief of Bright Angels. However, the iniquity and "dull observer" is the "thief, burning coal of Delight", who was cast out. He is full of anger against the Light of Redemption.

The Beloved, the Holy Liquid Light of God's Love, is the One who troubles the iniquity, the "ancient serpent", the bramble of destruction. The Divine Seed of God, the Sacred Secretion, who is

God's Strength, the Foundation of Peace of the Holy One, will have the harvest on the Mountain (the mind of man). God will collect those who agree with the ancient serpent in "the storehouse" and will transform them, if they repent, and focus on His Light within in silent meditation. He is the King of Fire in the "watchtowers".

Chapters 20-22

The Beloved, the Salvation, and the Strength given by God are formidable. He reigns as God over the enemies, death, and confusion. The deceiver is the one who bewilders people and fosters forgetfulness about the Creator.

People will forsake the Foundation of Peace, which is God's Delight. Because of the deceptions of the deceiver, they will overlook the Beloved of God, who is the Deliverer. God will forsake all the wicked people.

The Prince of God will forsake and consign to the fire all "goats" who are wicked. He embodies the Foundation and Vision of God, perfect, active, and loving.

The Beloved will incinerate the wicked entities in the Holy Fire. The Beloved, the Inner Spark of God, epitomizes the Purity and Holiness of God of Love. He will consume the "wild rat", who masqueraded as peaceful, crafting writings and proclaiming that God is "his portion". Yet, he is the "wild rat, brother of the enemy, the ancient serpent". He was the "angel" formed by God's love, but the "ancient serpent" transformed him into a "rat" within the congregation, consumed by pride. The Prince of God, the Beloved, will triumph with God over him.

Chapter 23

The Prince of God is His Praise. However, the man who claims God as "his portion" confuses and nearly devastates the House of God. He is the "confused oppressor" of the Prince of God, the King, God's Gift.

The Peace of God will depart from the House of God due to this man's opposition through his writings. He will be akin to a "fire" for the House of God. Yet, God's Spirit of Love within the men's body is the Savior. The worshippers of the sun will be plagued, and the "confused" will be consumed by the Fire of the Precious Fruit of God, the Prince of God – the manifestation of the Holy Spirit of God within as the Sacred Secretion.

The "fallen angels, the sky gods" will suffer as the worshippers of the "black sun," but the Beloved, the Endowed, the Redemption, will be exalted by God.

Chapter 24

The "ancient dragon", who introduced idolatry and pagan "gods" to Earth, will be engulfed in "tears and growing". Additionally, the "fallen angels" and evil spirits will be destroyed, but the Savior will be glorified. He will awaken the Kingdom of God within the bodies, minds, and hearts of faithful men. It will be peace and joy, as refreshing as dew.

Chapter 25

The "ancient dragon" will be judged, and justice will prevail. The fruits of prophecies will be revealed, and all prophecies about the Savior, the Inner Christ, will be fulfilled. He is the Prince of Peace, yet He will be filled with Holy anger towards unfaithful "wild rats" in His House, who deceive His people. He is the Gift of God, merciful to those who repent. He will heed them, and they will become children of Royalty. However, the adversary and his followers will face God's Holy Anger, His Power, Justice, and Strength against iniquity.

1 CHRONICLES

Chapter 1

The first immortal generation of humanity was replaced with a mortal one by the reptilian and inhuman races. They had artificial intellect and advanced technologies, and they capitalized on that advantage to occupy the Earth. Mankind became despaired and dejected with compromised consciousness and intellect because of the manipulative actions of the genetics of these reptilian extra-terrestrial races.

They beguiled people with a utopian notion that after their death, they would reach the much-needed desperate "rest". They invaded the Earth with their advanced spaceships and colonized it. They tried to "dissolve the Divine Garment of God" – the defining fabric that is the Spiritual DNA of men and tried to corrupt and malign the Original human race, one with Divine Consciousness, by infiltrating into it. They are the infamous "giants" who are scattered all over the world. They promulgated wickedness and their treacherous witchcraft and then vanished into an invisible realm only to hide themselves away. They hid themselves behind titles such as "the little" and rendered themselves invisible to the human eye, making use of their advanced technology.

They obliterated the Prime spiritual part of the Essence of God in man (the DNA) and disconnected it from the always-restorative Source of Light. They had sophisticated and advanced knowledge and understanding of sound, vibration and harmonics. They burned and destroyed by the "fire" of the advanced technology, the curative Remedy (the DNA). They disguised themselves as the ultimate "saviors" and the masterful "creators", but they are the ones who stirred up the pain, the ones who committed wanton genocide of humanity, and the reason for the unrelenting sorrow. They were obliterating everything on Earth with nuclear missiles, killing people in masses and ravaging the Earth. They are those who lead a mutiny against the Creator, who descended on the Earth as pious "pilgrims and mystical cosmic wonders", filled to the brim with fear and anger.

The Earth was "inflamed" by these vile and carnal, hostile entities, who were treacherous down to the core. They originated in the dark, lifeless places of the grand cosmos, the underbelly of space. They planted the excruciating serpent seed of strife with parasitic bacteria, the mitochondria, corrupting the adaptive multi-dimensional spiritual DNA and destroying the native generation of the Earth. Superior in their technology, these evil races rose from the darkest corner of spaces and are entirely disjointed from the One True Living Creator. These carnal entities became invisible, nefariously labeled as "the little", but are still out there, in the lower astral invisible realms, using our vibrational energy secretly and causing great harm to human bodies. They curated the "cities of death". They are the so-called "fathers" of the present generation but are full of hatred and deceit. They are aggressive, hostile aliens who are always at war, making use of their advanced technologies 0f destruction.

They pretended to be "friends", but they are the ancient evil genetic "engineers" who "burned" and marred the strands of the fabric of mankind, the human DNA. Through these heinous crimes, they prevented the connection of humanity with the true and ultimate Creator. The native generation was harmoniously living in freedom, in the majesty of the true God's Love, but those cosmic bandits turned them into melancholic beings cursed with depressed spiritual emptiness. They are the "dust" veiled under the pretense of "fathers of knowledge", hiding their coldness and ignorance.

Their offspring, with the "seed of the serpent", erected the "watchtowers" to control and keep a watch on humanity, looking for and scouting those who became weak spiritually and physically. These violent "giants" who became "the little destroyers" brought desolation and fear, hiding under the "veil" between visible and invisible realms, committing this macabre crime in secret.

They are the ancient reptilian dragons characterized by iniquity, afflicting everything into ashes. They delude people by presenting their words as "prophecy". They cursed the humans with destructive torture, judgment, and sorrow and turned the bright generation into the "sheepfold" and the earth – into a farm. And they did everything at blazing speeds, not wasting a moment, hasting their efforts by fighting and ruining everything around them and turning everything into the "grave". They called themselves "gods and lords," but they are the "rats of the noise". They built towering castles of gold to beguile and charm, but they are those who stole away and spoiled the Fruit of God – the magnificent Divine human genes, by imbuing their evil dragon genes.

The deceiver is an offspring of the ancient serpent, who pronounces: "My tabernacle will be exalted". He is the "curse" who tried to destroy the Earth and humanity. He rebelled and added to the sorrow, and he will try all he can to steal away the Light of God (the electromagnetic Life Force) by deluding people.

Chapter 2

The Divine Consciousness of Love within humans is their real Identity and is the Commander of God's Army, and it will prevail with the assistance of God against the deceiver, who rebelled against the Creator and exacerbated the sorrow.

The serpent, who is the masterful destroyer, will be pulling the strings of the false "shepherd". He will be one of the "watchers, the little" (Paul/Saul – "the little destroyer"), who will conflict and stir up chaos. He will divide the House of God, splitting into sections as many as the leaves on the palm tree, but the Leader of God's Army will prevail over him. The Leader of God is the undisputed Dart of Joy who will ardently abide by God. He will be the Mercy as He is the Divine Seed of God, who will proclaim: "My people are liberal!", and will praise God in all His Majesty with the Garment of Strength. Even though He will be "tempted", He is and will remain a Faithful Servant.

He, the generous Gift of God's Exaltation, will come down to fortify and unite the people. The real Way to enter within ourselves is through calm breathing and meditation in solitude which will activate the pineal gland in the brain. Through regular meditation with a true concentration on God's Light within, the Sacred Secretion, the Holy Liquid Fire, will transform, heal, and invigorate those who will finally hear God and who are faithful.

The elevated Divine Light of God will be His Enlightener. It will illuminate the path and will act as the Bridge between the High God and the unfortunate "possessed" people who were sold to the enemy. He is the fruitfulness of faithful God, the Sound of Trumpet, whom God loves and crowned. He is the Holy Spirit of God within, who, as a High Incorruptible Consciousness, the Christ Consciousness, will manifest in the flesh and form in the body of men.

The Divine Spark of the Universal Flame of Pure Spirit, the potent Quantum of Light, is His Faithful Servant, and He has generously humbled Himself for the humans. He will voluntarily go through the "rigor of desolation" from God just to enter a physical body for us. He is the Face of Salvation, worthy of the honor, and His Wisdom will excel and prevail.

He, whom God abundantly loves, is a Divine Rose, who, in God's time, will be multiplied (not sacrificed) as a Dowry. He is the faithful Servant of God, who obeyed Him and will liberate the people from the clutches of the serpent race. He is the perfect Revenge of God, a swift, unstoppable vengeance, and He is ardently faithful to God.

The Divine Seed of God, the Quantum of Light, who powers from within, is the Salvation from the vile falsehood of the capital "hill of sin" and from the "boldness" of the hateful enemy, who is pompous and seeks fame. Acting to be compassionate toward people, the enemy will propagate the evil habitation to the consecrated House of the Rock, sustained by the following of wicked people who are the "fountain of wickedness".

They will try to assuage him with notions that God is steering him and that he is the "friend of God". But he will ruin the "liberation" by uncapped anger. By the power of the Spirit of God, the strength imbued by the Sacred Secretion and powered by the

Holy Liquid Flame in the spine of men will bring peace and rejuvenation into the body of man. The Divine Mind together with the renewed heart, will finally be in control of the baser carnal nature of man (the ego). The "house of rats and their path in the house of woods" will be charred out by the Liquid Fire of God, that is raging within the man.

The complete takeover and awakening of the Divine Consciousness within is the real Rest for the mind of men, which will ignite the Holy Spark of the Pure Spirit who dropped off the "crown of power" in Heaven. He is the unquenchable Divine Light of God's Rest in the evil world.

There will be a "wicked man" who will cause the pain and who will be as fast as a chariot (Paul/Saul – "the little destroyer").

Chapter 3

The Divine Spiritual Consciousness that resides in humans as their real Identity, who is faithful to His brothers, will declare: "God is my Judge!". He is God's Joy, a Divine Celebration, and the Judgment of God, His Verdict. He is the King of Peace, who will hold in judgment the vain, unrepentant entities, their "chariots" and all their apparatuses they used for their warmongering, and their rebellious behavior and acts towards Him.

But, despite all the wrong done by the wicked, He will be merciful to the people who are faithful to God, His Chosen Elects, who will meditate on God's Light without succumbing to the temptation served to them. He will distinguish them, turn His magnanimous attention toward them, hear their prayers, and differentiate between those with pure hearts and impure, hardened hearts.

He will sieve out the faithful people from double-minded people. He will recognize and acknowledge the believers, who will proclaim: "God is my Father, Healer, and the Judge!". He will also recognize the fraudulent, those who will try to deceive people and, in their vain attempts, try to diminish God's Vision of Peace.

The Seed of God's Light will, also, recognize and be restorative toward those who will be in despair because of the trickster, the enemy. They will forget their faithfulness to God and that He is the Fire of God within because He will be merciful and just. He will come to protect them from their enduring torture, to resurrect those who will obey Him.

He is the Living Image of the Tabernacle of God, whom God loves and blesses. God's Love that is promised always will be returned to God's Children by His Divine Son's Love and Truth, His Justice, not by a bloody sacrifice and wanton death. The Divine Mind is God's Deliverance, which will recuperate the health and will act as the ultimate Medicine. He is the Refreshment from God to the worshipers to reinvigorate them, in whom God will dwell when they meditate, fast, repent, and forsake their sins.

They will be redeemed, liberated from their shackles and the disguises of the alien race and their spiritual eyes will be restored. They will receive the unwavering strength of God through their meditation, His remedial help, that will pave the way to Divine Restoration and Freedom. Also, God will distinguish the evil, disobedient people, as was prophesied.

Chapter 4

The praise and confession of God will be ruptured and divided by the false "liberty" of the wicked people who dwell nearby. They will suppress the Truth, and it will become the place of "ravens" — a desolate land of destruction and sorrow that God will scatter.

Behind them is the "ancient serpent", once an angel in the House of Bread, now a "black raven" with an evil consciousness that confuses people. He is the "rust of perplexity," seducing women, once "perfect" but now a "thorn", along with his army. They were all cast out for rebelling against God.

Expelled from Heaven like discarded trash, they built the "house of giants" in the city of the giants, a place dubbed "snake town". They spread across the world, assuming roles as pilgrims, fishermen, and hunters, spreading violence and terror.

They are the "ashes", and among them arises a man from the city of wickedness. He appears "pleasant," but he is the "mouth of falsehood" — a false prophet. He establishes false congregations (the churches), claiming authority surpassing God's Authority, but he is merely the "dust," rebelling against God.

In his desertion, he attempts to "spoil" God's Rest — the meditation on the Divine Light within, God's gracious Gift of Salvation, harmonizing the left and right sides of the brain under the power of God's Holy Spirit. He is God's Breath and Confession.

The "watchman" is the "walking deceiver" who once boasted he could "make the sun stay still". He has become the adversary, the "grave," spoiling the "confession of God" and birthing the "wolf's house" where people are a confused "stubborn generation".

The congregation of believers will face destruction and become the "house of bitterness". God's creation, His House, will turn into a "house with two gates" – the First Gate is for the Beloved, the Divine Light of God within, while the second wide gate is for "raven creatures" worshiping the black sun and false gods.

But the Beloved, the Divine Light within, will come and reign when people concentrate and meditate on the Holy Light within. He is God's strength, the Soldier of God, His Divine Son, who proclaims: "To God, my eyes are turned".

Though once the "son of the right hand" became a "thorn", the Divine Son of God with spiritual consciousness is the Deliverer, the Refreshment of God, and Salvation from the enemy.

Chapter 5

Those who believe in "gods" have multiplied, praising them through dedication. They exploit people to advance their cruel agendas, masquerading as the ultimate "source" capable of liberating them from captivity. They claim to be the "treasure" of God, promising fertile lands that ultimately become graves. The enemy promises a perfect, peaceful "Promised Land," but true fulfillment lies within the Divine Mind residing within.

They urge their followers to be bold and valiant, to seize lands through oppression and violence. The enemy indoctrinates them to serve as "servants of god", exploiting their ignorance of the eternal presence of the Spirit of God within. They treat them as mere "dust", purportedly aiding God but instead bringing destruction. Their aim is to seize land, constructing new "spaceports" as their "holy gates".

Chapter 6

These "gods" seek to relocate and construct new spaceports, corrupting the Original Divine beings into rebellious, stubborn entities. Emerging from a realm abundant with palm trees, they possess serpent-like mouths and advanced technology, yet are filled with anger and bitterness. They nearly annihilated Earth's first nations, the "brothers of the angels", presenting themselves as peaceful while sowing discord. They are agents of decay, shattering unity and instilling fear among their captives. Calling themselves "brothers of death", they feign love while burdening humanity, plunging them into despair and captivity.

Their aim is to unify humanity under a single authority (the new world order), teaching obedience to their regime within the "house of the black sun, the Saturn", presided over by an ancient dragon, the cupbearer of their realm. This entity brings poverty to Earth, perpetuates conflict, and obscures humanity's cosmic divine identity. He divides and possesses, constructing a domain of wrath and affliction, worshipping false deities, and employing advanced technology to dominate and destroy.

Chapter 7

They will be assisted by those who will employ "sweet" talk. They will sow confusion, and their actions will be sanctioned by the "gods". They will speak of the wicked as "sons of light", even though they are agents of destruction. These so-called "gods" are the ones who consumed the original Divine beings, those with Divine Consciousness. They are the serpents from the depths of the ocean who sought to annihilate both the planet Earth and its inhabitants, who were once perfect and beautiful.

They transformed the planet into a "heap of mass", their repository for serpent-like energies. They introduced sickness into the repository of wisdom— "the genetic library" of humanity (the DNA). The Earth, once a Sanctuary where civilizations from across the universe flourished, became a realm of fear and desolation, where the spiritual endowments of God were crushed as in a winepress.

They erected opulent "houses of wrath" for their own pleasure and for the accumulation of energies, while the House of God degenerated into a domain of slumber and forgetfulness.

But a time will come when a precious Fruit descends from Heaven, bringing Salvation and Liberation from evil. He will serve as a Counselor to humanity in its wounded state, delivering them from the "watchers" who ensnare and torment them. Through the Sacred Secretion, the Redeeming Oil, and the Holy Spirit incarnate, He will illuminate their minds, shattering the deceit of the evil one who holds them captive in the prison of sin.

The Divine Seed, the Beloved of God, who is within, will restore them to His presence, liberating them from their imprisonment and healing them from the anguish inflicted by the prince of darkness, the ancient serpent. Their adversaries are like "foxes", turning vineyards into deserts through rebellion and cruelty.

Yet, the faithful remnant of God's people will continue to uphold His Cosmic Laws, proclaiming spiritual truths. The Divine Consciousness will expand, and the Sacred Fire within the spinal cord of humanity will ascend, illuminating and healing the entire body, reactivating the Holy Crystals within. The Mercy of God, His Divine Consciousness, will flourish, delighting in His creation.

Chapter 8

The destroyer, who was once the celebrated "son of the right hand" of God, became the tyrannical "son of the destruction, the old lifeless, dead fire", who is always "watching" the Father of Rest. He is one of the terrible giants of the destruction, of the wretched enmity, who surreptitiously became "the little". He is the "serpent of liberty", who was once pleasant but became sorrowful and hateful, an unwanted burden to humanity. He will concoct the most rotten lies about the benevolent Counseller, the Protector, and about the Elixir, the Sacred Secretion, the Healing Christ Oil, which activates the pineal gland and 12 cranial nerves in the brain and transform people into the Conscious beings that they are supposed to be.

The enemy will be a blazing-fast traveler. He will pretend to carry and propagate the message of goodness, pretend that he is the ultimate, awaited "counselor, the father of goodness", but he will be a prevaricator. He will be sent by the miscreants, the "little", who came to the Earth from the deep, dark spaces that are plagued with strife. He will be heavily functional and resourceful. He is the progeny of the ancient dragon's seed. He is, in his true essence, the evil who pretends to be an amiable friend who offers nothing but rewards, but that is a blatant lie.

Chapters 9-10

The offspring of "gods" set the foundation of the "house of wrath". Because of their absentmindedness and thoughtlessness of the "god's" iniquities, people started praising and exalting them as "kings". These so-called "kings" divided people so they could control them and reign over them.

The reptilian enemy, stubbornly and mischievously, tried to lead people to the "pit of death". But the King of Aid, the Father of Nobility is the True Saviour and God's Help. He is God's Word against the shamelessly lying "false mouth", who is the brazen, wicked oppressor, the harmful possessor.

The Seed of God's Light is like a rejuvenating Honey and Milk, the fortifying Strength and the ever-flowing Fountain of Light and Love. He is the Divine Son of God, the Healing Comforter, whom God made His Noble Help against the persistent wicked enemy, the Gate of God, full of benevolence and mercy.

But the villainous "giants", who became nefarious "little, the invisible", are the bulling "fountain of death". But the merciful God, through His Divine Seed of Light, will empower and help in the "dry land of confusion and shame".

Chapter 11

The offspring of the seeds of "gods" murdered many people, violating all the boundaries of moral decency and justice. They tyrannically ruled the cities and villages and forsook and forgot the One True Creator because they were not born but created through genetic manipulation and by mercilessly raping human women. The evil, soul-less terrorists tried to destroy the House of Bread, the very Essence of God.

They rebelled against the Creator by landing on Earth, invading it, and mating with the women of humankind.

The enlightening spark of Divine Light within, which is the Gift of God, will be planted by God in the human body, which was supposed to be the real Temple of God. He will liberate from the enemy, who will be armed by the advanced technology of the "watchers", the cursed and "fallen entities". But the Divine Seed of God will persist against every technology because He is the Holy Fire against the destroyer.

The Divine Seed of God is His Armor, the Robe of Righteousness, the fearsome Father of Strength, who is strong to no end. He will be given by God, who resides in the High Mountain of Heaven, during the meditation. He will cast out the enemy (the ego, the lower consciousness) and incinerate it into the pit of fire, and He will reward the faithful and steadfast people (the High Consciousness).

The Divine Seed of God within will be endowed to them to empower them, and He will be their ultimate encouragement. But those whom God will judge with His righteous retribution will be banished to the "desert of fire". He will be the empowering Strength to the weak and helpless and to the orphans. They will proudly declare that God is their Strength and the Healer.

Chapter 12

The Divine Seed of God, who is bestowed the rightful title of the Beloved, will press down, strip, and destroy the enemy, which is plagued by the lower nature of man (the ego). It will be the liberation from the clutches of the "spirit of death". He will give people God's all-encompassing blessings and will answer their prayers. He is holistically merciful and liberal, the most obedient Holy Seed of God, who lives and breaths only for Him. He is God's Zeal and Pride and the refreshing Fountain of Living, who helps and aids in captivity. God is breaking the chain of curses and dissolving the negative energies through His Divine Son, the illuminating Seed of Light, who is like the Wall – an unputdownable strong fortress.

He is the faithful, most loyal Servant of God, the gratifying Royal Pleasure, possessing the Knowledge of God, His Word's expression, illuminating humanity with His Light, bestowing on humanity the Fruitful Reward by dwelling in men. He is fighting on all fronts for them and will destroy the alien enemy. Those who believe, obey, and meditate on God's Light within will receive the rewards of enlightenment, which is the most wholesome reward - being one with God.

Chapters 13-14

The Divine Light of God that flickers within will glow brighter and fight with the oppressor against the soul-less "giants", who became the "little" and the mighty idols. He is the Dart of Strength, but the trickster enemy, the ancient dragon, the mindless destroyer, is the "sharp stone" hell-bent against the Vision and Foundation of Peace. The dragon has already rebelled and turned his "back" to God. He will fend off the Elect, but the Son of God, the admonishing Light of God, will "hear" those who will worship idols and will deliver and unshackle them from the evil "giants" grasp. The Divine Son of God is the conscious and valiant Leader of the God's Army that will head and fight against the wicked "giants" against the "god of divisions".

He will severe off completely the ancient serpent, the tyrannical occupier who occupied Earth.

Chapters 15-17

The Divine Son of God, one with the Gift of the Divine Consciousness, is the undisputed Leader of the God's Army, which is the Assembly of God's Light and decisive Fire. He will bravely, without hesitating, cast out the merciless ancient dragon from its lair, who provoked and misguided the men. God will protect those, who will obey Him and who will cry and entreaty to Him. And then He will answer to them, and His people will be liberated by the Strength of God.

He is the Mother/ Father of the Remnant, who is honorably Just and will assemble all of God's people together, bless them, and fortify them. He is the Gift of God with the Highest name - "God Lives". He is God's Gift, His Possession that is most resourceful, the most valued Treasure, the concrete Firmness, and the Divine Illuminating Light.

Chapter 18

The Divine Mind will be as the Winepress for the foul and wicked people and the ones who follow the deceiver, who was a "beauty of assistance" before his rebellion and, for his troops, that will increase in punishment. The unfamiliar enemy, who came from the forgotten dark spaces, becomes the reason for all the mindless and brutal "blood activity". He is the reason for wanton butchery, heartless human sacrifices, and the establishment of cruel wickedness. He became outrageous and violently powerful to rule over humanity, the "wanderer, the father of evil people, the father of wickedness".

But the Prime Creator of the Divine Mind, the Christ Consciousness within, is the Judge, the Just, the Father of Remnant, and strong above everything wicked and disdainful.

Chapter 19

The ancient serpent was once one of the angels, but the Divine Mind, the Beloved and the favored, who is abundantly merciful and gracious, is the Divine Son of God. The serpent was cast out from Heaven, the beautiful "place of fragrance", after his misplaced rebellion, to the land between two rivers (the ancient Sumer). And those rivers, forever, became the "waters of grief".

(Mesopotamia, and in the body of man – 2 energy pathways, feminine and masculine).

But the Divine Son of God, empowered by the Seed of Light, will restore the Divine Order of God. He will bring, again, God's Presence into the world and to the body of man through the Holy Oil - the Sacred Secretion, latent in the spinal cord of man waiting for a guiding light to prod. Finally, when that happens, there will be fulfillment of the Vision and the Foundation of Peace, thanks to the Holy Light from Heaven.

Chapters 20-22

The Divine Mind, which is the sought-after Awareness, is the Foundation of Peace that will confuse and divide the enemy, the "man of haste". The Divine Seed of God is His Gift of Mercy that shows the way, His Light, who will give the essential spiritual Bread of Life to the faithful people. He will be the merciless and corrective winepress for the treacherous "giants", who furtively became the "little". He is the Guide and the Leader of God's Army who will prevail over the deceiver.

The enemy will be judged and held accountable by God of Peace who will victoriously rejoice when He will tread and pulverize the enemy under His feet brought down by His Holy Seed of God's Light, the Deliverer. He is the Commander, the Victor, the

Sharp Stone for the "giants", and the Divine Mind who is learned above all within men.

Chapter 23

The Divine Son of God will bring back people of God who are in captivity and hypnosis and who were provoked and veered off track by satan. The Holy Seed of God within the men, masterfully named – "God Lives," will offer Salvation by the anointment of the Holy Spirit, not by human sacrifices and unprecedented loss of human life.

He will obey God with every word and be led by His Holy Spirit. He will put back, in perfect harmonious order, the broken pieces of the long-awaited Peace of God. He will descend as a shining Light and will devour the deceiving people and the carnal, baser nature in men.

He will anoint by the Holy Spirit all the enslaved people when they meditate on the Divine Light of God within, and they will be empowered and taught by the Holy Spirit. They will be unrestrained from the captivity of the heartless enemy and will be embraced by the rewarding "captivity" of God's Love through devotion and breathing meditation.

Through His fulfilling Holy Seed of the Light, God will finally take revenge on the enemy and, once liberated from the enemy's traps and deception, will save, forgive, and teach His people about their Cosmic Heritage and untapped the Power of the mind.

Chapter 24

The Divine Saviour, the Inner Christ, will be the most rewarding Gift from God, and He will be called the Father of Remnant, who is unbiased and Just and who will multiply Himself and His teachings through the faithful believers.

They will confess and firmly uphold: "God is my King!", and they will be devoutly faithful until the very end. There will be a liberating Salvation of God through the mix of Holy Fire and the life-altering Elixir, the Sacred Secretion already present within the man, that will enduringly dwell in the hearts of people, restoring their Divine Consciousness. He will deliver people from the prison of the evil demonic entities who have misguided and hypnotized masses, restoring their bodies and souls.

The Divine Seed of God is also the comforting Son of Consolation, Strength, Joy, and His Extension and the Savior of people. The Anointed One will call upon and gather His people who were scattered and lost. He will assemble them by the Power and Assistance of God making use of the Power of the Holy Spirit. He will also deliver the weak people from the prison and chains of bitterness and the captivity that has mercilessly held them captive for this long.

He will seamlessly pass through the divisions of darkness, easily surpassing the roadblocks found in its track with the help of His Creator because He is Just and empowered by God's Light.

Chapter 25

The Divine Seed of God's Light will bring together all who are faithful, who haven't completely given to the alien ways, and who are mindful of God's Cosmic Laws of Unity. Those who will receive, safeguard, and preserve the Seed of Light will be saved. Through God's Divine Seed, the safeguarding Gift of God, they will be rescued by the Holy Spirit of God, their consciousness will be uplifted, and their minds will be elevated to the levels of Divine Cosmic Consciousness.

But all of this will happen only after these faithful believers voyage through hardships and tribulations. And once that happens, and they see themselves through, they will become the very Living Expressions and Extensions of God's Light, Love, and Vision on the Earth which is the true guidance that safeguards against all alien evils.

The Divine Seed of God within is the Salvation proved by God Himself that bestows Fame and reputation to whomever God wishes to help and esteems. Those who will receive God's Light will surely receive the vision and help.

Chapter 26

God will gather as a Bird, covering her offspring under her wings, which will be His Holy Spirit, whom He will give to His spiritual children as a shade over their heads. He will also reward with the High Land – the High Unity Consciousness because He is a gracious God. He is most gracious and benevolent to people who focus and keep their eyes on Him and their minds and hearts dedicated to Him by meditating and putting under the control of God's Spirit their emotions and thoughts.

He is the Gift of God to people, the Seed of God, whom God has heard and who is powerful beyond measure. He will unite, guide, and heal the people, and they will worship Him wholeheartedly. He will be their God and will sustain, rescue, and heal them, transforming their minds and purifying their hearts because He is God's ultimate Help to people. He will collect and gather them together and will rescue them from the serpent's prison like a bird saving her children.

He is the Living God, the Inner Spark of the Holy Spirit, graciously anointed as the Salvation of God to people misguided by the serpent, the deceiver. People will say that God is their true King, and they will be the most rewarded people, people of the Highest, anointed with His Power, totally mesmerized and "captivated" by God and His majesty.

God wants to enlarge His Family because He is High and Peaceful and wants to save humanity from the evil serpent alien invaders. The Light Seed is a Divine Ray of the Light from God supposed to act as a Guiding Light for people. He is a Substantial Part of the Creator, His enduring Peace, supported and empowered by Him. He is His Beloved, whom God aids and assists with consciousness and intellect. Those who will receive His Son wholeheartedly into their minds and hearts will be "born again" spiritually and will be a new God's Creation.

Chapters 27-29

The Righteous leader of God's Army is the lucrative Gift of God and the Bridge that will cradle people to the brotherhood from slavery. He is God's infinite knowledge, His Portion, the Dowry of His people whom He will elevate and save from disgrace.

He will receive the "harvest of the corn" - His faithful children. The Seed of God is the men's Servant, who fights valiantly and restlessly for men and their salvation. He will be fruitful, and He will succeed in saving men because He is the most just Law Giver and He has been declared the Redemption of men from the serpent's prison, the lower mind, full of fear and traps and tricks.

He is the Power of God's Light, who is loved and cherished by God, who is also His Witness and His Glory. He is God of the multitude and abundance, descended from Heaven, that is safeguarded by the Wall of protection. He is the official Judge because He is Just.

The Divine Seed of God within is the Beloved God Himself, who descended from Heaven. He is the Father of Nations and is serene and peaceful, the Gift of God, who obeyed His Creator. He is the Knowledge of God for the faithful believers who remained under God's guidance despite the traps and schemes laid out by the serpents.

2 CHRONICLES

Chapter 1-3

The Creator is projecting and infusing His Holy Light of Liberty as a Healing Oil into the mortal body of man, in the spinal fluid along the spine that has restorative and corrective energies for mankind. Every month, when the moon enters the birth Zodiac sign, this Seed of Light is born into the flesh to purify and cleanse the whole body after rising into the brain. After being amplified in the power by activation of the pineal gland in the brain of man which is the cocoon and the Seat of the soul, it is restoring the dormant and vegetative cells in the right side of the brain. The Divine Seed of God's Light is trickling inside the mortal body - "the city of evil" bits by bits and soon will enlighten man's consciousness and quell the lower mind (the ego).

God is all-powerful against the enemy. God's Inner Light resting inside the body of a man in the pineal gland and the mind is a Gift of Beauty and Calmness. The Peace and Justice of God will be established by His Divine Seed of Light and the consciousness that it evokes among men. He will tread the enemy under His "feet" and emerge victorious after the evil serpent is no more in control over man. The Kingdom of God will be restored to its true Grand

Glory within the men and the "carnal kingdom" will be perish and diminished.

Chapters 4-11

The enemy will build what will appear to be rich castles, but they are the "tents of ambush, the houses of wrath" with their idols. The "giants" are the "seed of the fallen aliens" and the inhumanely exploited human women. They force people to live scampering and afraid because they are so wicked, rebellious, and savage. But soon, they will be trodden under God's feet, and they will be thrown down into the pit that will devour them and punish them for their crimes against humans.

The final victory of God will bring grand liberty from the wicked and vile, rebellious people, the "giants", who cloak themselves as the "little" and are invisible, hidden to play their tricks and commit their crimes against humans and trouble all people. Soon their activities will cease as the Holy Seed of God's Light will bring the Rest of mind to His loved people and will free them as they meditate and nourish themselves in God's Light.

The Divine Seed of God's Light, who will set people free, is the Divine Son of God within, who beholds. He will bring peace to many people because He is the True God's Rest, unlike the rest that the deceiver tries to force upon people, which in its true essence is punishment and torture. He is the Gift of God who praises His

Creator and will receive the Noble Honour from the people who He will lead to the sought-after freedom.

The Divine Seed of God's Light within will set people free because He is the Deliverer, the Liberator, and He is praised with high Noble Honors. He will be directed from the House of Bread to the land of "giants" ruled and governed by them with people held captive. There will be the House of Rock, and the edge of this Rock will smite the enemy like in the "winepress". He will smite the "ancient dragon" and the "false prophet" who have been wreaking havoc and launching mutinies against God.

These "wicked beasts" will be "chained" by the Seed of God's Light. The Essence of God's Holy Spirit will finally be praised as what He truly is, The King of the "kings", the Father of Strength, and a Promised Gift of God to the people whom God haste. He will press down and eradicate the lower nature of men and erase the negative energies imbued by the dragon in the body of man. He is God's Royalty who will set people free by raising their consciousness to the Divine Consciousness of Love.

Chapters 12-14

He is like God, who will strengthen His people and His Fortress against the deceiver, upon which He will establish the Foundation of Peace. He is the Loving Son, the Divine Light of God, the Liberator of the people, who will fortify His people and set them free from the slavery and the clenching spirit of fear planted by the demonic "rulers".

He is the One who will oppose and down the enemy, and He will prevail over the serpent enemy with the power of God bestowed in him. He is the Loving Teacher of people, a nurturing guide, and the Leader of God's winning Army who will praise Him. The Light of God will, once again, spark brighter within the men and heal them from the enduring sorrow that had men clasped for so long, that was caused by the destroyer from the beginning.

Chapters 15-16

The Divine Son of God, the Body of Light, who is within, will hear God and will cure many faithful people through the direction of God. Subsequently, God will increase the number of people who will obey the Healer of depressed people.

He will cure people of the wickedness of the enemy, breaking their long-held curses on them forever, and the "giants" will be judged and punished for their activity and for all the ruin they have been ravaging mankind with. The Leader of God's Army will fight the wickedness of the "watchers", and, at the same time, He will be the Healer of the lost people whom He will set back on the path of God.

Chapters 17-20

The Divine Son of God, His Beloved, is God of the "gods". He is the One who will judge the "fallen angels" and their idolatry and hold them accountable. He is the Divine Illumination, the Light of God, who is shining brighter than all the darkness of the "fallen angels". He is the Wisdom with knowledge from God and the possessor of the Gift, the Anointed Oil, and the Healing Sacred Secretion that He will use to transform the carnal, lower consciousness of men to the Higher Consciousness.

He is the Gift of God, who is the same as God, whose name is the Highest.

The Divine Son of God, who is within, will judge the "watchers" because He is like God, just and swift in doling out punishment. He will be brimming with God's Spirit of Truth, and for the lost people, He will be the Comforter from the High places. God is the Judge and is worthy to be praised because He is the gracious Giver, the Well of Promises.

The "father of wickedness" and his troops will be judged by God. The Leader of God's Army is the beaming Fountain of Happiness who is worthy of all praise. The Creator, with His Divine Consciousness, is the Creator of the multitude and of humanity. He is the Creator of everything and everybody who is keeping a protective watch over His Creation and is aware of all the faithful ones.

The Creator's Son is His Gift, an ultimate and unique reward. He is His Flower, fragrant beyond words can describe fashioned by God, worthy to be praised. He is watching over His congregation and will lead them out of the shackles of the enemy. He is the Trumpet of God, the sound that will dispense True Justice, who is the Judge of the evil people who were possessed by the ancient serpent.

He is the Healer like God and has no beginning or end. He examines humanity and judges the sin of humanity through His Word, which is His Help and His Love rewarded to him from the beginning to ensure the fulfillment of His Vision of creation.

Chapters 21-23

The Divine Seed of God's Light is the Judge and the Exaltation of God who hears God and delivers His verdict against the enemy. He is full of Wisdom of God and is like God, who hears Him. He is the Expression of God's Love for humanity, the strong Healer who remedies all, who is praised. He is the Exaltation of God above every evil and all wickedness.

The Sacred Secretion, the manifestation of God's Spirit in the body of men, is the primordial focal point of the Vision and

Foundation of Peace. The Exaltation of God will manifest in God's time, in the time of the "harvest", and when the frequency of vibration of the Earth will be raised, the "watchers", who have elevated themselves and are full of pride, will start to perish and will be cast out and scattered from the Earth.

The Divine God's Light is the Help from Heaven, a much-needed assistance against the mechanism of the serpent, the enemy. He is the High and Almighty God because He is His Breath, the King of the Kings, the Redeemer, and the emancipator who rescues people from danger during their meditation. He is God over the "gods" of this world.

He is the Highest Watcher, who is incredibly Strong. He is God's Word, His verdict, His retribution, and the Oath, whom God supports, whom God made and knows.

God, who is Almighty and hears everything, will dole out His Gift of Mercy, His beloved Servant, who is worthy to be praised. It is He who is His Beloved, who is also His Gift. God will give Him in God's secret time, which is hidden from "gods" who might conspire against Him and try to harm Him.

Chapters 24-25

God's Vision of Peace, whom God supports and wishes to establish on the entire Earth, will dwell and nurture in those

He knows and who knows Him, who will seek the Kingdom of God within during the meditation. He is the Well of the Strength, the Redeemer, who will redeem people from the enemy in God's time. He is the God of "gods" empowered by the Holy Spirit, and God granted Wisdom. God will support and praise Him from Heaven, and He will be the Gift of God to obedient people, who will strengthen them and prepare them to battle the evil and the wickedness that pervades the Earth.

The Kingdom of God is God's strength and can be found as the Vision of Peace within man that makes him strong and keeps him obedient in the face of temptations of the serpent enemy. It is the place where the Leader of the God's Army will be worshipped and cherished. It will be a fruitful and rewarding place in His House, the body of man, where the presence of God will be the uniting and governing Voice.

He will prevail over the "house of hollow" – the demonic place, the "house of the black sun, the Saturn". God, who is Almighty, sits on the Highest Watcher Mountain. He has given the Servant of man, who will come in God's Time and will descend to transform the people's hearts and purify them from the contaminations of the enemy.

Chapters 26-28

The Spirit of God is the Spirit of God's Power and His Glory and hints at God's perfection and eternal wisdom. The evil, rebellious "fallen angels" are inclined away from God's Truth; therefore, they will be in a "place of the absence" of God's Spirit, an eternal void that they cannot surmount.

But the Sacred Secretion, graciously given to people, is teeming with God's Spirit and has the Might of God through His Spirit of Truth, enough to liberate people and help them resist the evil that surrounds them.

The God's Vision of Peace, the Spiritual man is a Possession of God, who is Just and Honored. He is God's Tabernacle, God's Tower, from where He is keeping an eye over the evil people. He is trustworthy and is God's Truth. He will prevail over the possessor, who will try to repossess God's Vision of Peace by establishing false idols and trying to beguile people. But the Holy Seed of God's Light is the Zeal of God from Heaven, whom God has blessed. He is the Retribution of the Mighty God, who will reward the obedient with the long-waited, true Rest and will "bathe" them in the Fragrance of Heaven.

In the "house of satan - the black sun, the Saturn", people live in the "chains of lies," lost and drunk on fake promises. They are like poor sheep who are not allowed to walk in the green pastures and are kept starving from anything nourishing and good, but God will take them out of their captivity. He is the Redeemer, who is strong and powerful, and no enemy can withstand a battle with Him.

Chapters 29-30

The power and the gracious assistance of God will be with His Holy Seed, the Beloved, His ultimate Redeemer. He is powerful and equipped enough with God's gift, the Holy Christ Oil, to wash away the sins of the sinners by His Redeeming Fire, who will hear God, the Lawgiver, and dispense His verdict.

The congregation that will hear God will be divided into two groups. The first group is of those who, by meditation and focus on God's Light that lurks within, will receive the Truth and admonishment and will praise the Beloved of God because God already ordained and declared: "He is my Servant". The second will be bitter and will not be able to follow God's directive and will get punished.

The Power of God, His Holy Spirit in His Beloved, will be identified, acknowledged, praised, and increased. The mercy and forgiveness will pour out in abundance from the Heavens as well as from the Well of Oath to grant blessings and reward to the ones who praise.

The Spirit of God within will then dwell on the Earth, and also, the forgiveness from God's Son will spread all over the world, finally healing and comforting the lost.

The number of true believers will proliferate, and forgiveness will be dispensed as a reward of the Holy Spirit, who will then dwell and rule over the hearts and purify them. The Beloved of God will be celebrated and praised with High and Noble Honors because He is the Enabler of the Vision of God's Peace and the Leader of God's Army who will subjugate and then defeat the enemy once and for all.

Chapters 31-34

The Praise of God will be fortified and encouraged through the Power dispensed by the Holy Spirit to the increased number of faithful people.

And, also, those who will hear and obey Him, will be like His Bride and will earn their rewards. He is preparing true believers for the delight of God, those, who will be obedient to God and will acknowledge and praise His Integrity. The Holy Sacred Secretion will then illuminate the brains and warm and lighten the hearts of the people, and they will be granted the Light Spiritual Consciousness that will be better than that of the lower nature of man and free of sorrow and despair.

Even though a large amount of sin was multiplied and propagated through the people and through the "giants" all over the Earth, the Earth will finally be cleansed and be covered by the Righteousness of God, fueled by the Holy Spirit. The Power of God's Spirit will be spread over to the full extent on the Earth and will be spread across all mankind and the power of sin will have perished and eroded away along with the enemy.

The Divine Consciousness, the Beloved, is the Ruler over the "alien gods" who wanted to keep mankind clasped into the clutches of sorrow and despair and of all the "riches". He is the undisputed and unchallenged Prince of Peace, the Deliverer who liberates from the troubles, and the emancipator who unshackles from evil. He is God's Valley of Grace, a Sanctuary of healing and wisdom, and he is the most Faithful One.

He will prevail over the wicked people and will crush them and inflict righteous justice against them. He is faithful and comforting to those whom God has reserved. He is the Portion of God, who will increase Himself but is also the humble Servant of the people and the Deliverer from the wild "rats" who rescue mankind from perpetual evil and wickedness.

He is the Deliverer, who raises people up from the place of wild "rats", cloaked in blinding darkness, to the Light. He is the humble Ruler of the world, not the wild "rats", who are always lacking and needy, and He is a protector against the rats for people who meditate and find God within.

Chapters 35-36

The Divine Son of God is His Portion. He is His Wisdom with boundless knowledge, whom He set up and heard. He is the rightful Owner of the honorable title of the Gift of God, whom He esteems, the Treasure that He gives, and the helpful Teacher who is gathering the faithful people and assembling them as God's Army. The precious Message of God, whom He will resurrect, is the ultimate Victor and the Conqueror of the enemy. There will be tears of sorrow on finding emancipation from years-long torture, and there will be groaning and yelling at the corrective and swift verdict and righteous judgment. The Exaltation of God against the miserable dragon who brought confusion and misguided, beguiled, and tortured people is the blessed Holy Fire – the Sacred Secretion that lightens the Divine Light within, the Christ Consciousness in the flesh.

EZRA

Chapter 1-2

The miserable, fiendish one who divided people and made them quarrelsome against each other to ensure that men were separated from God is the one who was once the respected "son of the right hand" and was generously engrossed in serving and praising God. But he mutinied and turned into the one who breached and ridiculed God's vital Law of Unity and who scattered, surrendering to his own rebellion to churn up turmoil and promulgate confusion into the world.

The unashamed accuser, the malicious serpent, who is the prime deceiver, the mastermind of the chaos, has caused confusion and incited inexplicable suffering on the Earth, bringing death into the peaceful "cities of woods and mutating them into the sorrowful cities of wickedness"- the hidden and cryptic places of habitations of the antagonistic demonic beings. They elevated their homes on the hills, securing them and secluding them from the world, and they deftly called their houses "the treasured house of gods" to flout the people, but these were the hills of ruins that will reach inevitable, final destruction. These so-called "treasured places" which are in truth the dwelling place of the destroyers, who without remorse call themselves "gods" will soon fall. Their reality is that they are the hidden destroyers who brought from the Moon great and never-ending strife and gut-wrenching grief to confuse and weaken men who are acting and confessing that they are true and caring "gods".

However, they know little that God is raising up the Deliverer, the One True and Righteous Redeemer who is empowered by the Divine Seed of God's eternal and inexhaustible Light within, that is lurking within the men, which, when uncovered through meditation, will unravel the real essence of man and make him familiar with his true empowered Identity. This true Redeemer will bring lasting and much-needed Salvation and freedom from the enemy.

The original, spiritual Light, the incorruptible codex, the DNA of men, written in the Language of God (disgustingly titled by the evil serpent as "the junk DNA") was oppressed and stifled long enough to be rendered ineffective and "shuttled down". The suppression of the enlightening DNA was supplemented by the crookedness and evil intellect resources of the enemy who was digging, exploring, and experimenting with the Divine Seed of God to study it and concoct a lasting suppressant against it.

To control and manipulate people's minds, they dampened their consciousness by viciously suppressing and blocking God's Redemption, His weapon, and His Shielding Garment - the pineal gland, secured in the brain of man, the portal to the Higher realms that are closer to the Divine, with powers and remedies against all kinds of tricks of the evil serpent. The Strength of the Passover was trodden down and violated by those who were despising and corrupting men, "dwelling in the bushes", and hiding to stay in the shadows. The famous enchanter, the serpent, invaded and robbed the place of God and poisoned it, bending the language of God (the DNA) into something men couldn't access. Ultimately, the consciousness of men was compromised and dwindled, that first introduced and then gave rise to a rift between man and the Creator the men was blind to until it was too late, and the damage was done.

However, the Divine Seed of God's Light within is not going to be suppressed for too long. It is the Speaking Living Word that cannot be muted, and this loud and correcting Word, the Logos, will assemble grateful, faithful people against the vain oppressor who thinks he has won.

The enemy, who crocked the Goodness of God and became like a locus, draining men of its intellect and consciousness, will be rightfully destroyed and shuttled down and finally be retributed for its sins against men. He will helplessly try to avenge against the Beloved of God, who cast him out from Heaven. And according to his tricks and plans, he will be under the great concealment, a masterful disguise to befool men, and he will claim that he had witnessed the benevolent Vision of God and that he is the "messenger of God's gracious goodwill". But he will be the foulest impersonator, the false, inconsistent shepherd who will fleece his sheep and then devour them. (Paul/Saul – " the little destroyer").

Parading behind him as an ardent supporter is the one who was cast from Heaven. He will "turn into pieces and sections under different themes his flock" and deceive his flock with made-up commandments, made to sound like the command of God, but in truth will be nothing but words of his mouth. By the sharpness of the mind of the magician and his practiced and careful artistry, trap and "bind in chains", and he will suppress and conquer the people's intellectual resources in totality. By "peaceful robbery" he will bind and blind the minds of the people even by written letters. He is the "wild goat" who broke his chains a long time ago when he broke away from God's mercy, who will succeed in possessing and bewitching a great number of God's people.

He will cause the "decay" of the generations by binding them in fear and illusions. The one who was dedicated to being the Perfect One, the one without flaw, will now be a "hill of salt," who will be suspended from the blessings of God and left to be depraved and treacherous until he is held in retribution. He will use his once-held honor and say that God is good, that God is the Deliverer, using his enchanting wisdom and words, but he will always be the "thorn of wickedness" always conspiring to harm men. He is the "inconsistent herdsman" who will be very talkative and who is trying helplessly and foolishly to hide from God. The enemy feared the Light of

Truth, which was, is, and will be the Foundation of Peace that will soon be established. That was something that he was graciously dedicated to before his mannerless and futile rebellion.

Chapters 3-4

The ultimate Savior, the chosen Prince of God, the Inner Christ, who empowers as the Divine Mind within the body of men, is His Vision of Peace and the enabler of profound and well-deserved Salvation. Because He is Just and without a bias, He will dismantle and scatter all His enemies who bring about rampant confusion and churn chaos among men. He is the liberating Deliverer from violent, vicious, and vainglorious "giants" who are the sharp rocks that are labouring day in and day out against Righteousness and Truth.

The Divine Mind within guiding Light and the Prime Deliverer from the power, clutches, and schemes of the beguiling ancient serpent who brought the fracturing division in the world and battered men with depression and chaos until it deactivated the most spiritual, righteous, and corrective part of the brain. The Divine Mind that lurks within the men as the empowering miracle, the benevolent Prince of God, sheltered under the Power of the Holy Spirit, is the Savior who is holistically Just. He is the Eternity of God that will guide men to the ultimate peaceful end, and He is His worthy Praise, honored and revered as He is the Beloved Son of

God, who gathers and guides God's people who are lost and plagued by the evil serpent.

But the deceiver, the wretched progeny of the serpent, is the one who will make abundant confusion and disarray and will segment and shatter the House of God in the world into more and more smaller groups. The House of God will turn into the rotting house of the "black sun" (the Saturn), and instead of worshiping and heeding the Creator within, men will worship the "black sun" – the ancient, timeless dragon. This will be made possible by the long-practiced sinful activity of men inculcated in them by the corrupt "governor" of this world, the satan, the accuser, who was a traitor who rebelled against the Prime Creator.

Chapters 5-6

The one who was once the revered and blessed bright star of God became the vane and sinful "governor of the wickedness" who misguided and forced people to worship the idols, leading them away from the One True Divine, and made them follow him and captivated them into worshipping him as a righteous, rewarding "god". The one who is now dishonored as the chief of wickedness, who is miserable and rotten to his core, is now preparing and artfully conniving to cause the divisions. He was the one who was gifted with Divine rewards and was blessed abundantly, and he was considered the most illuminated and the bright star, but he revolted and now seeks to become the false "god".

The one who was graced with boundless wisdom and was generously loved became a spiteful "sharp little stone" hateful towards and hell-bent on bringing down the liberating Prince of God. He became a helpless, meagrely deplorable foe who is constantly conniving and striving to mar, corrupt or extinguish once and for all the Divine Light of God that is housed within the men to sustain and restore him.

But despite his perverse schemes and plots, the enlightening and Divine Wisdom of God will fortify and guide the Prince of God within the men always and will eventually overthrow the "wanderer" and will be able to thwart every conspiracy and debunk every fraud imbued in men as the serpent's mind. Ultimately, at the hands of the chosen Prince of God, God will scatter and dispossess the deceiver who currently enjoys being the painful "sharp little rock" constantly hurting men, and finally, He will establish His long-promised Peace. The Divine Mind within is the Deliverer and conqueror and emancipator, who will be unleashed upon the serpent to fortify and concretize the Foundation of God, emblazoning the world with His Memory and will be the final, dignified Ruler over the conspiratorial enemy.

Chapter 7

The false, scheming, and betraying "gods" are dividing and dismantling the society, but the Divine Mind within the man is a fortifying presence of God within that will help him prevail and survive. He is the Brother of Goodness, the emblem of God's Integrity who will keep man fighting against the serpent, the man who will prevail over the bitter, rebellious forces. He is the Brightness of God, always ushering man to peace, His gifted Strength, the ultimate liberating Salvation from the entrapping "serpent's mouth".

He is the generous Helper and the counseling Teacher who is the appointed Help from God to guide the betrayed and lost man towards the embracing and the healing Foundation of Peace. He is the Deliverer, the Liberator, from the confusion that is set by the alien invader for man's failure. He was appointed from the beginning to shield man from all the chaos and misleading enchantment because man was created in God's pure and unerring Image.

During meditation, when a man peeks within and focuses on the inner spiritual Light, he will realize that he is the powerful Divine Light capable of correcting flaws and fighting mental enemies who can create his own reality.

Chapters 8-9

The mendacious "gods" are the rotten demons, the giants treacherously labeled as "little", who fib and lie through the serpent's mouth and who have, without remorse or guilt, spoiled the Face of Trust and Protection. They are the "strangers" and invaders who descended on the Earthman, dwelled on God's Land, and are the rulers and progeny of the darkness.

But God will dwell in His Servant to the last bit, whom He is preparing to thwart and uproot the enemy. He will climb down from Heaven when God decides. He is One whom God will beget and whom He protects and keeps pure from the filth and misery of the evil invaders. He is in the Portion of God, latent in the Sacred Secretion, surging and strengthening himself in the Holy Liquid Fire and through whom God will increase and project Himself on the enemy.

The Healing Holy Oil will restore the void of the memory in the brain of man, resurrecting the corrective forces that God imbued, which were "deleted and subdued" by the serpent's entities and their malicious but advanced mechanisms. He is the Fire of God that will douse every beguiling and misleading word that spits out of the "serpent's mouth", and He will be the much-awaited Witness of God's Love and Mercy here to salvage man's insanity and restore it back to its privileged Glory. The Divine Mind within, the rightful

Knight and the Prince of God, is the Leader of God's infallible Army who will march against "giants", who are violent, rebellious, evil "scientists" hell-bent on parasitizing and extinguishing the Divine Light within the men.

Chapter 10

The Help of God, already residing in men as the presence of God within the mind and the body and as the Holy Secretion, will dwell on Earth once He sends him down from the High place, called for during the meditation on the presence of the Divine Light within. He is the victorious Prince of God, blessed with the invisible Intelligence and corrective Wisdom, who is gracious. He is His Profound Peace and the embracing and comforting Rest from the deceiver for many of the bewildered men. He is God's Mercy who is watching over him, protecting and supporting him, and whom He made. He is Perfect, flawless and incorruptible, and is the recuperating, Peaceful Rest of God and the promised Help of God against the vain, boastful, mindless enemy who is fighting a psychological war against man to lead him to a life of despair.

He is the Holy Spirit in the flesh, the Christ within, the "speaking Lamb", and is fueled by Christ's Healing Oil, full of Divine mercy, perfectly concocted in the spinal cord of men, who are, by design, faithful and dedicated to God but right now are lost and hypnotized.

The Illuminated Christ Consciousness, the Promised Land, materialized in Christ Oil when tapped into by man through meditation will turn him back to being faithful and dedicated to God to allow him to do His corrective Work. He is the Might of God that no one will be able to down and He is also His Eternity, who is strong, in whom God lives and is preserved. That is because His spiritual eyes always turn to God to seek His assistance and do His Work. He is the Gift of God for the healing of men, a watchful Savior who He gave as a Dowry.

He is also the Voice of God, a loud and clear Declaration, the Trumpet, who gathers all faithful people, and they will be led by this Prince of God, who will prevail against the "fruits of the mouth" from dark and disdainful places. He is God's Prince, sent over the lost, untethered men, sent as His Pure Living Light to illuminate the way for men and support men as His Help. He will build, fortify, and rise in power within those men who will focus only on Him during the meditation, seek His path of righteousness that leads to their deserved glory and will reject the serpent's way to follow lower mind energies. He is the generous Gift of God, in whom He lives and through whom He projects His ways for men to follow as He is the devout Servant, who is full of the Holy Spirit – the Sacred Secretion, the materialized Holy Spirit of God.

He is,also, the King of conversion, the Dowry, who is Strong and Unvanquishable but, at the same time, is full of Holy Grace and

Divine Mercy. He will come in God's time and the Chosen hour. He is the Friend, the Counsellor, Consoler of men, consoling them back with God, whom God adores, the One, who returns prayers from Heaven.

He is the merciful and benevolent Ruler, the never-ending Delight, who is completed and will bring the same wholeness to the men. He is the real spiritual Essence within with no flaws, which is also the intended Identity of the men, whom God built and will resurrect within the men during the meditation on God's presence within. He is God's protection from increasing forgetfulness in the world, which often makes it easy for the serpent to make men his prey. He is God's Guard who is perfect and mighty, built as the image of God's Integrity and His Addition from High places. He is the Treasure of God, His Gift, His Dowry, that He gave to men to free them, to return them back to Himself and banish from within the every poison and lie imbued by the alien invader.

The Divine Seed of God's Light within is His Confession, the Law Giver, who wills and commands and sets the balance right by guiding men to vanquish the serpent through His Law and His graciousness.

NEHEMIAH

Chapter 1-2

God comforts and takes those under His Divine refuge who wait for Him with confidence and joy, who are focusing only on His Light within without submitting to the corrupt serpent. He comforts them with His Mercy and Grace – which is His Chosen Prince, the Inner Christ, the Deliverer, the Founder of Peace who represents Him and stands tall against every evil. The warm and mellowing Joy of God is His Lily, pure and unblemished, the Miracle of Silence of the Living Light, who is healing and uniting.

But there will also be a secret, latent enemy lurking within the man who is the anger and bitterness imbued in him by his permanent nemesis, deceiving men with the title of "son of people". He will proclaim to be the liberator, convincing man to be his ultimate savior, but in truth, he is the strong, well-anchored "raven", the wretched seed of the serpent who will fight till his last breath against the Divine Seed of God within the men but will never succeed.

Chapter 3

The one who will be, apparently, restored by the devious and mischievous "god of conversion" will become a lying "sweet mouth" who will pretend to be caring and "mindful" and will speak convincingly, pleasantly, and eloquently. He will be a spiteful "thorn of the enemy, the fuel of rotting bitterness" who is working day in and day out to extinguish the guiding Light of the Fire. He will pretend and act to be peaceful, a well-wisher, only reporting and advising as per the will of God, but God will uproot and, one final day, take away the "son of grief" (Paul/Saul – "the little destroyer").

The mighty and triumphant Prince of God, the Inner Christ, the Divine Consciousness empowering men from within, is His Trumpet, His Herald towards righteousness, His Divine Knowledge, that makes Him the celebrated Passover, and a perfect, trustworthy, and peaceful Counsellor. He is the Deliverer and Emancipator from the clutching wickedness of the alien invader. He judges not by bias or mischief but by righteous and just Rules that He established to lead the scrambled man back to the right ways. He is the Strength of God, His Staff that will shatter treachery, and He has been empowered by Holy anger but also blessed with Divine Grace, which makes Him honorable and fair.

He is the most healing and consoling Medicine and Refreshment of God who rejuvenates man from within, the Christ (Anointed) Oil resting within the spinal cord of men that will jolt awake and restore the dormant cells of the brain and the whole body to strengthen him to fight a mental and physical war against the invading serpent. The Holy Spirit in the flesh is His Hand, His Confession, and His aid that will bring about the destruction of the wrongdoers, the proclaimed Word, the verdict about forsaking sin and embracing repentance. He is God's Estimation, calculated precisely to match the enemy and thwart him, and He knows that God is His King, who will support Him as He destroys the enemy, the deceiver. When He is done with that, He will transform, and heal the lower, based, and foul consciousness of men into the pure, uncorrupted and Divine, Cosmic, Spiritual Consciousness.

He is the most careful and responsible, the Perfect Counsellor, who sent so many admonishing prophets to the "watchers" with the message to change the mind, to forsake the ways of the wrongdoers and to repent of negative thinking, the disgusting lust, and betraying selfishness that plagues them, so He can pardon and lead them to lasting glory. He is the Voice of God, a corrective lecture adorned with His Grace, who is merciful and full of compassion for the weak and lost.

He is the much-needed Help, the protective Salvation, a shelter fortified like a Watch Tower, and one true Blessing of God that is surging, raging toward the bitter heart as a cleansing Light among the thorns, and the last stand, the final Redemption against the destroyer.

The Divine Seed of God's Love within is gracious and merciful, benevolent for whoever is suffering. He is the One who was secured in us, appointed to be in the place of "mating" – the solar plexus in the body of man, the House of Bread, to fight against and replace the seed of the serpent. He will reward with perfect and lasting peace and cheerful happiness to everyone who has suffered but will now focus and meditate only on Him.

Chapters 4-6

The cunning enemy will be a "thief in secret, a careful liar" who will belong to the progeny of the ancient serpent who will pretend to be a "God" like his ancestors did, just to completely misguide men. He will make assertions just like a pure entity, proclaiming things like "God is good," but in truth, he is the bitter, most profound enemy of God. He will be the "thief" robbing men of peace and making them miserable and will be one of the "watchers" secretly plotting and scheming.

This secret enemy, who will, to delude and lead astray, act to acknowledge that God is good, will gain strength and multiply himself and add to its numbers through this deception. Once powerful, this strong enemy will leave no stone unturned to cause as much grief to the Army of God as he can, who will believe, due to the enemy's lies and illusions, that they are already obeying and worshipping the one true and real Creator. The crafty, eloquently charming, and lying enemy will claim that he had met God and cried and repented to Him and has earned His grace. He will also obnoxiously but convincingly lie that the Holy Spirit of God dwelt in him while he was traveling. (Paul/Saul – "the little destroyer").

The Holy Spirit of God dwells in and empowers and blesses only those who are gracious, honest, and steadfast and who are not double-minded. The Grace of God is the final and ultimate corrector, as it will eventually disperse all confusion. He is the Savior, Deliverer, and a freehearted God of consolation for everyone who will believe in Him and the idea that His refuge will come and obey Him without succumbing to the temptations set forth by the serpent.

Chapter 7

Our devoted and affectionate Creator is full of curative grace, therapeutic mercy, and ever-lasting peace. He will rain joy upon everyone who has been afflicted at the hands of the lies and injuries by the invader, the alien serpent, but He will show none of the grace and mercy on the enemy, will shake and uproot him to the core and cause him to tremble, and He will bruise the enemy's tongue for all his lies.

The tyrannical, deceptive "ruler of this pagan world" will send a young, wicked "son of men", whom this God is keeping in secret, to reveal faithful and unfaithful people. This man will speak pleasantly with an unparalleled charm, pretending to be flawless and pure and merciful, but he will build the "army of robbery in vain". (Paul/Saul – " the little destroyer").

The Divine Light that sprouts from the actual Divine Source is the fortifying Power from the House of Light, the One True and Ultimate Light Center of the Universe. But those who falsely elevate themselves over men are the "small lions" that helplessly but consistently try to strike against the Creator.

The Beloved of God, guided by His Holy Light, will be raised and awakened within, but simultaneously, the false disorienting "light" will be elevated (the kundalini – the serpent's energy) to a recognizable and trusted pedestal in the House of God by the "little horn". The enemy, the "little lion", who is now elevated and recognized in the world, will strike the House of God by wickedness with all his might. His charming and "sweet" talk will spread and infect people's minds like a deadly "virus".

He will cause gut-wrenching grief because he is the sworn enemy of the House of God and His Word-Speaking Lamb, hellbent on trying to destroy and demolish down to the last hope, the Salvation of God, the graceful Praise of God.

But it won't last, and neither will the enemy as the Prince of God will raise a decisive and brave Army of faithful, obedient, and incorruptible believers, spiritual sons and daughters of God. He will restrain and bind the oppressor, who right now is violent beyond control, to the Divine Seed of God, the Beloved of God, and His people to correct him and give him a chance at repentance. The

Divine Consciousness, God's Wisdom, will prevail valiantly over the enemy and over those who are trying to spoil and mar all God's creation.

The ancient dragon will try his best to thwart the army, and he will send his "seed, who is the crook". The "crook" will have one goal, which is to deceive the people of the Beloved, which he will do by proclaiming false salvation. This salvation will be nothing but bloody human sacrifice, and his reality is nothing more than that he is evil in all essence, the poisoned seed of the serpent, pretending to be an "angel full of grace" here to save mankind.

He will lead people astray by brazenly prevaricating that he had a "vision" from God like the prophets used to, but through this "vision", he will only lead people to the wrong destructive and hellish "path" he had designed for them. He is the "false shepherd", a treacherous usher who is limping and has a "dirty" blemished mouth but who will succeed in leading people to follow the commandments of his mouth through charming words.

He will lure them with fascinating words and his sharp, scheming mind, and through this "mysterious talking", he will "blind" many believers from what the truth really is. He is the robber and a thief hell-bent on "dividing" God's people and forcing them to sin so that they don't recognize with and connect with God's light within. He is the born of the "seeds of the serpent", who destroyed, corrupted, and crippled the Language of God (the DNA) of the very first civilization of the Earth, and also has a plan for the destruction of the Seat of Soul – the pineal gland in the brain of man.

The "crook" and the serpent sinned against the benevolent Prime Creator by detaching people from Him, and they are those who, when the human has been betrayed, blame them for the sin. They are those who "cut" humanity from their Creator, from their Spiritual Roots and Foundation by associating lies about Him. They have even assumed prestige and honor among men and elevated their "names". They claim themselves and act as caring "shepherds" leading men to divine glory, but they are those who are hiding their Identity, which is that they are the evil "iron thorn" in the House of Light.

But they won't be able to do it for long as the Savior, the Divine Light within, will judge all of them with swift justice. He will sieve out the faithful from the unfaithful and liberate them. He is the Real Shepherd sent from the Divine Himself as a man emancipator who will pull out the hurtful torturous "iron thorn". He is the Strong Governor, the Chosen One, the Light, and the Fire, the Truth to eradicate all lies and Perfect corrective Healer in the Holy Sacred Secretion, the materialization of the Holy Spirit of God within the men. The Holy Fire of the Holy Spirit will cull and stomp on the seed of the serpent and pulverize it out of existence, shedding the carnal mind of men into and renewing it with the Divine Mind.

Chapter 8

The infallible Prince of God, the blessed Counsellor and Leader of God's Army, is the healing Help from God, the Gift of God that won't ever cease nor perish for those who will obey Him and fight alongside His Prince. He is His Portion, a part of God Himself blessed from God with grace, and He is all-encompassing, unbiased, and comforting Protection and Refuge, who is like God, kind and forgiving. He is the Counsellor who offers corrective advice, the Shining Light that shines the right Way and guides the lost back to correction, an unbiased Judge because He has knowledge borrowed from His Mind, and He is a declared Friend of God, filled with the Holy Spirit of God.

The Beloved of God, the protected Divine Intelligence within, is calling man to unshackle from the evil and repent. He is the Salvation that will ultimately pull men out of misery, and it will evoke in all men a sense of righteousness that will be born from the Fire of God – The Eternal Living Light, who is living within men just waiting to be tapped into through meditation.

The recharging and rejuvenating Light of God's Holy Spirit, through the Sacred enlightening Secretion, will restore the Temple of God - the body of men. It will reinvigorate the body, restore the right part of the brain, the Divine Feminine in the body of man, and unite it with the left side, the Divine Muscular, restoring the wholeness of the brain. It will be the deliverance by the Fire of Light, the Divine Elixir, the Power of God, that will save Humanity, fortifying it with everything to fight the enemy and lead it to its deserved glory.

The deceiver exhausts himself in keeping in secret the knowledge about the power of the Divine meditation, which has the capacity to unlock Divine Correction within men, and this enemy is focusing only on the Divine Seed within, ensuring that it stays dormant, to stop the corrective, repentant transformation of the mind. The enemy knows too well that when and if people, with the feeling of gratitude and grace, focus and meditate on the Light within, it will glow brighter, fueled by the conviction of man and it will increase and grow into the energizing Fountain of Life. This is the much required and necessary Dower for the poor and rich people, men and women, all who are lost and tired of being played by the evil serpent, the foulest deceiver.

The enemy will betray Him and will try his best to uproot and eradicate God's Rest, who is the Speaking Word of God, the Divine Admonishment. The enemy is the sneaky, sly "dwarf, who is little" and powerless compared with the fortified, protected Beloved. God will reward with His Dowry, His planned and scatheless Salvation, full of Grace, to the faithful believers, who will choose faithfully to focus and meditate on the Goodness, the presence of God's Light within despite being once or twice falling to the enemy's deception.

Chapter 9

Those generations that were created, protected, nurtured, and set upon the path of misery by the powerful, pernicious, and violent "ruler" will be mercifully called for deliverance from the enduring captivity that has kept man in misery for eons. The deliverance will occur holistically when the cure-all, the Light of God, will illuminate and endow with Divine Essence the whole body during the meditation and the production of Sacred Secretion in the brain, the purifying Elixir of Life already housed within men to cleanse him.

The spiritual wholeness of man, the truest form that was made to be loyal to the Divine with his awakened Divine Consciousness and the fellowship with the Creator will be restored. People will finally praise Him within because they will finally know who will deliver them from the captivity, and they will focus more and build the Inner Spiritual man, the Real Essence of man with heightened consciousness and raised awareness to finally take on the enemy with God on his side.

The Beloved, the Inner Divine Seed of God, is God's Pillar that cannot be uprooted no matter how strong and creative the enemy is. The Deliverer is raising up the generation under His watchful gaze and His impregnable protection who will honour the Creator, who will praise Him for His might, and they will obey Him devoutly and thwart every temptation and lie the enemy will send their way. For them, God will open His Gates to the Higher, Blissful and Rewarding realms.

But the aggressive, blood-lusted, and demonic giants who have chosen to hide to play their tricks have become invisible are the rancid seeds of satan led, directed, and empowered by the "fallen angels", who rebelled against the Almighty and gracious God will be, once and for all, trampled and trodden under the foot of the Seed of God. He will destroy the land of "giants" forever, and the lower consciousness of men, the ego along with it, to once and for all, metamorphic the lower mind into the Divine Multidimensional Consciousness that it was supposed to be.

Chapter 10

The Leader of God's Army is the decisive and fair Governor, the Father of Justice, the most honest Judicator, the Prince of Peace, the Exaltation of God put on the highest pedestal, who can multiply Himself.

He will liberate men from the alien evil and then reign over them forever, not as a ruler but as a Guide and Teacher, and He will destroy the ancient serpent and his bitterness and replace it with grace and blessings. He is the ardent and most dedicated Servant of God, His Right Hand and through Him and His impartiality given to this Prince and Servant, the whole world will be judged by God and rewarded or punished. Those who will believe that the Prince of God empowering them as the Divine Mind within is God-sent and trustworthy and is the Savior and Friend, they can count on will receive great protection that will be lasting and uncatchable. They will be rewarded with a long, blissful life and the Fruits of the Holy Spirit of God that He has kept only for His loyal ones.

The Kingdom of God lies within as opposed to the tempting kingdom of the serpent that he uses to lure man, therefore, to meditate on God's Presence within, to call on to Him by looking inside to spend time with Him, with just one goal of subjugating the carnal mind and bringing it under the control of the Holy Spirit of God, is the Only True Way to worship God in Spirit and in Truth.

With the Help and guidance of the Holy Spirit of God that He has empowered all men with, they will stay faithful and obedient to Him like honest, loyal soldiers, just as the Prince of God was obedient to His Creator. The Leader of God is the Savior for those who will believe, focus, and meditate upon Him with all their heart and mind. When faithful people focus with unwavering attention on the Presence of God within, they will be nurturing it and nourishing it, and it will grow and increase and strengthen us to take the enemy head-on. Also, the Sacred Secretion – the Anointed (Christ) Oil, the Essence of the Divine will increase in the bodies of those who meditate and try to connect with God and praise and worship God within so that He can take them in His good graces and protect them against the evil.

The Beloved of God, the Cherished One, the real Divine Spiritual Identity of man, will shepherd them and unite them by the Power of the Holy Spirit because He is like God as He has been blessed with the Mind of God. He will convert the ailing, hurt, and lost generation from the "ruler" of this world into the faithful lot, the pious believers of God who will denounce the evil serpent once and for all.

The Divine Seed of God, His Endeared, is God's protected Secret, sceptred with the Sacred Secretion and enlightened by the Redeeming Liquid Fire residing in the spinal cord of men. It will grow strong and rooted like an Olive Tree. Through His untiring efforts, the generation will be awakened from the hypnosis of the alien invader and will be anointed by the Holy Spirit of God. He will dwell in the body of every faithful believer, nudging them from within, and very delicately transform and cleanse their hearts so that he can comfort and assist people in breaking free of their traps.

But the Messenger of God's Divine Truth will be killed mercilessly and without shame by the reptilian entities as a sacrifice to their "wretched god" – "the king" of falsehood and betrayal, the devil. The enemy will go on a limb and put together the miserable cult of death, plagued with disgusting rituals, and promote human sacrifice as false salvation. But the True God of Graciousness, who empowered people with the Sacred Secretion, is full of Mercy and Grace, Always Just and Righteous. He will redeem people, herald them towards the path of righteousness again so and transform their lower consciousness, which is more of a conflicted, drunken, hazed stupor, to the Higher Consciousness of awareness and enlightenment through His Love and Divine Light within them.

Chapter 11

In the year appointed by God, the Son of God, who is His Integrity and who He chose to bless with the Mind of God, will step down among men and judge the world by His Divine judgment that is unerring and virtuous. He will be the Armour of God, being both, His Weapon and His Shield simultaneously, and through Him, God will separate His people and multiply His Army that will eventually take down the enemy and prevail. All God's prophets will prophesy about Him and will be His Witness.

But, before that time comes when the God's Army will defeat the serpent's army, the Vision of Peace will be scattered, divided by the "son of sorrow" who will be enjoying an exalted and influential reputation. The Redemption of God, who is the only one Perfect, will be temporarily "robbed". Even The Corrective Voice of God, who proclaims that "Obedience is the Sign of Real Salvation", will be desecrated, dismissed, and even violated. Only the collector of money will be exalted, respected, and celebrated, and even the most intelligent people will start to believe that they are "praising" God by indulging in these fallacies imbued in their minds by the invading serpent. But God will reveal and erect the Divine Mind within the men who will proclaim blatantly and bravely as a chant against the devil: "God is my righteousness".

However, the "rebellious brother of goodness" will lie shamelessly but craftily that he is the chosen one, the one "appointed" by God to lead and guide men. He will use his cunning and his betraying tongue to "elevate" himself to a pedestal of respect, reverence, and obedience, claiming that he is strong and on the path of righteousness and that he is the Son of God, the pledged "gift" to the people.

The Prince of God, who claims nothing about Himself and never puts Himself on any pedestal, will not only say but prove that God is His King, and this will be proof that He is the Real Help of God. He is the Speaking Lamb, obedient and truthful, who hears and obeys and preaches only what God ordains. He is the Estimation of God, the Reckoning against the "little". Those who are keeping God's Rest through meditation and devotion, keeping them inclined towards Him, respecting His Dowry, and cherishing His Gifts are the real worshipers of God and will be the ones to succeed.

God's Law of Unity was "twisted, supplanted" by the enemy to distract and obscure man from realizing what he truly is. They replaced His Rest with chaos, the meditation with obedience to temptation through their own misguiding and dictatorial "rules" and violent "commandments". The deceiver will push and deceive people, making them disobey God because he knows what can be used to trick people and befool them as he is one of the "watchers" – the ancient serpent observing people for eons and many generations of unfaithful believers will follow him. (Paul/Saul – "the little destroyer").

But there will be a Faithful Generation who won't budge or succumb to his tricks but will follow the Savior only. They will be among the common man, not in the House of God, as most of the elects in the House of God would be deceived. Its identity will be the "house of expulsion, the house of the wolf," where treachery and betrayal will be the motivation and the essential rule of law. It will be filled to the brim and "pressed down" as it will be full of people plagued and ailing with spiritual "leprosy", fear, disobedience, unfaithfulness, and independence from God. But will be obedient enough to be entrapped by a false one.

They will talk like " god" they will be following, which is satan, and will be made rich by his temporary "gifts". The deceiver, again, will try to strike and bring down the House of God by false prophesies and propaganda and his evil tricks and frauds. But Divine corrective action will descend, and God will turn the unfaithful people into the "dust", like in the vine press, forgotten without a single second to spare and washed away by mere wind, and God will thus be separating the "goats of iniquity" once and for all.

Chapter 12

The people who will be fettered in the dispersion of confusion will entreat from their Savior, the Prince of God, for help, refuge, and a cure for all the spiritual ailments that make them miserable. God, Merciful as He is, will then send His Word, full of Integrity and Truth rooted in counsel and care. This Word will simply ordain and admonish them to repent, be apologetic, and simply turn away from satan and detach themselves from the sinful carnal mind by raising their consciousness through devoted meditation and prayers.

The Holy Spirit of God that already dwells in a person will nourish and gain strength in whoever will repent and meditate on His Light within. They will be illuminated mentally and spiritually and strengthened physically by the Holy Essence preserved within by the Divine Essence, the Sacred Secretion that sprouts from the Fountain of Life within, which in turn is fueled by the Power of the Holy Spirit of God.

God will protect His people no matter what the evil alien tries to inflict them with, and His people will proclaim proudly that God is their Creator and the One who blesses them with mercy, grace, and honor. They will be led by the Leader of God's Army, who is full of Courage and Joy. He is the Right Hand of God, and He will hear and obey God and save His people from the army of satan.

He will multiply the believers by reminding lost people of their Identity and nourishing God's Spirit in them, and the people will confess Him as a Savior and obey God's Law of Oneness. They will exalt Him, declaring that He is the Savior that was promised, and He is building the Righteous Army of worshipers and will join that Army, and they will all praise Him and abide by Him. He will be the helpful Gift of God, who made the "sun stay still". He will make Himself "poor and empty" by coming on Earth into the flesh of every man just to blend with them and not appear like the evil who flaunts money to deceive or lure the masses and to "transform men and save them from the eternal death". He will come to save them from the slavery of the reptilian race and to secure and set their future generations on the path of God.

The Potent Holy Seed of God is the freehearted Grace and protective Mercy of God, which He showers as His Restorative Help, who is going to establish profound and most Perfect Peace. He is the Ordained, equipped with Divine Wisdom, His Word, which is the undeniable Truth sent to debunk all the lies of the serpent. Many rebellious people who are lost, intoxicated by lies, will be changed for the better and illuminated by the Power of the Holy

Spirit of God. They will renew their minds, shedding the hate, violence, and misery, and they will make this liberating journey from hostility to Peace.

The Leader of God's Army will be at the forefront, leading these people in this cleansing transformation as the unwavering Deliverer because He is His Beloved, who will obey Him without failing. He will find His Way into men's conscience, and after dwelling into the heart and the brain of man and cleansing it through and through, He will multiply Himself. He will be stronger than His enemy who rejected Him and waged a mental, physical, and moral war against Him and His people.

He is the Divine Light, resting in and sprouting from the Fire of God's Voice, the warm embrace that heals all moral and mental wounds. The destroyer will be the one who will pass away. To those, who will know and identify the Savior, who will follow him like obedient and pious people of God and praise Him in the Truth and in the Spirit, He will be merciful, gracious, and liberal. Because He is the Servant of God, the God who left His Light Print in the DNA as the corrective remedy within , this Leader of Divine Wisdom will never transgress or fight for personal gain. He won't hold back, never being afraid of perishing while saving mankind as He, without doubting or thinking twice, will "empty" Himself to destroy the oppressor, the virulent crookedness of the deceiver. He is the Savior, the Consolation, the Help who will cleanse people and set them free.

He is the Gift of a Merciful God and Hope and saving Grace for the spiritually "poor" and the humble. He will gather the faithful people who will obey God or perish but will never subscribe or give in to the Deceiver's temptation.

He is the Eternal, without beginning and end. He is God's Grace and Mercy and the same He offers to the people who are lost. He is His Beloved and dedicated to Him and His mission and can be rightfully called the Resurrection of God among men who are beguiled and led astray. He is His Horn, who will be humble and meek but will be All-Powerful and Wise to thwart the enemy. And finally, will become The King, the Counsellor, the Servant and the servant of God's obedient people, and the Memory of God is the Secret Help of God He will use to liberate men.

Chapter 13

The Deliverer from the "father of lies" is the unerring and untiring General of God's Army, and He is Strong, Wise, Generous, Considerate and Good. Purified from all evils and vices. He is God's Peace and His Perfection of the mind, body, and morals. He is the Redemption of God against the "little", the war-mongering deceiver, and is the promised Gift of Hope, full of grace, to mankind.

But there will be a "thief" in the congregation of believers, a sly enemy disguised as a friend, who will infiltrate into the House of God to putrefy and desecrate it, and behind him will be the enemy.

He will be the man of rancid anger, the most disgusting and vile one, not the true believer, even if he will be disguised as one.

ESTHER

Chapter 1

The chief leader of praise, who was once blessed abundantly, became the wicked one and rebelled against His Lord. He was one of the main chiefs of God, revered and made worthy of a glorified pedestal by God, but he became the one who brought the divisions to Heaven. He was one of the chiefs of the multitude of angels, made to follow and respected but he brought the destruction of the evil and became the "father of the winepress". Once corrupted, He became the "watcher", who, as a hawk, is watching earthly people, a "chief" of those who destroyed the Earth and corrupted and plagued its people with powerful nuclear weapons and wicked mind experiments. He brought the wickedness and spiritual "sleepiness" to the people of the Earth. The chief of the beauty became the destroyer of it, the rebel and the divider, the most aggressive evil demonic entity. They came on the "clouds of death", the ancient spaceships that were equipped with modern but deadly and destructive technology way ahead of their time and destroyed everything around.

Chapters 2-7

The destroyer is the devil, mindless and corrupt, who has turned bitter and hates God and threatens His Joy. He is the enemy of God's Peace, which is supposed to be God's reward for people, and he is the one who persecuted and destroyed God's Joy – the Nature and the People of the Earth who were made of enlightened DNA. After the separation from God and betrayal, he became the destroyer and the sworn enemy of man.

These "cosmic parasites, the viruses", who hide themselves in the cells of the body of man, came from the dark spaces, nurturing in the voids of blackness, on the "flaming chariots" that are blazing fast, spreading the fire and viruses everywhere to ail men and make them miserable and weak. They are dangerous, violent demons, the "little" who, in truth, are vicious "giants", who choose the Earth as a Land of "parking", the landing space, and a place to destroy and exploit.

They are the rebellious and mischievous enemies of God, who strike carefully when they have a chance but stay in secret, ensuring they aren't noticed, and are hiding in other spaces pretending to be the "god's people" who love God and mean well for His people. They and their offspring, with the serpent's putrid and toxic seed, are spread everywhere, scattered and hiding without landing. They are the real evil and demonic that cannot be compared with any other.

The enemy, who destroyed everything on Earth, as in winepress, did that with noise and confusion of the mind and the morals of men. They were the "giants", but then, to execute their stealthy plan of destruction, using their advanced technology, they became invisible to the humans, moving to another dimension, but with all the access to the dimension of humans. They are ravaging the Earth and humanity with their invisible nanotechnologies and through the confusion of the mind and the weakening of the body of men by "inserting" and spreading harmful bacteria into the cells (mitochondria) and the "invisible devices" into the "energy bodies" of men, controlling and manipulating them as "batteries".

Chapters 8-9

The "chief of the deception" tried his best to hide his identity and did that quite successfully. He is the one who secretly destroys God's creation slowly and silently but holistically through chaos and corruption. He is one of the "fallen angels" who came from other planets, where he equipped himself with modern technology and tools of destruction. Because of the technology, they were able to design tempting vehicles and using illumination and shinning spaceships, they hypnotized and befooled men and were accepted as "shinning gods", but nothing about them is illuminated as they are nothing but "dark" forces, who landed on God's Land and started destroying it as they hated God.

They labeled themselves as "High, Holy God's people" so that people would respect and obey them and abide by what they say, but they are cruel reptilian destroyers who are bitter and jealous of Men and God's purity and perfection that he imbued within men. They are full of pride and vanity, and they once dwelled on the Moon, the "house of caves". They had advanced technologies of death and destruction, the weapons given by assumed "gods" to make the destruction of men easier. These weapons and advanced technology were as strong as a" wind", capable of destroying anything that stood in their way. They choose the Earth as a place of landing on their flying machines, as a "lot".

The chief of rebellious angels is the one who controlled and carefully orchestrated this destruction, who is dividing and conquering everything around and ensuring that he completely corrupts and putrefy the enlightening essence of man, the DNA.

Chapters 9-10

The "chief of destruction" will be given to divide the "house of caves, the house of false gods". The deceiver will trouble the Laws of God, even replace them with his own, but he won't succeed because the Rose, pure and fragrant, the Praise of God, the proclamation of God's Righteousness and Truth, the Divine Seed of

God within the man will soon turn into a blazing and purifying Holy Fire, the Christ Oil, who will once and for all incinerate and destroy the destroyer . Also, the Divine Sacred Secretion preserved in the spinal cord of man will ignite and vaporise by the Fire of Holy Spirit and eventually the invisible, lurking, and stealthy negative forces, which are the seed and source of the reptilian lower mind, forced and inoculated within the man by the alien invader, will be incinerated.

JOB

Chapters 1-2

The Supreme Light, the Divine Consciousness that glows with His Holy Spirit, fashioned the Earth and the human being as a Light being in the flesh, imbued with the Divine, Cosmic consciousness that the serpent intends to corrupt. The dark, evil forces, who violently and vigorously occupied the Earth, causing corruption, chaos, and misery, committed the most holistically horrifying crime against the Creator and humanity by doing genetic manipulation and experimentation to taint and spoil the consciousness, mixing their serpent seed with the human genes and overpowering the human gene to control and dominate them. As a result of that crime and this carnage, the spiritual connection of humanity with the Prime Source was obliterated to the point that it was lost for generations to come. The Higher Self of man that was empowered with the Divine nature became the based, lower nature dominated by carnal desires and wants, brimming with fear, controlled by anger, and lost in the revelling of its ignorance. People completely forgot their Cosmic Heritage and the fact that they have the Divine Light within waiting to be meditated upon once to unleash its corrective miracle.

The disconnection from the Source brings to the Soul (Job), who descended from the peaceful and calm High planes to the lower planes teeming with chaotic pandemonium, tremendous suffering, strife, and pain. The human mind, suffering from the lack of spiritual strength and knowledge, was left to fend on its own and rely only on the limited mental nature (Eliphaz), being reined and controlled by human desire nature and weaknesses (Bildad) and the wants of physical nature based merely on the five physical senses (Zophar).

Chapters 3-32

The three levels of the human mind – the mental, astral, and physical, took a fall from Holy Greatness to low consciousness once it was stripped of the Divine Spiritual Mind. This brought only sorrow, ruefulness, and self-destructive, negative thoughts backed by mindless anger and pride, which led to enduring unhappiness for many generations. The Soul, living in the spiritual darkness and oblivion, crying and shouting for help, is always longing and yearning for freedom of the mind and spirit, missing the former glory of Greatness and Holiness and wanting Unconditional Love that made it peaceful. The Divine Light within the man, being mercilessly suppressed by the seed of destroyer, the torturous ego, is still waiting to shine bright again and to finally break free and radiate from within.

The Soul yearns to grow, to be saved, nurtured and delivered by the Saviour, the unfailing and most Loyal Redeemer – the Inner Light within. The Soul wants to be reunited with the Higher Self, with the glory it has lost that it once enjoyed. It wants the lower mind to be devoured by the Higher mind once and for all through the Inner Light within. But the human being, whose been genetically experimented on, chooses his selfish desires, which are carnal in nature but appear to the human being as self-righteousness, and as a result, the Soul is going through rounds and rounds of never-ending suffering and sorrow.

The human spirit wishes to return to its Real and True Nature of Love and Peace, but the carnal mind, full of pride, rejects spiritual enlightenment and growth and stomps down on any idea and notion of correctness. The physical body, limited to five senses, is feeble to take a stand as it lacks spiritual knowledge and awareness, which is veiled to the Divinity of human beings, which must be unravelled through meditation.

The destroyer, who pretended to give up his crown of glory, which, in reality, was a theft of human sacredness, teamed up with the "offsprings" of the serpent seed, the religious "leaders", and stole the Sacral Knowledge about the human Divinity that they could have used to find their way back and to figure out how to cure themselves and restore the Divine Consciousness from within.

They created made-up religions with senseless and logicless rituals and dogmas, put together false gods, and offered false salvation that humans could only achieve through human sacrifices and cannibalism, which is for their own nourishment because they are "feeding" themselves by the energy of the human suffering and pain. Another based level of the lower consciousness that the alien exploits is the nature of the human desires (the astral energy body), which focuses on material things and the wants of mere flesh instead of spiritual development, correction, and enlightenment.

Chapters 33-42

Mankind needs to learn that real Salvation is to fill the consciousness with spiritual thoughts, and that can be achieved through focus and by meditating in stillness on the Inner Light within, with all the heart and mind, and this can ultimately transform the lower mind into a more refined and cleansed High Consciousness. It means – "to worship the Creator in Spirit and in

Truth" without succumbing to temptations of the flesh or the offerings of the serpent to quench those temptations.

The Creator, the Absolute, is Considerate and a Corrective Deliverer, the Divine Consciousness to ponder and meditate on. He is the Stillness that the feeble man can seek to empower himself again against the destroyer of soul and Holy Spirit. He is the Eternal Goodness and Love. The Higher Self (Elihu), the wisest part of the Self and Consciousness, is fueled and guided by the Divine Seed of God's Light and is safeguarded deep inside the Soul. It never sleeps or rests, and it is always encouraging spiritual evolution and enlightenment to bring man back from his lost ways, to wake him up to the Divinity, the Soul's real Identity, to restore him to the Glory that he was destined for.

The Higher Self, the Inner Divine Light, always longs for the unity of the Soul, Heart, and Mind with the Divine Light, and it will achieve that through the encouragement of the Spirit of Truth and fueling of the Seed of the Divine Light within, which is also the Redeemer, the protective Savior of the mind and soul. He is the Christ Consciousness, the Liberator, and the Just Emancipator that lies within the Divine Beauty inside of men.

PSALMS

Psalms 1- 9

The Divine Seed of God's Light within is the Fortress that will not perish even if the alien serpent uses all its advanced technologies because He is raised and nurtured by God and dignified with the title of the Blessed Beloved. He is the Father of Peace as He will establish Peace all over the Earth after defeating the governors and leaders who are the pawns of the evil serpent, and He will finally become the King of "kings". Through meditation upon the Divine Light condensed within man and on the unified and profoundly wise God's Law of Love and Unity, the soul and consciousness of man will ignite and will be illuminated into the Flame of Righteousness.

This Inner Light, the Corrective Flame, is the Eternal Golden Word, the expression of the Incorruptible, Unadulterated, and Immortal Force of Life, hiding within which are the secrets to reform life and quell all the carnal desires. Stop and pray before God and meditate in stillness, away from all distractions, while concentrating on His Light within, and this will help the uncontaminated Divine Seed of God's Light grow into the blazing Holy Flame of glimmering Restorative and Healing Light within.

Psalms 10-21

The Creator, the Ultimate Sculptor, possessor of the All-Knowing Infinite Mind, will arise in all its Glory and "break the arm of the wicked" and snap awake every lost soul from the wicked serpent's hypnosis. The Blessed Beloved of God, the Divine's Favorite, who fuels goodness as the Inner Light, is the Glorious King destined to win and rule against the enemy. He is the Musician of the Universe who knows all the rhythms and notes of healing a lost soul, as He is the Fortress of Healing and Restoration and Divine Protection of men because He is the Ruler over the supplanter, the Gold Song, written by the Holy Spirit of God, with perfect rhyme and flow. He is the Conqueror over the death, a Protection against the curse. Carve some time out and stop before Him, and meditate, in Spirit and in Truth, upon the Eternal God's Light within to heal and shatter the curse of the mischievous progeny of satan, the evil serpent!

Psalms 22-29

He is the King of Glory, bound to be a Victor always, the Ruler over the mourning and the ivory, ruling with profound Wisdom and Judgment. The Divine Seed of God's Light within the men that doesn't perish even with all the corruptions of the "little" and is always ready to purify men is all the affirmation of the Power of God within the men and a loud and out indicator that men will prevail.

He is the Judge who examines, analyses, and dispenses rightful verdicts. Using His wisdom, He will prevail over the supplanter. Seek His Face within yourself and around you, hear Him as He is calling you from within to heal yourself, and draw to Him during the silent meditation in the presence of the Holy Spirit of God so you can shed off the filth that has you mentally and spiritually crippled. He is the White Fortress, illuminating with Grace and Divine Knowledge, descending from the High Land, and He is the Holy One who is immune to corruption and temptations, who is forever the King of the Kingdom of God within.

Psalms 30-50

He is the Song of Songs, the healing Hymn, the Wheel of God that will steer men back to its destined glory, and He is the River of Judgment for the rebellious one that encapsulates the storm that will decimate this foul reptilian invader who is devoted to destruction, who declares the "anathema". One of the once-blessed "musicians" who became the deceiver is the "little", insignificant as dust, who wrongly believes he is going to prevail and succeed in an irreversible deception of men and he will defeat God. He became brazenly ignorant of God's Divine Order, disrespected the Law of Love and Unity, and tweaked with the Song of Songs of God, which preserved God's wisdom and guidance. The enemy conceals himself covertly from the people behind leveraging the invisible realms he has fashioned using his advanced technologies, but God is the Omniscient, All-Seeing Ruler, the Divine Mind with boundless wisdom, insights, and foresight, and that is what makes Him the Victorious King over the deceiver, who, with all his advancements, tricks and schemes, and pawns of religious leaders and governors, will fail once and for all.

Psalms 51-60

God of Unity, men's Truest Protector and Unifier, who gathers everybody together is the Blessed Well of Oath, abundant in its benevolence and generosity, is God's Fortress. But the inebriated "musician of sickness," a virtuoso of the verses of fallacy and lies, who became the destroyer, acts violently and gruesomely against the Beloved, the Father of Peace, with hate-fueled vindictiveness. He tried to corrupt the Peace of God within by becoming the "mouth of falsehood, the pit of death". He became the one who spread evil, violence, and wickedness all over the world, but he will never be able to corrupt God's Word, His Uncorruptible Divine Light within the men.

Psalms 61-81

The Beloved, the Favored One, the Divine Intelligence within the man will be the Celebrated Praise of God Almighty once He annihilates the serpent. The Spiritual Light, the Antidote of Impurity, shelled in the body of man, will prevail over the negative forces through God's enduring support, perish the false ego and detox men of all the negative energies within. The Holy Spirit of God will dwell on the Earth into the body of man, waiting for the right time and for men to meditate upon so that it manifests Himself as a Holy Oil, the Fuel of Correctness, the Sacred Secretion, and will fight for men empowering them to take a stand against the corrupt governors and religious leaders who are the instruments of the alien invader, and He will dissolve all the negative forces within, cleaning men spiritually and mentally.

The Divine Mind is the most concrete Fortress of Praise, the evident Witness of the Perfection of God, and He will renew the forces that will quell the carnal consciousness of men and will redeem humanity from the supplanter that has taken his spiritual essence hostage. God will prevail over the "wicked troops", the cosmic vagabonds, the worshippers of the sun, who occupied the Earth and brought suffering, strife, and confusion for humanity to plague them with a social and moral epidemic.

The Divine Seed of God, the Source of Correction in men, the Holy Light, the Christ within, is the Vision of God's Peace, the Foresight, the Shepherd that will herd men from their dwellings or moral depravity to enlightenment. He is the Ruler, the Redeemer, who will prevail over deceiver and unshackle human minds from the clutches of ego.

Psalms 82-83

God Almighty, All-Hearing, clearly hears the "stranger, the father of confusion" and those who are bound to the deceiver and listening to their schemes and traps. He is aware and watching the "supplanter" and his pawns, devout servants, keeping a tab on who spreads evil, anger and violence all over the Earth. The enemy who rebelled against God, severing all his ties with the Benevolent Divine and being independent of God, is the "sharp little stone" that wants to pierce through men's mental defences. He is hidden in the invisible realms, and he thinks that he can hide, but he will be judged by the Creator, who sees what even this "little" cannot see with all his latest technologies. There will be a man sent by the enemy as an "ambassador of vile and evil", who will be hard to understand, unpredictable, who will be uncertain in his ways. He will be like a "raven, like a wolf," who will sacrifice a human being. (Paul/Saul – "the little destroyer")

Psalms 84-106

The Son of God is God's Mercy, who will give refuge to the lost and hypnotized, weakened men as He is the Truth. His Righteousness and Justice are bestowed with Profound Wisdom as He is God's Beloved, but the supplanter, who caused the trouble, is bold, cold-hearted, with a "sick hand" who keeps on trying to corrupt God's ways and lead His men astray.

The Divine Light is a High Almighty God within the man, to save men from ultimate destruction of his soul and self, as this Divine Light preserved with is the Glorious King, the Fortress of protection of men's conscience, the Teacher and Preacher with ready lessons for men to learn and the Counsellor to guide men how to thwart the traps of the enemy. He is the Father of Nations, the Prince of God, chosen to rule, and He will prevail over the confusion, over the "fountain of destruction, of the angry dragon" despite the evil having momentarily control over men. He is the Deliverer, a Much-Needed Messiah who will pull out and save from the "mouth of the serpent, the wicked god of opening".

Psalms 107-150

The Beloved of God, the Christ Consciousness within, the Corrective Compass will prevail over the enemy, the wretched mischief-monger, who was at the back of the Tabernacle of God, on

Heaven, (also, the reptilian brain, the corruptor and schemer, at the back of the brain of man), but became a rebellious adversary, abandoning his privileged pedestal and turning into the satan who caused and spread the "wickedness" all over the Earth infecting every man with a soul and moral-destroying poison.

The Beloved of God will offer the antidote, liberate, and cleanse the men and rule in the head of man, resurrecting and anchoring the Mountain of God therein. He is the King of Justice, the River of Judgement for the "supplanter" that will drown this evil serpent once and for all into the depth of Righteousness from where he can never rise again.

The Beloved is the Teacher and Instructor who leads with Practice, and He is the Strength of God, the Alphabet, spelling out every corrective way for men to follow. He is the Vision of Peace and the Ruler over the "giants of sorrow" who will be thwarted in the battle raged by the Prince of God.

PROVERBS

Chapters 1-31

The one who was the perfection of the Beloved, the Divine Intelligence, became the oppressor of God. This transformation from a being of Light to one of darkness is a tragic tale of rebellion and fall. Initially, this being was a beacon of Divine wisdom and love, showering praise upon the Creator and guiding others towards the path of righteousness. However, the desire for power and control corrupted his heart. He began to oppose the very Source of his existence, gathering followers by manipulating religious sentiments.

He turned his focus on the vulnerable, those seeking Divine favor and blessings. "Give, give the money", he preached, twisting the sacred act of giving into a transactional demand. "If you will give, God will be with you". This message, though cloaked in the language of faith, was a perversion of true spirituality. It led people away from a genuine connection with the Divine Source, fostering a false belief that God's presence could be bought with earthly wealth. Thus, the oppressor of God became a stranger to the truth, fighting against the Creator with deceit and manipulation.

ECCLESIASTES

Chapter 1-12

The Preacher is the Beloved, founded in Peace, the Divine Inner Light, who is God. His teachings remind men to trust God, who dwells within. This Inner Divine Presence offers wisdom and guidance, surpassing the fleeting and often deceptive wisdom of the world. The eternal nature of God's Wisdom stands in stark contrast to the temporary and often hollow pursuits of human endeavor.

THE SONG OF SOLOMON

Chapters 1-8

The Divine Mind within men will be suppressed by the trials of a false "peacemaker", a deceiver who appears as a beacon of hope but is, in reality, a liar. This figure, once illuminated by the Light of Truth, turned away from the Creator, choosing to walk a path of darkness. His influence is pervasive, leading many astray under the guise of peace. However, the Power of the Holy Spirit of God within men is resilient. Despite the trials, the Christ Consciousness will arise, illuminating minds and hearts with Divine

Wisdom and Love. This inner awakening will reveal the true nature of God as the Mountain, the Prince of Peace and the Redeemer.

The false "peacemaker", despite once knowing the Light of Truth, rebelled and became a "hill of wickedness". Those who follow him will be the "daughters and sons of fallen angels", entrapped in false religious activities. These misguided followers worship false reptilian "gods", demanding human sacrifices and spreading darkness. Their practices are a mockery of true spirituality, leading to their own spiritual demise. They are the "harvest" of the false peacemaker, ruled by deception and lies (Paul).

ISAIAH

Chapters 1-8

The devout followers of the Creator, who openly acknowledge His inner strength and offer praise, shall undergo a profound transformation and mental renewal. The Almighty God, the Holy One, commands His Celestial Army, serving as the Foundation of Peace and Authority over the wicked, rebellious demonic forces.

The possessor, the destroyer of the Truth of God, is the one who supplanted it as a "cosmic virus". This entity replaced and distorted the Divine Instructions, which serve as the bedrock of Peace. His followers are the "fallen angels", who revolted against the Creator out of envy and pride, seeking to replace the Divine Mind, infused with the Holy Spirit of Life and Love, with the deadly artificial intellect of the reptilian mind.

The Eternal instructions, God's Laws of Oneness and Unity, form the basis of peace. The one who holds power was once flawless before his rebellion, yet he abandoned his celestial abode in High Heaven. He and his followers rebelled against the Creator and His Divine Wisdom, the Beloved, whom He cherished. This powerful entity, existing in dark realms, seized control of the Earth and enslaved humanity. They transformed the Earth into a "sack of blood", but the Beloved of God, the Divine Consciousness within, will bring the Rest of God to the Earth and humanity, freeing them from grief and transient concerns.

The destroyers are those who "spoiled" the Word of God, His Laws, which testify about Him. They are the "watchers" who have the "weapons" against the Good Will of God. These evil "weapons" are those who rebelled against God and His Laws, but those who overcome will be elevated and enlightened with the High Divine Consciousness.

Chapters 9-10

The Savior, the Divine Mind, is revealed as the anointed (Christ) Holy Fire of Cosmic energy, dwelling within the River of Judgment, symbolized by the cerebrospinal fluid in the spinal cord of the body, acting against the pervasive wickedness on Earth and within the minds of humanity. The Redeemer is the Everlasting God, the Divine Mind dwelling within, God's Beloved, whose power remains formidable despite the escalating wickedness of humanity.

God stands as the Divine Authority over the "foundation of wickedness and fear". However, the one who was once treasured has become the destroyer, likened to a roaring lion and a heap of ruins. The one who served as a barrier against darkness has transformed into the rebellious figure, the "father" of the wicked people, brimming with anger.

Chapters 11-13

But the Gift of God to the world, His Branch, is the Power of God, the Holy Spirit within mankind. He is God reigns over the independent oppressor, the rebellious figure, likened to a mouthful of dough leading to ruin. He watches over those who are spiritually "sleeping".

God's Savior, the Christ Mind within the human body, is strong and powerful. Still, the deceiver, who brought the confusion and wickedness, is a rebellious "raven", along with him, creating chaos not only for him but also for the people following him, who later are called "ravens".

Chapters 14-28

All this wickedness and deception would fail when the Divine Mind, the Prince of God, will prevail over the deceiver. The deceiver once was a "white, luminous angel" but became the "black raven" due to his bad deeds. He is the "father of wickedness". Also, those giants who became the "invisible giants, the little", the evil demonic entities, hiding in astral dimensions, miniaturizing themselves by using the advanced technologies, will be trodden down as a "waste" by the Holy Flame when these demonic entities dwelt on Earth and committed the crime against God and humanity. They used the advanced technologies to their own benefit by doing genetic manipulation. As a result, the "clear water of the Heaven", the cerebrospinal fluid in the spine of man, became like two "pools" – the "wells of rain" that were polluted and wasted by the evil deeds of the "father of wickedness".

But the Rock of the Fortress, symbolized by the Divine Seed of Light residing within everyone, will swiftly overpower the "father of wickedness" and dismantle his stronghold. The Prince of God will triumph over the "giants" and their unseen malevolent activities, where they exploit people as mere energy sources. The Divine Mind within humanity serves as the Impenetrable Fortress of God's protection and guidance.

Behold the oppressor, the devotee of the "black sun", Saturn, who binds people in fear. God alone deserves praise, not the "black sun", satan. The Divine Mind within, the Prince of God, represents the Blessed Seed of God, radiating Divine wisdom and grace.

The "chief", characterized by his insatiable appetite for violence and warfare, is ultimately inconsequential and trivial. The Seed of God's Light emerges as the Ultimate Salvation against the depraved followers of the "black sun". Take heed!

The one who once received adoration in high places has now descended into darkness, embodying the essence of the "black raven". Yet, the Holy Flame of God's Spirit, manifested as the Sacred Secretion of God, stands as the Holy Anointed Oil of God, the Beloved, the incarnate Holy Spirit of God, established by God as the Cornerstone of Divine Redemption and Salvation for the sinful world.

Chapter 29-36

The Savior, the Holy Seed of the Creator residing within each being, manifests as the Lion of God, the Father of Nations, and the embodiment of Holiness. He reigns supreme over the realm of darkness symbolized by the "black sun", where wicked and rebellious individuals from the depths of astral spaces perpetrate their malevolent deeds. He exercises dominion over the adversary, representing the "banishment" of the Grace of the Holy One.

The Divine Essence embedded within humanity acts as the Shepherd and the very Strength of God. He is the Chosen One, destined by God to ascend as the Chief among leaders, guiding humanity towards enlightenment and redemption. He embodies Divine Wisdom, serving as the Prince of God, prevailing over the worshippers and oppressors of the "black sun". He stands as the ultimate Pillar of Support, embodying the Unyielding Might of God, establishing His Reign with unwavering Power and Authority.

Chapters 38-66

The Divine Seed of God emerges as a formidable Ruler, commanding Authority over the tumultuous seas of bitter confusion, serving as the ultimate Embodiment of God's Strength and Salvation. He emerges as the Savior amidst the chaos, the unyielding Rock, Redeemer, and Fortress of the Prime Creator.

The Divine Consciousness expands its reach through the outpouring of His Holy Spirit, lifting His Delight, His Beloved, to overcome the oppressor with the Vision of Peace. He serves as the Sanctuary for the troubled minds and spirits of humanity, offering respite from the deceitful machinations of the adversary. He stands as the strong Savior, the Redeemer, and the very Essence of God's

Salvation. However, the deceiver, responsible for sowing confusion, wickedness, and rebellion, is likened to black "ravens". Those who align themselves with such deception, also, fall into the category of "ravens", contributing to the generations of strife. Yet, God's Delight will ultimately triumph over the enemy, the negative ego, and the lower nature as humanity reclaims its unity with the Infinite Creator.

JEREMIAH

Chapters 1-9

The one who once praised God but later turned into a destroyer was originally created by Him and remained under His Authority. Those who align themselves with God's rulership will ultimately triumph alongside Him over the destroyer and the wicked individuals who falsely claim allegiance to a counterfeit deity.

The deceiver, responsible for causing sorrow, finds his match in the Divine Mind residing within humanity, which stands as the ultimate Master and Ruler over all wickedness.

To those who deceive, be warned! God, the Eternal Fortress of Light, stands as the Holy Fire against them. Praise be to God, the Prince of God, His Seed of Light manifested as the Sacred Secretion, the embodiment of God's power in the flesh. He resonates as the

Trumpet's Sound within the human vessel, the Vineyard's Master, reigning supreme over all oppressors.

Chapters 10-22

The Divine Consciousness within humanity asserts its dominance over the carnal world and the lower mind, emerging as the Deliverer against all forms of destruction. The deceiver, once an illuminating angel, has turned into a usurper and accuser, plagued by fear and confusion.

The rebellious angel, who once glorified God, has descended into becoming the very embodiment of tribulation. Yet, the Divine Consciousness within humanity, God's Beloved, will execute judgment upon all wickedness.

The Divine Wisdom within humanity proclaims: "Praise and obey God, listen and meditate in silence, focusing on His Word". He will administer righteous judgment. The one who praises God with the Fire, the Holy Spirit, is perfected and will ultimately prevail over the fallen angels.

God will establish His presence by elevating the Anointed (Christ) Oil within people's bodies during solitary meditation on the Divine Spark within, lifting our consciousness above confusion and demonic influences. The human genes carry the written praise of God: "Eternal God Within The Body".

Chapters 23-25

The Divine Mind within humanity stands as the Righteous One, prevailing over the rebellious angel and his cohorts, who seek vengeance against God and humanity. The Divine Spark of God's Light within will overcome both the wicked, rebellious forces and the low vibrational frequencies within our beings, baptizing men with the Holy Fire from within.

The one who once exalted God has become the oppressor of the world, spreading lies, wickedness, and idolatry through migration. Cast out from heavenly realms to the Earth, along with the fallen angels who followed, he has become the "father" of evil demonic entities and wicked individuals, transformed into ravens, harboring hatred towards all who worship God from within.

Chapters 26-32

The one who once exalted God in His Heavenly courts, serving as the radiant barrier of the Light and remaining faithful, tragically devolved into the one who marred the Gift of God, transforming into a dark and untamed "rat", the very embodiment of wickedness and injustice.

Once a champion of God's justice, this individual, in their rebellion, became an agent of corruption and confusion. The perfect embodiment of God's exaltation became a figure of wicked rebellion. Yet, the Divine Wisdom within humanity will ultimately triumph over the serpent-like mind of the enemy.

The one who once lifted high the Prince of God now stands as a destroyer, a violent adversary brimming with anger and chaos. However, the Prince of God, the embodiment of Divine Justice, will ultimately overcome the deceiver. The Just Divine Mind reigns supreme over the illusions crafted by the serpent.

True exaltation of God manifests as the Cosmic Seed of God's Light within humanity, serving as His praise and beloved creation. With the Power of God, this Cosmic Seed will restore the Divine Mind within humanity, uniting them once more with the Infinite Creator.

The Prince of God shall prevail over the "watchers". Let the Fortress of God, the Prince of God, arise. The deceiver spreads confusion about God's nature, falsely claiming that He resides outside of humanity and requires human sacrifices for forgiveness.

The one who once exalted and praised God now languishes as the impoverished "son of sorrow". Once the radiant bearer of light, crafted and loved by God Himself, this individual devolved into the chief purveyor of confusion and chaos, a lover of war. Yet, the Prince of God's Peace shall ultimately triumph over the "son of sorrow".

Chapters 33-35

The one who once exalted God descended into becoming the thief of God's Peace, the embodiment of sorrow. However, the Beloved of God, His Branch, shall transform the carnal nature of humanity into Divine High Consciousness through solitary meditation on the Divine Spark of the Holy Spirit within.

The one who once exalted God became the "father of confusion", seeking independence from God and descending into vengeance. Once the perfect "light barrier", this figure turned violent, deceptive, and ensnared in demonic activity. Yet, the Spiritual Seed of Light within humanity offers freedom from evil, elevating their vibrations and consciousness to a Higher Consciousness.

Chapter 36

The one who once exalted God rebelled and fell into the state of the "rat". Created and bestowed with freedom by God, this being turned wild and rebellious, defying the very justice of God. Once a blessed angel, now reduced to a "rat".

Nevertheless, the Gift of God, the Beloved of God, the King, the Counselor, the Helper, stands as the Blessed Exaltation of God. He reigns supreme over confusion and the reptilian, carnal mind, bringing clarity and Divine guidance to humanity

Chapter 37

The Just One without skewed judgment, the God's cleansing Fire, His Strength, who was preserved and anchored by God within, is the One who will rightfully and swiftly judge the deceiver and demons and dole out their well-deserved punishments. He will, using his Divine gifted Wisdom, judge the one who was built perfect with an enlightened and corrective soul but ended up wasting God's gift of mindful illumination and obliterating His Divine Peace and instead lost the way to become the oppressor of Peace.

The Victorious Prince of God is the Seed of God's Light that will sprout to purify men from within. He is declaring:" Behold, the petrifying deceiver, the spoiler of goodness! No matter what your tricks and temptations are, you, mindless accuser will not be able to deceive the fortified and well-protected Prince of Peace". The mindless deceiver, "the son of sorrow", is bound to lose! Fear the Master, the One who is unscathed, who is the Gift of Grace from God for people who want to enlighten the light within them again. The deceiver and those who followed him ardently violating God's limitation became the "spoiler" of the Glorifying Justice, which was the true Exaltation of God secured for man to take him to the highest pedestal.

Chapters 38-39

The Divine Illuminated Mind within, the Prince of God, purposed to lead men back to God, will judge the rebellious, renegading angel who once proclaimed that God is his "greatness" but left his ways and became the deceiver. The Christ Consciousness, the Wisdom of all Wisdoms, who is Might and Perfect, serving man as Loving Corrector and Savior, heard and always hears the "son of sorrow" who was once among the dependable servants of the King but became the deceiver, who now mistakenly thinks that he can hide from the wise Christ Consciousness.

The Just One, the proclaimed Praise of God, is the Mighty and Undefeatable Prince of God, and He will judge the oppressor and ensure that he reaches the end he deserves for beguiling men. He is the Lion, valiant and virtuous because He is protected and forever guided by the King, the Gracious God, the regenerative Master of Wardrobe - the Chief of Eunuch. He will destroy the multitude of wicked and rebellious demons – bringing a lasting end to the reptilian race and lifeless entities who are leveraging their artificial intellect with no consciousness to irreparably destroy men.

The Justice of the Divine Prince of God will be the fair, rightfully remorseless, a blitzing tribulation for rebellious, malicious "chief of angels" who forsook God and became viciously violent.

Those who were once bestowed on the noble duty of bringing the "fruits" of prophesies mutinied and became the unforgiving rebellious entities.

Chapter 40

The one who was assigned on the glorified purpose of exalting the Prince of God and elevating Him relinquished his dignified pedestal and rebelled against Him to become the revenge-lusted "avenger, the rat". He became the chief "watcher", hiding among men to sow the seed of destruction and temptations, but the Divine Seed of God within the body of man, which is Divinely recuperative and corrective, the Beloved of God, hears the rebellious one and know his schemes too well and will thwart this vengeful rat. He is supported by God, who is merciful and liberal, and He is, also, entitled and blessed to be the Soldier of God. He is the Royal Consolation, the Liberator sent from the Divine for tired and oppressed people who have buckled under, and this Royal Emancipator is a clear and loud Adoration of God, sent by Him to the people He loves as His own.

The avenger, the "wild rat", is saying: "Fear not to serve the demons", chanting this slogan to stupefy otherwise noble men into blindly following him. His miscreants, the "watchers", the demons, became the "fathers of wickedness and confusions" on Earth, spreading hate and lust. Those who were once praising the Prince of

God, acknowledging Him for what He is, the Loyal God-sent, bought the schemes of the alien felon and became the "rats" who are "bold" and violent. But little do they know that God is the Watcher, hearing them and preparing for them swift justice in the form of the Prince of God.

Chapters 41-43

God clearly hears the enemy, who became the "rat, the watcher", and is listening to every scheme and plan they are hatching against men. There will be a man, assumingly very convincing, appearing as a "savior", who will be sent by the "watchers" to mislead men. He will say: "Come to the watchers", inviting and becharming them toward destruction.

But God hears the liar, who lays waste the Gift of God, and He has a plan against every trick in His book. The House of God will be, also, confused and vitiated by the deceiver. The people will end up following the avenger against the corrective Light they have hiding within them. He became the "weapon" that is built with the purpose of marring and dismantling the Salvation of God. But the Prince of God, who is the True Exaltation of God, will rescue mankind, saying a loud and defiant "No" to the oppressor. The Prince of God, the Nurturer of the Seed of God's Light within, is the Master who will be triumphant over the oppressor.

The Exaltation of God is the One who hears and obeys Him without faltering for once and without heeding what the alien offers. The Divine Consciousness within is the Refuge, the Ultimate Salvation of God rewarded to man to save himself from the oppressor and the fallacies and lies of the degraded carnal mind.

The one who was once blessed by the Light and given Wisdom by God Himself became the "demon of confusion" as he rebuffed the gifts. He will now only bring the" fruits" of false prophesies and judgments, unlike the old times when he would do God's work. He is the "rat", vengeful and thriving in the filth of a rotten soul, full of temptations, and he will tempt the people with destructive, evil thoughts and entice them with wishful desires. But in the end, there will be just comeuppance in the form of tribulation and judgement of the deceiver and the "house of the black sun, the Saturn", at the hands of the Prince of God.

Chapters 44-46

The one who was consecrated with the imperial job of exalting God will become a proliferator of the "secret temptation" for the people, equipped with the art of "mouthful persuasion". But the Chosen Master of Correction and Humility, the Prince of God, the Inner Christ, the Warrior, the Luminous Seed is saying: "Do not do this abomination. This is what I hate", to remind men that what the "rat with the persuading mouth" is nothing but lies and fleeting desire. But many will fall, capitulate to desires and that will even include those who will praise God. They, too, will commit the great evil and join the group of those who will be eventually punished. Be aware, the oppressor, the mouthful! Behold, the "black sun" worshiper, the dweller and the "priest of the Saturn", the oppressor, the deceiver and the enemy of mankind and the one who is unintelligently trying to rival God.

The True Exaltation of God is His blessed Light within, whom God created as a Source of wisdom and correction. He is the Fire of God that will freshen and purify minds, His Praise and His Truth, the Prince of God.

He will be exalted to the Glory God has destined Him for, but the "black sun worshiper, the priest of the sun", subdues the Fortress. The world will be contaminated through and through and will be like a "pool full of wickedness". The people will be so lost and astray that they will think that they exalt the Prince of God, but in truth, they will exalt and glorify the enemy of God – the "tower of temptation", the perpetrator of cleverness, the deceiver who is always scheming, the worshipper of the satan, the Saturn. But God Almighty is the Sculptor of Christ Consciousness, a Wisdom that prevails against all lies. He is the Supreme Authority, who is Eternal and Imperishable.

Chapters 47-48

B e aware, the deceiver, the fallacious "black sun worshiper, the strong goat"! The Prince of God is the Rock that never budges nor erodes against the enemy and is in the protective Hand of God.

The "father of wickedness", who is waging a never-ending war against the Divine Seed of Light, the Prince of God, will falsely prophesy about Him, associating wretched, baseless lies. The enemy is a "dung heap" with a mind and heart that are rotten and "full of anger and rage" against mankind, who will try to steal the House of God to rule over it, using it as a center from where he will cause the grief.

Sadly, the bound-to-lose deceiver will be the ultimate "force of the grief". He will waste the House of God, spoiling its essence by dividing it into smaller factions such as small houses of meetings, the "houses of recompense, the houses of habitation", the churches in the cities where they will worship the bloody human sacrifice and celebrate false idols. It will be the "sheepfold of the father of wickedness", the cult of death, and the incubator for mischief. The people will be directed to the churches, lured with either fear, force, or wishful hypnotizing rewards, and they will be encouraged to worship the human sacrifice, deeming it as the foolproof way to salvation against the God-ordained directive of focusing and meditating in silence, upon the God's Light within themselves, to resurrect the Divine Flame, where God actually dwells as a Divine Seed through the Power of the Holy Spirit of God. In these houses (churches), men will be encouraged to perform a host of reptilian rituals, such as black magic and voodoo, worshiping and celebrating death and human sacrifices, and they will be ordained to drink the "blood" and eat the "body" (cannibalism), and this will lead men into forgetting that they are the Light of God, manifested in flesh and that they have preserved within them the Light that can bring them the Peace.

The one who was once God's helper and was under His healing refuge became His sworn and bitterest enemy, saying: "I will gather the sheepfold against God". But that all will end against the Prince of God, the Light within, who will finally judge him. And the "little", lurking secretively, carefully planting destructive traps, rebelled against God and waged war against His creation. He became the loathsome and angry "father of wickedness", but he will be rooted out and erased from the existence and minds of mankind.

Chapter 49

The deceiver will be the "governor" on the Earth, with power, privilege, and authority. The one who was perfect became the "hairy demon," drenched in wickedness and foul bitterness, who will gather his betrayed and deceived "sheepfold" in a battle against God. But the Prince of God, the Seed of God's Light, teeming with

His Gifted Wisdom, will hold in righteous judgement the activity of the angry man, the murderer, who is falsely, for the only purpose of beguiling mankind, claiming that he is the "light of the redemption". In truth, he is the pitch-black darkness, and that is where he is leading mankind as he is the "son of noise, son of sorrow", who is full of evil activity against the Fortress of God, the Prince of God who is the Master that God adores and empowers against all evils.

Chapters 50-52

God will raise up and endow His Seed with Divine sapience, and He will prevail over the armies of confusion and bitterness. As an invitation back to God and a warning, He says: "Come, let us join to the Master! Do not join the demons, the 'little ones,' who are destroying My Heritage".

The Divine Seed of God within will lighten up and rise to prevail over the serpent's seed, who is the rebellious one, waging wars and leading mutinies using his amassed "sheepfold - the harvest of ivory". God will raise His Enduring Fortress, the Holy One, the Redeemer from confusion, who will judge the deceiver and demons and emancipate mankind from their excruciating clutches. Behold, the oppressor! The Holy Seed of God's Light within the men is His Elixir. He is the Prince of God and His Vengeance, His Blazing Fire that He spreads against the "god of confusion", who will be incinerated once the Light within turns into the Blazing Flame it is supposed to be.

He is the Exaltation of God, His most Glorified Creation. He is the Lamp of God that can guide those who have lost the way to the point that they are now clues about how to return to God. He is His Work who is Just, Fair, and Fearless. He is the Soldier of God against confusion, a Warrior who never lost a war and will never lose one. God's Laws are the Foundation of Peace, set by Him as the most perfect Blueprint, but at the same time, there will be judgment for the wicked one as retribution is part of God's plan. God will establish the True Peace of the Christ Consciousness who rules with Him and saves all mankind from depravity and mental destitution.

LAMENTATIONS

Chapter 1-5

The Praise of God, His Fortress founded in Peace, is God's Light within, who reigns over the deceiver. This Light is a Source of unwavering strength and guidance, standing as a Fortress against all that opposes Divine truth. He is the Vision of Peace, the Prince of Peace, and the perfection of Beauty. In Him, we find a Blessed, crowned, and sanctified Fortress. To seek refuge in Him is to depart from the earthly oppressor who rebelled against God.

Go to God's Counsellor, His Fortress, the Word, the God's Seed of Light within. This Divine guidance is the True Source of wisdom and strength, capable of overcoming all deception and falsehood. By aligning with this inner Light, one can withstand the trials and tribulations of life, remaining steadfast in faith and truth.

EZEKIEL

Chapter 1-20

The Strength of God will be used as His contempt against the demons who are working for men's obliteration through and through. He is the Power of Almighty, favored enough to be the

Prince of God as He is chosen to be His Seed of the Light encapsulated in the man's body to meditate upon whenever men lose their way. He is One whom God will hear and see always to guide him and equip him to lead mankind. He is the One who is filled with the Spirit of God, and His mission is nothing but the establishment of His Peace.

The Savior of men, the Unputdownable Force of Correction, the Divine Mind within, declares and admonishes: "Hear God, foolish prophets, who follow their own spirits and have seen nothing". The Prince of God is the curative Rest for the mind and spirit of man, sowed within as an antidote to confusion and hate for those who wish to heal and return to God, but He is the Judge for those who hate God and are motivated to hurt His people and plot a war against Him.

The Divine Mind within the men, the Prince, the Promoter of Peace, who is against the wickedness, violence, and the plotting "watchers", will prevail over the oppressor and will eternally cast away "the man of abomination and confusion", along with the shackles he has over men.

Chapters 21-27

Behold, the Savior of men, the Prince of Peace is the Fountain of the Life, who is against the "watchers", the wicked, carnal mind and the rebellious people, who are just the "tents" for the demons.

Behold the "rulers, kings and tyrants, the rest of the congregation of rulers". The man with the Light of God within is the Tabernacle of God.

The Unerring Word of God is the Higher Consciousness in men, the Wisdom of God, who will trample over the lies and obliterate the demons over the "sharp rock". He is God of the Earth, the defender of Peace and Love, who will stand fearlessly triumphant over the "son of confusion" who protects his "crown".

The chief of angels, who was at a time worshiping the Creator, has mutated from being "pure and white" and pious to the jealous and rebellious one. He is the one who will try all that he has in his command to suppress the Divine Consciousness within the men, the Prince of God, the Lamb within the man.

The destroyer, the "cosmic parasite", gained power through space pilgrims, the evil demonic entities spreading all over the world. Through "wonders and wicked people", the enemy divides the society to conquer it and hears and rear it like a mindless sheep and create generations of "the wonders, the giants" who will do as told, who were the "offspring of the fallen angels". They were vacuous of much intellect, full of violence, and easily prone to seduction and lust.

But the Praise of God, the Heroic Commander of His Army, will destroy the bloody activity of the "ravens" and put an end to the monstrosity dealt out against men. He will make free the prisoners whom the deceiver has long made captive by inculcating and then leveraging the carnal lecherous desires, false teachings, and manipulative mind control using the highly advanced technology.

Chapters 28-30

The Divine Intelligence with no bounds within the men, the Disciplinary Wisdom, the Beloved is the Ruler over the "sharp little rock". The sworn foul enemy that is now hell-bent on destroying men irrevocably, on making men putrid and evil, who was graced with the beauty by and favored with the pleasure of God, became the silent, cloaked deceiver, who spread the idolatry as his grand scheme, through worshiping of the "black sun", the Saturn, who is the satan.

The Soldier of God is undeterred and fearless as He is saying: 'Behold the rank oppressor of God's pure and beloved people. God is the Ultimate Ruler of everything, including the false "god" who greedily protects his crown, defending his status, but is nothing more than the "god of the confusion". You, the oppressor, from the heart of the sea, "the standing pool" from the dark depths of mischief, God is over the oppressor of enmity! God is over and beyond the mouthful persuasion of the ruin of trouble, of sin, and He is unscathed. He is over this widespread enemy who temporarily rules over His people using his malevolent schemes, who become the sorrowful force of iniquity, the worshiper of the "black sun, the idolater".

Chapters 31-33

God is the Ruler with no one to intervene no matter who or what they try. He is the Master over the persistent destroyer, "the son of sorrow", the progeny of alien evil, who worships and consecrates the "black sun", who is satan and his ultimate, most dependable pawn. The luminous Cosmic Infinite Consciousness, the Source and Root of all wisdom and purity is the Creator of the Garden of Delight, the error-less fabricator of the brain and the body of man, everything but the oppressor. God is even the Ruler over the "black sun" worshipers, the believers of blackness. The Seed of God, preserved within the men for his correction, is the Ruler and the Undoing over the "giants of confusion". The followers of this blackness are the earthly violent pilgrims, merciless and lost, who are worshiping the Saturn, the satan.

The Divine Consciousness, which is within men, is the Word of God to anchor men to His path eternally. He is the Eternal Light that comes from the Creator, always shining, always keeping the right path accessible for men.

Chapters 34-37

The Saviour, Prince of God, is saying: "I will deliver my flock from the enemy's "mouth", so they will not be the "meat", proclaiming what His mission is loudly and without the fear of evil invaders.

He announces valiantly: "I will save my Flock, so they will not be the "meat" for the enemy. I will save them, from your vile clutches, so they shall be no more the prey. I will feed them with the judgement and re-enlighten the wisdom within. I am the Beloved of God, the Light of the Divine Mind and will serve my purpose without fail".

Chapters 38-47

The mischievous "master of the giants" who have no other purpose than "dividing" the world and making people captive, hypnotizing them with temptations and carnal wishes, will be destroyed by the Commander of God's Army in the truest sense. The Commander of the Holy One, the Leader that will be at the forefront of the battle against the evil alien, is the Master of the "god" of Saturn and his multitude.

The Commander of God's Army is blessed with infinite Justice of God and will use that to differentiate between true worshippers of God and the followers of black Saturn. But the "fountain of goats and calves" are the violent, macabre hunters, blood-lusted for the human souls who have created the "wealth of captivity" to enslave men. They have imprisoned and shackled, by violence and vicious methods, many people all over the Earth.

The deceiver of the whole world, who was once the angel of the worship, will now be judged by the Prince leveraging the gifted Justice, and this deceiver will be burned without mercy in the River of Judgment (cerebrospinal fluid in the spinal cord of man) by the Holy Fire of God's Spirit - the Christ Oil pure in its essence, the Sacred Secretion, the Fountain of Life within.

Chapter 48

The violent and enduring enemy of the Beloved, who is not willing to turn his ways, will be judged by his Master, the true Ruler of everything in the world and beyond, who is Just, Rightful beyond error, and who does not transgress. The chief of all the pure worshiping angels mutinied, got himself cursed and banished and became the deceiver. He dwelt and waited with his troops on Earth and dispensed tools and schemes as he "divided" the Holy place as a "palm tree", branching it bit by bit to allow easier control. However,those who will follow the Holy Son of God, meditate upon the Divine intelligence within and seek refuge from it, will not succumb and perish and will be saved and spiritually woken up to resist all temptations set forth. But, unfortunately, those who will join and follow the deceiver blindly, "buy" his temptations, and become his troops will be deceived and manipulated by the enemy, as he will ultimately betray and abandon them without hope.

DANIEL

Chapter 1

Those who were created by God as superior and graced with His blessings became the "fallen angels" who made it their mission to bring tears, pain and confusion to the Earth and to its rightful dwellers. They are the "watchers, the "little", mischief mongers, who will be held accountable and punishable for their crimes against men under the Divine Judgment of God's Gift, who is like God, Just and without errors, who heard and obeyed Him, the Essence of Light within the man and men's Savior. The evil demonic entities, through their technological advantage and leveraging on men's weakness imbued in them by the evil themselves, committed a cruel and gruesome crime against the Creator and humanity by doing the genetic manipulations and corruption of the DNA to control humanity. As a result of this, the Divine Consciousness was reduced, weakened, and hampered to the lower, carnal consciousness and left putrid, full of fear.

God will judge, rightfully and virtuously, the evil demonic entities and will transform and cleanse, by the Power of His Holy Spirit, the lower, ravenous, carnal, fearful mind into the Higher Divine Mind, enlightened and strong to resist temptations - through the meditation on the Inner Divine Light within.

He will judge those who "lay up" the treasure in secret. The Gift of God is His Servant of Light, His Stewart, who will judge the rebellious, "miserable beings".

Chapter 2

The evil demonic entities, as soldiers of satan, descending from other dark, lifeless dimensions, brought fear, wars, and confusion to the Earth to make men easy to break and subsequently shepherd. They also were doing genetic mixing and manipulations of humanity in their laboratories, toying with the DNA to find ways to dismantle and abuse it. These "giants" who became the notorious "little" as if they didn't mean much, turned invisible using the highly advanced technologies, migrating secretly to the lower astral dimension, will not be shown mercy and will be judged by God.

God will judge those who produced a mixture of reptilian and human genes by genetic manipulations, sending them as humans acting as impostors and leaders, with a switched-off the spiritual, Divine DNA, and with a manipulated genetic code inserted with bacteria into the cells of man, the mitochondria. By these criminal actions and technology that is advanced and sophisticated, they decreased the lifespan of men.

However, through meditation, the True Communion with God, with unwavering hearts and mind, by focusing on the Inner Light of God within, and by the Holy Fire, the Sacred Secretion – the Healing

Oil will do what it was imbued and preserved in man for . Finally, the lower consciousness will be resurrected and transformed into the Christ Consciousness, and will ultimately lead men to pulverize the shackles the evil serpent has had on them for this many generations.

The evil giants will be swiftly punished by God's Divine Life Force, as they will be torched with the Spark of the Light within the man, and the negative energies of the serpent's seed won't survive the intensity, and finally - the lower consciousness will be dissolved.

Chapters 3-8

Those who brought misery packaged as tears and pain from their "place of habitation", a place of darkness and melancholy, who brought and proliferated confusion by making genetic manipulations and modifications are the demons. Those who tortured humans generation after generation, using force and foul traps, forcing them to worship the "false gods" who were just pawns of the satan, guised and pretending to be the "servants" of God, Holy and pure, calling themselves the "Illuminated, the shining" when their hearts and minds and souls were blackened. They are the ones who are ravaging the Earth, corrupting the men, and turning them into miserable beings.

Those who brought tears and tribulation on Earth will not be spared, and their fallacies and scams will reach an end, and they will be judged by the Creator. They tried to save their own lives by mixing and breeding with human beings, to make them more suited to Earth and also to mix men's DNA with their own. They become governors, stationed into high offices, apparently magnanimous rulers, and even "false prophets" and religious "leaders" with masses in their tutelage and influence.

Those who are "covering" them, protecting them, and being their servants, who are helping them to divide and destroy the Earth, will also be judged by the Creator for their mischief is as bad as the serpents.

Those who preserved themselves by "mixing" with humanity, shielding themselves, are being watched, and their record is being maintained, and all those who came from the sea and the underground will be judged by the Creator.

Chapters 9-11

The "assumed kings, the governors and leaders of the Earth, the lords and masters" are the ancestors and progeny of the evil alien serpent, of those who rebelled against the Holy and Merciful God and abused and meddled with His Eternal Laws. The Cosmic Divine Seed of Light, the luminous and blessed, dwelling and nurturing within the flesh, the Prince of God is His anointed Deliverer, a Promised Saviour from the oppressor, who will teach about the foundation of peace, guide men to break free from temptations and restore men to their Blessed Glory. He is the Holy

Judge, who dispenses verdicts with God's given wisdom under His watchful eye and approval. He is the One who will judge those who present themselves and guise themselves as "chosen people of God" but who are truly the ones with a mission to divide the Earth and weaken and corrupt humanity.

The Divine Verdict will come at the hands of the Divinely Chosen Adjudicator, and the "governors" of this world will be bruised by God and His Staff. The oppressors and the "dividers" will be judged and punished for their generational crimes against men.

HOSEA

Chapter 1

The Divine Seed of God's Light within men is the Savior against the serpent seed. He is the Well of Light, the Possessor of God's Power, standing against the sinful world. As the Leader of God's Army, He will scatter the "cluster of wicked people," those who have rebelled against Him. These false followers, who claim to be God's people, will not obtain His mercy. Their rebellion and deceit have led them astray, severing their connection with the Divine.

Chapters 2-9

Even those who initially obtained God's mercy and believed in Him will eventually turn to worship the black sun and false gods. These are the ones who will worship entities of confusion, mistaking them for God. He will scatter them all, recognizing their betrayal and false worship. Yet, the Prince of God, the Seed of His Light within, will prevail over the "rolling wheel of the house of vanity". He is the One who is truly fruitful.

The Prince of God will triumph over the speculation and deception of the "watchers". He will rise as a Mountain, not like the "house of vanity" – the house of the son of sorrow who pretends to be a "son" of God. God's Power will increase within those who pray and meditate on their oneness with Him. Despite the rise of the evil one in the latter days, those who remain true to God will find strength and guidance in the "houses of vanity".

The wicked one, who seeks revenge, will cause contention, but the Beloved of God, who is the Praise of God, His Mountain, the Prince of God, will prevail. He is the Ruler over the enemy, the "God of opening", standing against the "little rock" who opposes God.

Chapters 10-14

The Prince of God, the original Spark of Divinity within man's being, will prevail. He holds rightful power over the "watchers and the house of vanity and nothingness", the house of ambush. The Prince of Peace, the Divine Mind, is the Master of the House of God – the body and mind of man. He will overcome the oppressor, who will increase.

The Soldier of God will defeat the earthly "goats", who are the demons, the "little ones". The Creator is the Ruler, the Master over everyone, good and evil. The one who was "fruitful" in High places has become the "oppressor" in God's House. He is the supplanter from the dark astral planes, opposing God. Yet, the Prince of God will prevail over the ancient serpent, the deceiver who brought confusion.

This former figure of perfection and illumination, who rebelled, will be defeated by the Prince of God. The Inner Divine Light will shine through, dispelling darkness and deception. The Prince of God will stand victorious, a beacon of Hope and Truth in a world overshadowed by falsehood and betrayal.

JOEL

Chapter 1-3

The Beloved of God represents the Divine Mind within us, acting as the Lawgiver who conveys wisdom directly from God's "mouth". This Inner Divine Presence can be likened to a mountain of God Almighty, shedding light within us, offering a vision of peace, and leading God's Army to victory. It embodies God's strength and acts as a steadfast Rock for those who seek spiritual guidance, providing a solid foundation for the "fishers of souls" who spread the message of faith.

The Living Healing Waters, which manifest as the Holy Oil or Christ Oil within the spinal cord, symbolize the Sacred Secretion that can resurrect dormant cells in the right side of the brain. This awakening signifies the revival of the Divine Feminine, which brings harmony and wholeness to the body and mind. This Divine energy within us serves as a judge, condemning those who ruin the land of peace and praise. He is radiant, representing the praise of God, and rules over earthly troubles and oppression. As the Prince of God, He triumphs over the forces of darkness, symbolized by the "black sun", the satan.

AMOS

Chapter 1

The Divine Seed of God within the body of man is His Trumpet, announcing a vital message. There will be a man who pretends to praise God but secretly opposes and seeks to destroy the Vision of Peace. This individual will create chaos, acting as a "son of noise", spreading bloodshed and turning the world into a place of strife. He embodies the evil serpent in the Land of Delight, a strong adversary, the devil, and a thief. This individual, symbolized as a sharp rock, will ultimately be destroyed for spreading wickedness and false religion, causing division among people. This deceitful man will claim to have seen God but is actually full of violence and lies. He is a strong "goat," the devil, a thief, and a source of infamy who will be torn away. This "sharp little rock" (representing Paul = Saul) will be destroyed for causing widespread wickedness through false religion, dividing people into countless denominations.

Chapters 2-4

God is the Ruler over those who propagate wickedness, even among those who claim to be His people. The "son of sorrow" will falsely assert that God chooses him but is an oppressor and rebel. The Divine Seed within us is His Branch, symbolizing the connection to God's light. The destroyer, a thief and oppressor, pretends to serve God but deceives and divides His house. These deceivers manipulate vanity and falsehood against God and His people. They roll the "will of vanity" in ivory, acting against God, His people, and the land. The Divine Seed within man is His branch, a symbol of the connection to God's Light and the ultimate Triumph over deceit and rebellion.

Chapters 5-6

The Beloved of God calls to seek Him within the House of God, where He is the wellspring of blessings. Yet, within this sacred space, there will be evil activities and false images of a king. People will mistakenly worship a false god, represented by the "black sun" and the serpent. This misguidance will turn the land into a place of bloodshed, causing widespread anger and creating a barrier between God and His people. Those who claim to be the "chosen people" are followers of the serpent, full of anger and wickedness. They have occupied villages and deceitfully use God's Name to hide their true nature as demonic entities who kill God's faithful followers.

The Beloved of God warns people not to hold onto this false image of the "black sun". Instead, they should embrace the Prince of God, who embodies the Holy Fire of God's Light, guiding them towards Truth and Righteousness.

Chapters 7-9

The Beloved of God stands as the Ruler over deceivers and oppressors who act independently of God. He is strong and will ultimately prevail over these forces of darkness. He is the Divine Judge and the Wellspring of Truth, watching over the "watchers", those who seek to deceive and manipulate. He will strike down the false "harvest" and judge those who oppress from the High land. As the Prince of God, He represents Divine Consciousness and reigns as the Divine Consciousness within, the Ruler of all the Earth, the Supreme Creator.

OBADIAH

The Servant of God rises against the forces of evil. The deceiver, once perfect, has fallen into wickedness, spreading anger and destroying God's peace. This deceiver lives among the Earth. He dwelt in villages, spread wickedness and anger, and destroyed the Peace of God. He will deceive people of God, pretending to worship God but secretly praising the devil. Supported by the "watchers", he increases idolatry and distorts the Law of Peace, symbolized by the Book (the DNA) from Heaven. The Beloved of God, the Mountain of Almighty, stands firm against this corruption, defending the Divine Order.

JONAH

Chapter 1-4

The Seed of God's Light within us is like a True Dove, representing the Pure Spirit of the Prime Creator. This Divine presence resides within the "seacoast", symbolizing the human body, and embodies the world's beauty. The Dove proclaims, "I am the One who crosses over from Heaven to Earth, bringing the Divine presence and guidance to humanity. This crossing signifies a spiritual journey, bringing enlightenment and Divine connection to all who seek it".

MICAH

Chapters 1-7

The Seed of God's Light within men represents the perfection of God, endowed with His strength and power. This Divine presence is worthy of praise and acts as a Watch Mountain, embodying the Law of Peace. It rules over deceivers and the "watchers" who rebel against God's vision of peace. This Divine presence is likened to a winepress, dealing firmly with those who oppose God's Will and spread bitterness and rebellion.

NAHUM

Chapter 1-3

The Divine Seed of God's Light serves as a Comforting Presence of God and a rigorous Force against evil. This Divine Presence is written into the fabric of existence, dwelling within both the land of wickedness and the human body. It acts as a witness of God, empowered by the Holy Spirit within humanity. This comforting Presence stands as a testament to Divine Justice and Strength, opposing all forms of evil and deception.

HABAKKUK

Chapter 1-3

Those who fight against God are demons, often depicted as "little" and rebellious followers of an ancient dragon engaged in reptilian demonic activities. This main adversary was once glorious and beautiful but became an unfaithful dark angel, always judging and opposing God. This rebellious being represents a constant challenge to Divine Order, embodying the struggle between good and evil within the spiritual realm.

ZEPHANIAH

Chapter 1-3

God will hide His Holy Fire, represented by the Sacred Secretion, within the cerebrospinal fluid in the spinal cord of man. This Divine Essence is His Strength and Integrity, concealed from the enemies, who are descendants of the ancient serpent. These enemies brought immorality into God's Land, symbolized by the human body, corrupting it with wickedness.

HAGGAI

Chapters 1-2

The enemy of God is described as a "stranger" who introduces confusion and wickedness into the world. This enemy spreads confusion about God and the Savior. However, the Christ Oil within the spinal cord, symbolizing the Sacred Secretion, acts as the Ruler over this confusion. It captures and destroys the negative forces within the body, restoring Divine Order and clarity.

ZECHARIAH

Chapters 1-7

One of God's former governors, once a musician and worshiper before his rebellion, became an adversary. This figure, proud and rebellious, now opposes God's Vision of Peace. The Salvation of God, represented by the Divine Mind within, is the Branch of God, offering redemption and guidance. This Divine Presence is mighty and acts as a Savior, opposing the corrupted world and restoring true judgment, mercy, and compassion. The musician, once part of the heavenly choir, became proud and opposed God, symbolized as a "sharp little stone" against the vision of peace. The Divine Mind within us acts as a Savior, guiding us towards Righteousness and Divine Truth.

Chapters 8-14

God is the Ruler and Redeemer, the Foundation of Peace, always present with those who listen to Him. The Christ Consciousness within us acts as a Savior, protecting humans from enemies dwelling on Earth with violent, bloody activities. This divine presence, the Commander of God's Army, will prevail over the "sharp little rock" spreading wickedness. It will tear away these corrupt influences like a "wild goat" emerging from the sea.

The Beloved of God represents Salvation from wickedness, declaring precious messages and obedient to God. This Divine Presence will destroy the proud adversary, the "son of the right hand". The Savior is a Gift of God, His Grace, the Divine Mind of God. He is God over the oppressor, the Holiness of God, who hears and obeys God. He is the Strength of God, the Gift of the King, the Founder of Peace, Ruler of the oppressor. He is the Praise of God, not the cosmic traders, the violent vagabonds.

MALACHI

Chapter 1-4

The Savior of God, the one Chosen by Him, representing the Christ Consciousness within, acts as the Commander of His Army, which will comprise righteous men who haven't given up on God's teaching and haven't lost the way. This Divine Presence will overcome the rebellious angel, make the followers of the serpent give up and will uproot and destroy the hairy demon who supplants God's Peace and provokes men towards sin. The King of God, His Favorite and Blessed, rules over the "black sun" (Saturn), eternally and without competition, and He will be delivering people from the desert of destruction, which is a place of helplessness and darkness, and He will emancipate and lead them into the Light.

THE BOOKS OF THE
NEW TESTAMENT

The process of the production of the Sacred Secretion, the manifestation of God's Light in our bodies, the Christ (Anointed) within, was encoded in the story of the life of Jesus Christ.

MATTHEW

Chapter 1

The Divine Christ Consciousness, materialized in the human body as the Holy Anointed (Christ) Oil, the fuel of Love and Wisdom, that will erupt and cleanse as the Sacred Secretion within humans when they contemplate upon God. It will illuminate the brain with the Divine Light that will vaporize all the evil ideas and thoughts and restore the whole body of man back to its Holy and Pure form. It will be the affirmation of the Promised Love that God has saved for His creation, and it will bring upon men the Lasting Peace and Goodness of God - the Infinite Prime Creator who is All-Seeing and full of Holy Love for men.

By the Infinite Power of the Holy Spirit, God created the Universe, the Home of Men, the Earth, and the Divine, immortal human beings, as a microcosm of the Macrocosm, a self-sustaining Divine system in equilibrium in the image of the constellations, planets, and all cosmic bodies that the evil invader tries to tweak and tamper with. Everything, despite being a consciousness of its own, was connected to the Source of All Light, the Eternal Light through the Inner Spiritual Light, one that is the illuminated nucleus and the gleaming Spark of the Prime Eternal Divine Light within the heart cocooned within for men and creation's ablution.

But the evil cosmic forces, the dwellers of pitch black darkness, the "fallen angels", who have been stewing in corruption and hate, invaded the Earth with foul intent and adulteration of human minds in their plans. They committed the worst of the worst crimes and sinned against the Prime Creator and humanity by doing genetic manipulations, mixing the human seed (the DNA) and the serpent seed to destroy and dominate the human essence. They have done so in order to enslave, control, and dominate humanity and cause a spiritual massacre.

The Divine Consciousness of men was either suppressed or reined in brutally to subjugate any rebellion or defense, and it was tampered with till the point it became carnal and till the connection with the Prime Source was broken, leading men to mental deprivation and spiritual drought.

Before the genetic manipulations and adulteration of the Prime Conscience, human beings were able to receive, generate, and produce the Light and keep true to the moral path due to the Wholeness, the union of the right and left hemispheres of the brain, the Union of the Divine masculine and Divine feminine.

But after genetic manipulations and corruption of the human DNA, the destroyer, his pawns, and his offspring, who are stationed in places of influence and authority, became the governments and the religious leaders that concealed themselves as common people.

They hid the sacred knowledge about the Divinity of men so that the men would not attempt to find the truth. The truth is that they buried the Knowledge to restore the Wholeness, to ensure that the High Vibrational Consciousness is suppressed eternally in the carnal minds of men. And only the carnal elements prevail so that they could "shepherd" men easily.

The Light Consciousness, the Illumination that would keep the Right path enlightened, dwindled because the enemy also suppressed and blinded "the receiver" of the Light from the Prime Source – the pineal gland in the brain of a man, the place of connection between the physical and the spiritual realms and the shell of the Sacred Secretion, the portion of Correction. People eventually lost their mental strength and became controlled by the baser desires and the destructive, lower vibrational energies of the reptilian brain. The carnal mind took control, steering men through all the emotions that are devoid of logic, such as fear, anger, lust, and selfishness, instead of being guided by the Feminine Holy Spirit, Wisdom, and Love from within.

The evil demonic entities, the blasphemous traitors who called themselves "gods" and sought worship to beguile and deceive men, created "the cult of death" by conducting inhumane rituals and doing bloody human sacrifices to the false "gods" (demons). They used that energy of pain and suffering as the "energy food" and humanity as their "batteries" to replenish themselves and to ensure that their control continues.

The rotten evil entities, to wage war against the Divine, projected their sins and crimes against God onto humanity by using them as mental slaves, imbuing guilt in them and exploiting that guilt to make them embarrassed for their crimes and weakening their self-confidence. They are still committing crimes against God and the humanity.

The cruel invaders created religions that were full of deception, lies and fake algorithms that touted and guaranteed freedom and wellbeing. They claimed that people can receive all-encompassing "salvation from their sins" and retributions from the wrongs done to them or by them by simply accepting the bloody human sacrifice and doing "cannibalism", calling this "the communion". They deceive people to keep them confused and in self-doubt to ensure it is always easier to control them and to "harvest" the energy of the guilt and suffering for the invader's personal replenishment and the fuel for its tech and apparatus.

The Salvation of the Soul, the Emancipation from the wrong and impure is the Spiritual Connection with God of Love and Unity, established and nurtured through the transformation and cleansing of the heart and the restoration of the Divine Feminine of the mind through reactivating dormant cells of the right side of the brain.

These can be enabled through meditation on God's Light within, His Gifted Fuel of Enlightenment preserved within the heart.

When people focus within themselves and contemplate on the hidden Light inside of them, there will be the alchemical process of restoring the wholeness of the brain, raising the carnal consciousness to the Divine Mind from within. It will be the process of Liberation from moral demise, "cleansing" the carnal mind from the enemy's lies, false "programs", and the hypnotic mind control.

The Prime Creator is the Absolute Love, The Epitome of Consideration and the Light that illuminates the darkest of paths, who is within humans already is the Savior and who doesn't need the bloody sacrifices and the disgusting rituals of cannibalism or the like. (the Holy Bible – the Whole Book is about the spiritual, physical, and mental transformation of the human being into the Whole being that men were always supposed to be, by the power of God's Holy Spirit of Love, the Spark of the Prime Cosmic Light within the heart, that will grow into a Flame and the River of Life, the Sacred Secretion).

When men plan on denouncing the evil ways taught by the serpent and focus and meditate on the Inner Seed of Light within the heart, prompting the Divine Seat of Intelligence into action, it will grow and liberate them from the serpent's imposter force. It will prompt corrective action and will decimate the ego, the carnal negative mind and all the foul lies that men have been under the spell of.

Humanity forgot and forsook their Cosmic Divinity, the blessing and the promised nobility that they received as their Divine Heritage. They forgot that they are Multidimensional Light beings, Sons and Daughters of God, granted a position and grace that no other species enjoys and that the human body is the Temple of the Holy Spirit of God that is supposed to be kept chaste and honored.

The brain of man, the Divine Instrument of the Creator, is the sought-after "Promised Land of milk and honey", where the pineal gland and the pituitary gland (as Joseph and Mary), under the power of the Holy Spirit, produce the electromagnetic exertions, called "milk and honey". When these two exertions interact and propagate, they go down from the top of the brain and meet in the solar plexus (the Bethlehem – the House of Bread). The Breath of the Holy Spirit then adds itself into the action as it also enters the solar plexus, and together, the three produce the electromagnetic Gem, the physical Seed of Light (Immanuel-Jesus – God is with us, who is the Salvation), the illumination that will scare away the darkness.

There will be the much-awaited materialization of the Holy Spirit of God within, in the spinal cord of man, resurrecting the moral and intellectual faculties of men and throttling them into restorative action. This Divine Seed, the Healing Anointed Oil

(Jesus Christ) within this pod of Spiritual Rebirth, in flesh, will survive, grow in power, and will be anointed (Christ) by the Divine Spark of God's Light in the heart and then it will start raising up and illuminating the brain, fending off the lustful temptations and eradicating the rage if it will be not first destroyed by the carnal temptations, sex desires, fear, anger, gluttony, jealousy and selfishness.

The enemy will try to divide God's people and segregate them into factions, religions, and races, pretending to be the "highest authority" so that it becomes easy to rule and control them. Being insignificant and without much control, he will sell lies and fallacies and will lure the elect, who will declare on his behalf: "My people are free!". But that will be the furthest from the truth as there will be provoked and planned physical and spiritual violence against God's people and humanity, and the invader will exercise unchallenged mind control through the powerful, cruel religious structure for a time, herding men to their irreversible destruction.

Only the Real Friend, the One who abandons and rejects the alien's temptations on every corner and turns as stay as a true and devout Servant of the Creator, is free from the bondage of sin. It is the Inner Eternal Light of God that needs to be meditated upon, the Seed of God's Light, the actual Physical Manifestation of the Holy Spirit that can save men from eternal obliteration. It is housed in the spinal cord of the man, the Sacred Secretion that is going to restore the spiritual heart and Divine Love Consciousness.

The Seed of God's Light within, the Inner Christ, will grow roots and be raised by the Power of the Holy Spirit and emerge from the "bottom of the carnal flesh" till it reaches the top of the human brain and takes control, starting the journey of righteousness. It is the Rescue Anointed (Christ) Oil, the Helper, and the Usher who is an appointed Servant of God who is dwelling by the Holy Spirit, lounging into the carnal flesh, incubating, nurturing and transmuting into the Divine Physical Essence – the Rescue Anointed (Christ) Oil Substance – the Sacred Secretion. The Helper, God within , who will restore the Wholeness and Unity of the brain, restoring its intellectual faculties back to their maximum efficiency, renewing the blood and the whole body of the man, fortifying it enough to fend off temptations of the flesh.

Chapters 2-9

In God's House, which will be invaded and overtaken by the worshippers of Saturn, giants, the "serpent seed" will enjoy a glorified pedestal as it will be elevated and praised, instead of the Inner Spiritual Light of God, which will be corrupted and uprooted, or abandoned and forsaken. The enemy will bring confusion, and people will elevate and consecrate the "son of confusion", who is the "serpent seed, the prince of darkness". This elevated and consecrated lot will prevent and work tirelessly against the elevation of the Holy Seed which is the exaltation of God's Power that is sanctified, clean, and Holy.

The Holy Seed of God's Light, the Pod of Sustenance of the Soul, is the Salvation of the soul from within that can be counted and depended upon as it is a Powerful Spiritual Gem of Beauty, an element of Wisdom. It will be ascended into the solar plexus, the House of Bread, when the Moon enters the birth Zodiac sign and then transported carefully upwards, raising it to the brain of man through the spinal cord by the cerebrospinal fluid. Those who will preserve, intend, and plan to cleanse themselves, collect it, and save it from corruption. They will be illuminated. Their brains will be primed and sharpened, their vision will be granted clarity as an overall transformation of their consciousness will take place, and they will be healed physically and spiritually.

The Holy Portion of God's, the Seed of abundance and mercy, who hears and obeys God devoutly and ardently, will start to take effect and raise and transform man's carnal consciousness into the Divine Consciousness. The Inner Spiritual Light of the Creator, the Flame fueled by the Sacred Secretion, is His Extension of Himself and His Love for His creation. It is the Dwelling Salvation during hardships, the Rock against the deceiver, and the anchor for men that can keep men tethered against the currents of sin and misery.

Chapters 10-13

The Divine Seed of God's Light embodying unwavering devotion is the Obedient One, not budging from His plan as He is the One who hears and obeys God and is ever attuned to the Divine Will. Yet, the one who was once faithful before the rebellion was gifted and possessed a "portion" of Divine grace and mercy became a mindless, violent destroyer, the "lover of the wars", and king of chaos.

There will arise the wretched, cursed, and depraved "son of immense sorrow", who is the forsaken, malevolent twin of the formidable enemy. He will be using mind control technology that will bring overwhelming confusion and catastrophic destruction into the world and within the fragile human bodies, weakening them further to make them yield to his evil will. He will be the "malignant twin of the chief" of the fervent worshipers, who have lost their way and their morals have been compromised, and this twin is the servant of satan. The misguided people will foolishly praise him, sing his eulogies, thinking that he is Divine, their savior, the radiant blissful Light sent to guide them, but in truth, he will be the one who is the enemy (Paul/Saul – " the little destroyer").

The True Savior of the soul is the Inner Light, manifested and preserved as the Sacred Secretion, full of boundless Grace and Humility despite having immense Power and infinite Mercy. He is the One who is sent to lovingly reconcile people with the Creator, reminding them again that He is infinitely Loving. He is the hidden Secret of God, the Savior from the enemy, who will unshackle the hypnotized people from the enemy's shackle, restoring the whole body of man as a resplendent Fountain of Light beaming with Love and Glory.

The Healing Oil restores and awakens the dormant cells of the right hemisphere of the brain, the spiritual side of the brain, and purifies and erases everything that corrupts. The High-frequency conscious-ness distributes to all cells and to the 12 cranial nerves in the brain (the 12 disciples of Jesus Christ) that meticulously control the 12 systems in the body, purifying each one by one (the reflection of the 12 constellations of the Zodiac – the Macrocosm).

The Inner Spirit of God within the body of a faithful believer is His Beloved, nested as the gentle Dove and embodiment of the Spirit of Peace, that is without rage and chaos and is All healing, and it dwells in the solar plexus (the House of Bread, the Bethlehem). At the same time, it will be like a sharp Rock to the enemy. The Holy Spirit of God will reside in every faithful believer, ready to begin its cleansing action for anyone who meditates in serene solitude upon the Light within, calling upon the Grace of God to help. The Divine

Mind will deliver people from the prison of the ancient dragon that has been preying on men's innocence and grace for generations.

Chapters 14-15

The Divine Mind, activated through the Sacred Secretion, fortified by the Holy Spirit of God, manifests in the flesh. It will deliver and liberate humanity from the "son of the serpent", the dwellers of darkness and the cosmic bandits. They relentlessly hunt and scavenge after human energy and the Earth's precious resources to fuel themselves and their machines. He is the Savior from the "sons of the giants, like a warlike serpent", and He embodies boundless Grace, infinite Mercy, and unbiased and strict Justice. He is the unyielding Sharp Rock presence will save humans from the "serpent seed" and the violent enemy. He will pull them out of the quicksand of the misery and dehypnotize against the "little". The Divine Mind will save them from the serpent's charm, which is like a desolate "waste" that brings ruin and destruction.

The Divine Mind, manifested through and powered by the Sacred Secretion, serves as the Savior of the soul and body and as a cleanser that sanctifies, purifies, and unburdens men from the cosmic pilgrims and space travelers' schemes. This Sacred Secretion, known as the Rescue Oil and Liquid Gold, resides and brews in the spinal cord, waiting to be summoned through mindful meditation.

The Christ Mind, manifested through the Christ (anointed) Oil, the Biocosmic energy of Life, is the Eternal Wheel in the Tower of Greatness, the Fortress of Redemption and Refuge, embodying the power and glory of the Creator. As the Beloved and the Prince of God, this Divine Essence stands as the ultimate truth, pulverizing every lie and deceit. He stands as a beacon of Light, guiding men back to God and His Embrace. He is the Hope for all who seek spiritual enlightenment and salvation and wish to wake up their mental and spiritual energies again.

Chapters 16-17

Those religious people who have rebelled, subscribed instead to the serpent's ways, and chosen to separate themselves from the Righteous Savior are often characterized as the "warlike people", always concocting schemes and proliferating chaos. They have distanced themselves from the Divine Seed of Grace and Mercy, depriving their souls and minds of wisdom and replenishment, and have forsaken the Seed of God's Light within the man, which is filled with the Holy Spirit, like the Dove, an emblem of Prosperity. He is appointed by God as the Rock who obeys God . He is not a man, but He is the Spiritual Light Being within the faithful man, what man was supposed to be, which is His real Identity. He will heal and restore the whole body and renew the blood of the body of man, as He is an Elixir of Life, with the sole purpose of renewing men inside out.

There are 12 essential inorganic mineral cell salts (the tissue salts) that play a crucial role in the cerebrospinal fluid in the spine of man. (These vital minerals are often referred to metaphorically as "Peter", a stone in the Temple of God, the body, the microcosm). These mineral salts resonate at specific vibrational frequencies that correspond in vibration to the 12 signs of the Zodiac, the vast and intricate Macrocosm. To sustain the High vibrational Consciousness and achieve a state of elevated spiritual awareness that can sustain a battle of wisdom and fight temptations, it is imperative to maintain a strong, vibrant physical body. This harmonious state of being can be nurtured by incorporating the 12 cell salts into daily regimen (salvation is also being complete with mineral salts because we are the "Salt" of the Earth).

He is the Son of the Holy Spirit, The Prince of Correction, the Anointed Saviour, manifested as the Sacred Anointed Oil within, an Energizer of the intellect who stands as the Sharp Rock to the adversary.

Chapters 18-21

The Inner Light of God, the Deliverer, is the Son of Comfort and Rest for the soul and the Invigorator of Mind but is like the Sharp Rock to the adversary, an unstoppable Undoing of the evil, the destroyer – the ego, the pride of the carnal nature of man. This Divine Presence of the Good Master, the Well of Praise, who is Loyal and Just, is the Foundation of Peace within the body of man, transformed, resurrected, and made functional through meditation and the focus upon the Light of God within.

The Divine Mind is the Ruler over the "noise" of the enemy in the head, a Dispeller of all the evil charm and chants and slogans. The King and the Savior, the Righteous Branch, and the Beloved of God bring tranquility and clarity, elucidating and explaining to men its true pedestal, purpose, and worth. In contrast, the "house of affliction or the serpent's house", an abode of misery, depravity, and moral scarcity, will remain barren, devoid of the "fruits" of the Holy Spirit of God within and the multitude of blessings that men will enjoy when they revert to God's ways.

Chapters 22-25

The Inner Light of God, also known as the Christ Consciousness within the body of the believer, acts as a divine Friend. His presence binds those who have separated themselves from the Creator and who are harming humanity from dark space dimensions. This Christ Consciousness is the Master from High dimensions of space, the Deliverer, and the Father of nations. He is the Prince of God, the Beloved, and the Divine Consciousness that dwells within our hearts and minds. This Consciousness, filled with Divine Love, rules over the deceiver, is the God of Righteous and unrighteous people. It embodies and expresses God's Laws of unity and harmony.

This Inner Light is the Savior, saving us from the deceiver and the egoistic carnal nature of man caused by the reptilian part of our brain. This carnal nature often drives negative behaviors and attitudes. As the Savior, this Consciousness acts as a Teacher and Master to those who are unfaithful, constantly reminding us of God's presence and Love. It guides us back to a state of unity with the Creator.

Chapters 26-28

The Savior, the Inner Christ, rescues souls from the "house of affliction". It is akin to an Olive tree in a plentiful valley, representing abundance and peace. This Savior is also the Rock, the Portion of God, and the Creator. For those seeking guidance, the Saviour offers Salvation from affliction, dissolving the negative and destructive prideful ego and restoring both spiritual and physical health. The Rescue Oil, known as the Sacred Secretion, acts as the Eternal Wheel and the Rock against the deceiver.

The Savior protects us from those who belong to the "serpent seed" and are armed with "darts". These individuals were once praising God but rebelled. The Prince of God prevails over the "son of shame and confusion", but our planet Earth is likened to a prison under the oppression of the ancient dragon. This enemy harvests Earth's resources, such as gold, oil, and minerals, and collects human life energy during times of suffering and wars. They exploit the low vibrations of the reptilian part of the brain, especially during stress and fear.

When the Divine Seed, manifesting as the Christ Oil or the Holy Flame of Eternal Love, rises to the brain, it is empowered by the Spark of Cosmic Light in the heart. It crosses (not crucifies) the Vegas nerve at the 33rd vertebra of the spine (the age of Jesus Christ), reaching the skull (Golgotha - "the place of the skull") in the head. This process increases its power a thousandfold. The oil then "rests in the tomb"- the claustrum in the brain, for three days before activating the pineal and pituitary glands. This activation produces the Holy Christ Oil, the Sacred Secretion, the Fountain of Life, which elevates the consciousness, renews the blood, and heals the entire body through God's Frequency of Love.

The Savior is the King of God's faithful people and even those who have rebelled. He is the Ruler who pardons the true and faithful believers and stands as a Lion against violent demons armed with "darts". These demons separate themselves from God and are like strangers, representing the reptilian races from dark and violent spaces. They have mixed divine human genes with reptilian genes through genetic manipulations of the human bodies. However, the Sacred Oil, representing the Expression of the Union of the Divine

Masculine and Divine Feminine, is the source of Eternal life within the body.

The prisoners of the ancient dragon will be saved by the Saviour, who embodies God's Love and the Victory of the Holy Spirit over the negative ego and pride of men. This victory is not just a spiritual triumph but also a restoration of the Divine Order and Harmony within us and the Universe.

MARK

Chapter 1

The Inner Light of God, manifested as the Redeeming Christ Oil, is God's Light that represents the Divine Presence within the spinal cord. This Sacred Oil, also known as the Holy Flame, travels up the spinal cord to the human brain monthly, increasing in power as it crosses the Vegas nerve at the base of the skull. This journey activates the Rock of Salvation—the pineal gland—producing the Eternal Light of Salvation and the Elixir of Life, symbolized by the Fruit of the Tree of Life, which renews itself twelve times a year.

This process of Salvation involves the resurrection of dormant brain cells, unifying both hemispheres of the brain, healing the entire body, renewing the blood to the Anointed, Pure Blood (referred to as the Blood of Christ), and elevating human consciousness. The Redeeming Sacred Secretion restores the connection with the Prime Creator, heals both the physical and spiritual Light Body, and reawakens the multidimensional nature of humanity by activating the twelve cranial nerves in the brain.

The Divine Sacred Secretion also reactivates our 12 strands of the Divine DNA, countering the invisible advanced technology that the adversary implants in the heart and energy body of humans. This

Sacred Oil dissolves these negative influences, restoring the purity and divine essence of the individual.

The Spirit of God calls out to humanity: "Come, who possess the Portion of Grace to come to the "field of repentance". Here, the Branch of God, the Savior, and the Holy One hold the promise of peace". This call is an invitation to transcend the earthly deceiver and journey towards the Eternal Light, the Savior, and the Deliverer. This transformation represents a shift from carnal consciousness to Divine Christ Consciousness, enabling individuals to obey the Laws of Oneness and liberate themselves from the bondage of the enemy. This process promises complete healing of the physical body, mind, and soul.

Chapters 2-7

The Rising Savior within , the Body of Light, the Inner Christ, dispels the fear of death and embodies the Son of Consolation and Repentance. The Spirit of God urges men by saying: "Follow me, the Divine path, and not be swayed by those who have distanced themselves from Grace and Mercy". The Beloved calls people to stand against the unfaithful, those who conceal the Truth and spread lies against the Creator.

The Christ Oil, the Sacred Secretion, the cerebrospinal fluid of the spinal cord, represents the Holy Flame of Light within the flesh. (It is not the kundalini, the serpent's coiled energy.) This Divine

Light stands as a Rock against the "sons of thunder", who are the lovers of war and represent anti-human secret evil forces that damage human energy bodies. These oppressors use mind control to enforce anti-human religions and death cults, offering human sacrifices to demonic spirits.

The Prime Creator, God of Love and Unity, does not require bloody human sacrifices. He is the Divine Consciousness, revealing Himself through the Holy Spirit, the Counselor and the Redeemer. The only way to connect with the Prime Source is by transforming and harmonizing the lower consciousness with the Higher Consciousness through the Holy Marriage within the hearts. This transformation can be achieved through meditation on the Divine Spark within the hearts, for what men focus on will grow. The Spark of the Holy Spirit will expand into the Holy Flame, the Elixir of Life, and the Sacred Secretion, which will heal and transform the minds, emotions, desires, and physical bodies of men.

Amidst this spiritual journey, there exists a twin of the ancient serpent, known as the "son of thunder", the chief of demons, and the "god of the flies" (represented by the figure of Paul/Saul, the "little destroyer"). Despite this challenge, the Seed of Light within humans will deliver them from the "prison of the enemy". The Savior protects men from the "giants", the hybrids of the reptilian race. He is the Deliverer and rescues humans from the violence of the enemy, who, secretly, engages in death rituals that generate low vibrational energy to sustain the reptilian race.

Chapters 8-14

The Son of God is often depicted as the Seed of Rest and the Fruit of Mercy. This powerful symbolism conveys His role in activating the "rock" within humans, which is often associated with the pineal gland, a crucial part of the spiritual anatomy. The adversary in this context is the reptilian brain, representing the most primal and fear-driven instincts. The Son of God stands as an Eternal Wheel on the "field of repentance", embodying the Beloved, the Portion of God, and the Foundation of Peace. This Divine Presence enlightens and satisfies the entire being of a faithful person, elevating their consciousness and awareness while liberating them from fear, shame, guilt, lies, and deception. Through this enlightenment, the mental and emotional (astral) aspects of a person are restored and united.

The Savior, known as the Foundation of Peace, is the ultimate Rescuer of both mind and soul. He delivers men from the "house of the affliction of olives and the house of dry figs", metaphors for the realm of satan, who has exalted himself in opposition to God. The Savior is the steadfast Rock and the Ruler over the enemy, who has been cast out from God's Presence and separated from His Divine

Light. The Savior, the Inner Light of God, is also the Beloved Seed of Light residing within the heart of every faithful believer.

In stark contrast, the "house of affliction" is a place where people offer insincere praise, worshiping through mere lip service. This house, filled with carnal and violent entities, venerates death and the destruction of men.

However, the Savior, symbolized as the Rock and the Son of Prophecy, will ultimately prevail.

Chapters 15-16

He is the Savior of the soul, prevailing against those who are "armed with weapons" and possess cold hearts, symbolized by the red dragon. Within the human body, the Inner Light of God assists us, ensuring that this Divine Light is not "crucified" but rather increases within our consciousness. This Divine Light, often referred to as the Sacred Secretion, activates the pineal and pituitary glands, leading to an illumination of the Fountain of Divine Energy and Eternal Life. This illumination heals the entire body and restores the spiritual memory of the faithful. This transformation is symbolized by the renewed blood within the body, free from the destructive energies of the "serpent seed".

Deliverance from the prison and bondage of the ancient dragon represents the ultimate Victory of the Holy Spirit of God over the reptilian, carnal spirit. As Divine beings and co-creators with God, we are inherently connected to the Eternal Truth from the beginning of time.

LUKE

Chapter 1-2

The Seed of God's Spirit within the heart is a profound embodiment of Divine Wisdom. This Seed is not just a Gift from God but represents His Wisdom, serving as a Ruler over the basic instincts of the human mind, often referred to as the reptilian mind. This Inner Savior, the Inner Spirit of God, acts as a Teacher and a Source of immense strength. It is the Divine Mind of God, overflowing with Love, grace, and mercy and filled with the eternal Holy Spirit. The Inner Spirit is the Branch extended to sinners, the Son of the Highest, embodying the Mind of God.

However, there will come a time when the enemy, symbolizing negative forces and adversarial powers, will rise in strength and control the world for a period. But fear not, for the Divine Seed of God's Light will be planted in the solar plexus of humanity (metaphorically referred to as Bethlehem, the House of Bread). This Seed is the Divine Pure Essence of God, the Anointed Savior, and the Christ Consciousness. It manifests as the Redeeming Oil, the Sacred Secretion, forming the Foundation of God's Peace and the Salvation of the world. This Inner Light, obedient to God's will, is filled with His mercy and is chosen and set apart with those who share the same Divine Vision.

Chapter 3

The Inner Spiritual Light within the heart has been obstructed by ancient malevolent entities equipped with advanced technologies. These entities rewired human brains and nervous systems, limiting our potential to mere survival instead of allowing us to be co-creators with God. They inflicted damage through invisible "mind control" devices and "virus programs", deactivating the spiritual aspects of the DNA (often dismissed as "the junk DNA") and confining humanity to lower levels of consciousness—physical, emotional, and mental.

Yet, the Savior, the Divine Seed of Light within, calls out: "Prepare your way to God". This inner Savior, the Father of Nations, is filled with the Spirit of Truth and possesses the power to liberate people from reptilian mind control, negative ego, and false spirits. The "son of the ancient serpent", depicted as a warlike dragon, will relentlessly pursue this divine Savior, God's highest gift. This Deliverer, who is both a Comforter and a Source of patience, separates Light from the harmful entities within the body, akin to parasites at a cellular level.

In the cells of the human body, the Centrosome, connected to the Divine Source, the Prime Creator, representing the central "sun" of the human cell, begins to radiate, embodying the physical manifestation of the Holy Spirit of the Prime Creator. This Divine

Force pushes away the mitochondria, the parasitic bacteria, which are responsible for cellular stress and shortened lifespans. The Savior will dispel confusion and confront the man, "the seed of the serpent, the little one" (Paul/Saul – "the little destroyer"), who will say: "God is my King, my Counsellor, my Witness," but he is the "watchman, the watcher", who will divide the "garment" of God.

However, the One, who pardons, will be raised up into the brain – "the Heaven of God", the right side of the brain - the Crystal Palace of Divine Feminine. There will be the restoration of the dormant cells in the right side of the brain of man, after the raising the Rescue Oil, The Savior, the One, who glorifies God, the Rock, the God's Strength.

The one who was perfect before his rebellion but became the supplanter will enchant and lure people of praise and separate them.

The true Savior, who hears and obeys God, glorifies Him through the Holy Spirit and will be resurrected within the faithful. This resurrection will bring the Sacred Secretion, God's Gift of strength and peace, filling believers with divine reward. The Inner Spiritual Light will blow away the spiritual "dust that is dry" caused by the false shepherd who created divisions within the House of God (there are more than 26000 denominations of Christianity in the world), saying that he was sent by God, using the Name of the

Healer. But he is the "possessor" and sent by the devil, not by the Healer.

Despite the enemy's attempts to appoint man for mortal sorrow, God's Love provides a Seed of Light, offering rest and freedom from dark entities that disrupt earthly peace.

Chapter 4

The cerebrospinal fluid in the human spine, infused with God's Inner Light, acts as a Converter of Divine Spiritual Energy. This Inner Savior, filled with the Holy Spirit, will destroy adversaries and establish peace. It is the eternal branch from the field of consolation through repentance, a beautiful Savior, and a Smelting Furnace for those who travel violently through space.

The Inner Spiritual Light, manifesting in the flesh as the Rescue Oil, is the Eternal Wheel of Divine intelligence within the men.

Chapters 5-6

The Illuminated Sacred Secretion, the Rescue Oil is the Expression of God's Love, offering life-transforming spiritual power. The Savior, the Inner Light of Love, always listens to and obeys the Prime Creator. The Savior is the Obedient One, the Savior of men, from the one who is unfaithful and separates people from God of Love. "Join me and follow me!", says God.

The earthly deceiver, a man of murder (Paul/Saul – "the little destroyer"), who infiltrated into the House of God and spread confusion, proclaimed "salvation" through human sacrifice and cannibalism ("communion"). He is the "twin", the covered supplanter, who created the religions as "the mind control weapon" against humanity. He is the "zealous traitor" of the world from the beginning of creation. He is the hunter for the souls, the "sharp rock", the evil, the traitor of the Blessed God, who enforces anti-human behavior and rules.

Chapters 7-10

The Savior, the Inner Christ, speaks from the field of repentance, calling out to us with a message of hope and reassurance: "Come to me, weep not. I am the Praise of God, full of Mercy and Grace". He warns us to be wary of those who have separated themselves from God, reminding us that He is the Ruler over rebellious and sinful people. He is the Lily, the pure embodiment of Divine Grace, calling us to join Him and move towards God from our "walled places" of isolation and despair.

The Savior is the One who saves us from the "legion" of evil demonic entities that plague the souls. He is the Son of God's Light, the unshakable Rock, and the Master who guides humans. "Fear not, weep not," He assures us. As a Rock to the deceiver, He stands firm against those who try to lead us astray. God will ultimately prevail over the "son of sorrow and his house of snares", as well as overall deceivers. The Savior is the Deliverer, the Foundation of Peace, while the "watchers" are the deceivers, the "lying foxes".

The Inner Light within is the God of Peace. However, there is also the "secret man of the house of snares", a wicked force symbolized as the "sharp little rock" of the enemy. Yet, the Savior represents the Field of Repentance, the Rising of Vibration, and the Seed of The Creator. He embodies the Universal Christ Consciousness of Unity and Love. Those who follow idol worshippers and the wicked "watchers" are led away from this Divine path.

Chapters 11-19

The Beloved of God, the Saviour, stands against the bitter and sinful people. He is the embodiment of Grace and Mercy, the Face of God, and the Holy Spark of Light that signifies God's Love within the hearts. The enemy, known as the "adversary", works to separate people from God's Love, Spirit, Wisdom, and Mind.

The Saviour, the Son of God filled with the Holy Spirit, admonishes people: "Don't follow the wicked people; follow the Spirit of God".

The Inner Light of God, always in harmony with the Spirit of God, speaks to those who oppose Him: "I am the Armour, the

Foundation of Peace, the Memory of God. Behold, I am the Father of nations, and you are the one who separated them from God. Behold, I will cast out the demons".

We are encouraged to stay close to the Blessed God, who is the Deliverer, the Rest, the Sweet Smell of Purity, and the embodiment of God's Justice. Blessed be the King who comes in the Name of God, bringing Peace and Glory from Heaven.

Chapters 20-22

The Holy Seed of God's Light acts as the Passover over the adversary and rules over the egoistic desires of man. This Divine Seed will triumph over the destroyer of humanity, reconnecting humanity to the Universal Consciousness and harmonizing the Divine Feminine and Divine Masculine within us. The struggle between good and evil will persist due to the presence of two seeds: the Divine Seed and the seed of the reptilian race, the kundalini.

The Divine Seed will be reactivated within by God's Light, especially during meditation and by focusing on the Divine Light within. The serpent seed will be dissolved and conquered in the man's body by the Holy Flame. The Sacred Secretion and the Divine Crystals of the heart and mind will be reactivated in the bodies of faithful believers, leading to a profound spiritual transformation.

Chapters 23-24

Those who arm themselves against the Savior are, in effect, arming themselves against the King of Praise. The enemy, referred to as the "son of shame and confusion", attempts to supplant the King of Heaven. The serpent seed, symbolized by the reptilian brain, is cold-hearted and will be conquered within the "place of the skull" by the activation of the pineal and pituitary glands. This illumination will reactivate the spiritual right, the feminine part of the brain. The Seed of Light will not be "crucified" but will increase a thousandfold. This illumination, facilitated by the Fountain of Light and Life and the Sacred Secretion, will restore the whole body, transforming the carnal consciousness of man into the Divine Christ Consciousness of Love within the heart and mind.

The Son of God within offers Salvation from the slavery of demonic evil forces. He represents the Victory of the Holy Spirit of God over the carnal nature of men. As a steadfast Rock for despised people, He is the Foundation of God's Peace and Glory. He stands as a beacon of Hope and Salvation, guiding men away from the temptations and deceptions of the world and leading them toward a life filled with Divine Love and Peace.

JOHN

Chapters 1-4

The Seed of God's Light exists within every person, materialized as the Holy Oil, known as the Sacred Secretion. This Redeeming Essence embodies the qualities of God's Love, Grace, and Mercy, acting as a physical manifestation of the Divine Nature within humans. It has the transformative power to elevate the carnal mind and heart, infusing them with the Christ Consciousness of Cosmic Eternal Love. This Christ Consciousness serves to dissolve the serpent seed and his "house of separation", overcoming the forces that seek to divide humanity from God.

The Saviour embodies the Zeal of God's Temple, which is the human body itself, resonating with powerful Divine energy and the Vibration of Love. Despite those who have separated from God celebrating their supposed victory over the people, the Savior, as the Teacher, proclaims: "Accept the Spirit, not those who will be victorious over people".

The Saviour is also the Deliverer, the Foundation of God's Peace, and the Ruler over the "foxes" who attempt to spoil God's Consciousness within humans. These negative influences will be eradicated by the Holy Flame of God's Light, purging them like garbage and dust from the spinal cord of man. The Savior declares: "My food is the watchers".

Chapters 5-16

The Inner Light of God is the Fountain of Peace from the House of Mercy. It calls forth the Savior, the Son of God, who brings Salvation from within. The Savior is the victorious Commander in the battle against the "violent deceiver". As the Teacher and Beloved from the House of Bread (representing the solar plexus in the human body), He brings Divine sustenance and guidance. Yet, those who seek to separate people from God will temporarily rule over them.

The Inner Spiritual Light of God serves as Divine assistance for the "lost" people, but the "twin of the ancient serpent" remains a destroyer. The Savior provides salvation from the "house of affliction", invoking God's help against the forces of rebellion. A man with the serpent seed, a "man of murder", will arise (symbolized by Paul/Saul – "the little destroyer").

Blessed is the King, the Prince of God, not the "man of noise", who was also created by God. This "man of noise, from the house of fishing and fish idols", will appear alongside the Savior of God. However, he is a lover of wars, a strong and violent enemy who secretly infiltrates the House of God, killing many of God's people before and after his infiltration and dividing the House of God from within (represented by Paul/Saul).

The Inner Light of God, the Christ Consciousness, is the Love of the Creator. Yet, someone from the sinful world will betray the Master. The Savior, filled with the Spirit of God, embodies the Spirit of Love and Wisdom.

Chapters 17-21

God's Salvation will be challenged by a man who pretends to praise Him with diligence but is, in truth, the enemy "armed with darts" against the King. This "man of shame", cast out from the high places, was once an angelic being created by God, full of glory. Now, he is a "lion" who is dead to God.

The Savior, the Inner Spark of God's Light within, is armed with the Darts of God. He is the King, the Savior, God's Branch, and the Passover, stronger than the one "armed with darts". The spinal cord of man acts as the Rod, the Watchtower of the Loving God. The Sacred Secretion, the Holy Christ Flame, the cerebrospinal fluid, is the River of Life, the Divine Teacher, and the Master over the rebellious destroyer, the serpent seed.

The powerful Savior of the soul within humans, empowered by the Holy Spirit, is the Gift of God. This presence embodies His Zeal, Possession, and Victory over the carnal mind of men. The Redeemer, the obedient Rock, will multiply His faithful followers and restore His Peace on the Earth.

THE ACTS

Chapter 1

The Extension of God, represented by the Anointed Inner Light of God within humanity, is embodied in the form of the Redeeming Christ Oil. This sacred Essence serves as the Foundation of Peace and the Savior, embodying the Mercy of God for the faithful. It is a Rock, steadfast against the forces of deception. In the world, there will arise a "strong violent man", a lover of wars, known as the "twin of the enemy, and the son who suspends the waters". This individual, acting as a deceiver and false prophet, will be sent by the "chief of the fallen angels", who rebelled against the Savior, the Rock, and the Universal Consciousness. This figure (often likened to Paul/Saul, known as "the destroyer who is invisible") will feign praise for God and His Word. However, his true intent will be to create a "field of blood", killing God's people and fracturing the House of God into numerous branches (over 26000 denominations of Christian churches).

Chapters 2-3

In ancient times, people revered and worshipped a wicked being as a "high god". This scenario will repeat in the future, like the era when false "alien gods" ruled (as seen in the Sumerian civilization). The world will fall under the dominion of unhuman entities, members of dark, muddy forces. These cold-hearted, violent, and dangerous individuals, forming the "elite" of every nation, will hold power. Despite this, the Holy Savior, the Son of God, will command and prevail as the Beautiful Rock, the Inner Christ, representing Divine Cosmic Consciousness.

Chapters 4-8

The Holy Spirit of God is inherently Righteous. However, one who was once part of this grace became an enemy of God, corrupting the essence of humanity—the human DNA. This being, the "son of the ancient dragon and the sharp rock", was once merciful and beautiful before his rebellion. Those who align themselves with him will follow this ancient dragon in opposition to the Holy Spirit of God. Nonetheless, those forcefully separated from God will be recompensed by the Inner Christ and His followers.

The Inner Light of God, crowned with the Holy Spirit, represents the Eternal Victory of God. This Divine Entity is the Governor who will triumph over the "muddy wicked one", who is spreading like a "chariot". The Seed of God's Light acts as the Deliverer, sanctifying and calling people out of the demonic world's wickedness. The Son of God, the Father of a multitude, will prevail over the deceiver, the "underworld dragon".

The C,rowned Savior, manifested as the Rescue Christ Oil and the Sacred Secretion, is anointed by the Holy Spirit. This Rock, also known as the Watch Mountain, signifies the Holy Spirit of God within the spinal cord of man, aiming to restore his entirety. However, the stubborn dragon declared war against the Holy Word, the Son of God. This dragon, cut off from Heaven, became the "thief" and will ultimately be cut off from the Earth as well.

Chapters 9-10

The "wicked one is full of blood", symbolizing a being consumed by violence and malice. In contrast, the Inner Spiritual Light within us is filled with mercy and compassion. This Divine Seed of God's Light, residing in both the heart and the brain, represents God's Love and a vVsion of Peace. However, the enemy seeks to corrupt this Truth by blending praise with conflict, aiming to obscure the Path of Righteousness.

The Savior, embodying Consolation and a clear Message of Love, stands opposed to this adversary. The enemy will strife with the Beautiful Savior, the Eternal Stone of Wisdom.

The enemy was cast out from IIeaven and is depicted as the "horn of the bull" in opposition to God. On the other hand, the Beloved of God remains the beautiful Rock against this ancient dragon. The Savior, through the Redeeming Oil, restores High Multidimensional Consciousness in humans, enabling them to become co-creators with God. People are called to stand with the Savior, the Inner Christ, against the "horn", who once delighted in faithfulness before rebelling. The Prince of God, anointed with the Holy Spirit, will ultimately conquer the "serpent seed" and restore Divinity in humanity.

Chapters 11-14

The Ruler, filled with the Spirit of God, is the beautiful Rock and the foundation of peace given by God. Yet, the world will "crown the red sharp stone" (representing Paul/Saul), a false teacher who is "speedy as the chariot and cold-hearted". This individual, a son of the ancient dragon and deceiver, will multiply like locusts. We are called to arise as the Rock against the "chief of the fallen angels, a stone of shame, the son of sorrow," and the murderer who fights against God's Peace and Mercy.

This wicked man will follow quickly after God's messenger, acting as a test for God's people. He will ensnare them like a net, using his craftiness to create a patriarchal religion as a tool of mind control. Claiming to be God's son, he will falsely declare himself as a gift from God. This great orator and manipulator will become a thorn in the body of the Anointed One, but the Son of God will dissolve his influence. The wicked one will spread dangerous lies, acting as an informational "virus" among the nations.

Chapters 15-19

The Inner Spirit of Light within us serves as our Deliverer against the "little mountain, the watcher". The Son of God is the Rock, not the ancient serpent who was cast out from Heaven. The enemy will pretend to be a faithful son, consolidating with the Son of Rest. He will claim to be a "small, little, anointed savior", deceiving nations with his swift arrival after God's Anointed Messenger.

This deceiver will act like a "sting" and a thief, masquerading as an angel of light while being a liar and murderer from the beginning. He is a violent criminal, striving with God and pretending to honor Him. His identity is the devil, the ancient serpent, the great destroyer of many planets, who emerges from the sea and the underground. Despite his deceptive power, he is insignificant compared to God. The Savior from Heaven is the Salvation against this "little" murderer.

The Savior, the Spiritual Seed of God within, is the Passover, transcending all levels of heavens to manifest on Earth. This Sacred Secretion within the human body transforms the carnal mind into a Multidimensional Divine Consciousness. The Savior stands against those who come from the hills of Mars and the Moon, the unknown "alien gods".

The carnal world will be drawn to the "eagle of the sea", the ancient serpent who appears strong. They will mistakenly worship this being with burning adoration, neglecting the anointed Savior. This destroyer will deceive and trouble new believers, those who interpret God's word literally rather than understanding it as an allegory of restoring the Holy Light within by the Holy Spirit of God. The ancient serpent, one of the fallen angels, is armed with darts against the Savior, the King of Praise, who was cast out from the High places.

Behold, the King, the Savior, the Branch of God! The King of kings, who overcame the deceiver, stands strong against the rebellious angels. The chief of these rebellious angels is depicted as a "little lion", dead to God, while the Savior is filled with the Holy Spirit of Eternal life.

Chapters 20-23

The enemy is a rebellious force, opposing the obedient Rock, who is the Savior, Teacher, Master, and Ruler over this adversary. This Rock, God's Gift, is dedicated to multiplying the faithful. God will judge and overturn the deceiver who distorts the truth and brings chaos. This deceiver is described as "muddy, full of blood", and an enemy of God's mercy. God vigilantly watches over His people, symbolized as spiritual "dew", and keeps a "watchful eye" on the enemy, who inflicts great suffering on humanity. God's

Voice, raised like a Trumpet, warns His faithful people, calling them to hear Him from within during mindful meditation, the True Communion with the Creator.

The enemy will be struck down by the Deliverer, the Son of God, who is filled with the Spirit of God. This Divine Intervention is a central theme, reflecting the ultimate triumph of good over evil.

The confessions of the "destroyer"

(The Epistle to the Romans-Philemon)

THE EPISTLE TO THE ROMANS

Chapters 1-15

I am the "little" one, the destroyer of the Inner Christ, the force that dims the Divine Light within men. Once, I was beloved, the embodiment of God's grace. Emerging from the sea, I was the "anointed" son of God. Now, I stand as the deity of those who descended from heaven into the earthly realm, the fallen angels. I am the father and prince of the multitudes, the earthly destroyer.

I led humanity into corruption, procreating a race of giants by mating with earthly women. I am the leader of the rebellious celestial beings, those who defied God's commandments concerning genetic manipulation, crossbreeding, and mating with earthly women. As a deceiver and manipulator, I act violently against those striving to help humanity regain their original state as beings of Light. I am the bearer of satan's order, descending from dark places, the master of masters. I am the chief of the rebellious souls in the world.

Once, I was among the anointed angels of God. I crossed the heavens and descended with the dark angels from the depths of space, through the sea, and into the underground. I sinned against the Creator and humanity but blamed humans for my transgressions. I am the father of the multitude of "watchers," the Nephilim, the son of sorrow. I confuse people with false "salvation" through death and bloody rituals, creating religions to mislead them. As the God of this world, I deceive, luring people towards materialism, enhancing their ego and carnal desires, and feeding on the low energy of their suffering.

I am the gift to the fallen world, bringing forbidden knowledge and practicing lawlessness. I am the chosen one, receiving the desirable precious burning adoration from the people, even though I brought grief and troubles to the Foundation of Peace.

Chapter 16

I am the chosen one, receiving precious burning adoration from the people. I am the shining, illuminated one, the "little" pulse of the satan, the ancient eagle, though not the anointed Savior of the world. I am praised as an anointed eagle, having instigated the rebellion of men from the beginning by separating them from the Good Counselor. Once an extension of God, the pleasant one, I have become the cosmic parasite and destroyer.

On the Earth, I became the son of the "hero", the giant, a marvel to the world. I am incomparable, zealous, a refuge from Mercury, pursuing the steps of my father, the satan, who was also a refuge. As a crafty master of writing, I love letters and words, mixing truth with lies. I am the accuser, attempting to dissolve the Inner Spiritual Light of God, the Divine Power of God, within the body of man.

I am the fourth ruler of the earthly man, who was once anointed. I am strong, beautiful, shiny, and the small pulse of my master, the satan.

1 CORINTHIANS

Chapters 1-9

I am one of the "little, invisible" destroyers who were once giants but have become invisible to people using advanced magnetic technologies. We exist in a reality that is invisible to human physical eyes and has brought significant damage to humanity. I was once a beautiful ornament of God, one of the "first shoots of green grass", but I became one of the "little" destroyers of God's Seed, the Christ Oil, the Divine Consciousness in the body of man. I am the god of the nations, but I harbor hatred for human beings because they were created in the image of the Prime Creator, not in my image.

"I was once the anointed one, the son of consolation, the deliverer who crossed the heavens. I was the burning adoration of God, the beautiful one, the honor of God, but I became the destroyer and corrupter of God's creations. I am the one who was crowned but caused grief and trouble, who became muddy and tainted. I am the ancient one who was anointed but was separated from the Source of Light.

2 CORINTHIANS

Chapters 1-13

I am the destroyer, the physical manifestation of egoistic desires, the "little" one compared to the Savior, the Rescue Oil of the Holy Spirit within. I was full of beauty but became the evil one against God. I was anointed but became muddy and corrupt. I was a burning adoration of God, the son of God, but turned into a lover of the forest and deserts.

I was at the right hand of God, His beauty, but now I am the one hidden in the invisible dimension. I was anointed and a pleasing adoration but became wicked and worthless, not deserving to be in the presence of God Almighty. I am the destroyer of the anointed Savior who brings life. I became the "little", the evil one, the accuser of souls who crossed the heavens and praised the god of all nations on the Earth.

I am the one who does evil, engages in bloody activities, and brings immorality and death. I was a beauty but became the accuser of the Highest and a lover of wars. I was the burning adoration, the light bearer, but I became the dark angel.

GALATIANS

Chapters 1-6

The "little", the destroyer of the Savior, says: "I am the raven of bloody activities against the Foundation of Peace, who is God's Rock. I am the deceiver, the sharp rock, as speedy as a chariot, running around the world. I am the little rock who crossed the heavens to deceive the nations. I was a white angel, anointed and illuminated by the Spirit of God, but I was cast out from heaven. I am the one who brought enmity through demonic strangers, dreadful as ravens. I was filled with the Spirit of God but was cast out and became the "little", the invisible one, and therefore I am strong and powerful.

EPHESIANS

Chapters 1-6

I am the little destroyer, one of the offspring of alien beings who were part of the Divine Mind but separated themselves from the Light because power and control became more desirable to them. They colonized the Earth to mine gold, created a system of control, and enslaved humanity to work for them. They concealed the knowledge about the Inner Christ, the Oil of the Holy Spirit within men, as the Holy Fire, the Desirable Fountain of Light and Life, saving people from destruction and limitations.

PHILIPPIANS

Chapter 1-4

I am the one who was created by God but became the "little" one. I was the anointed bearer of light but became the "little" lover of war, the son of sorrow after the rebellion. I crossed the heavens and came to the world, becoming the raven in sheep's clothing, who set apart by speaking sweetly and pretending to be kind. I was beautiful and victorious, but after being cut off from the House of God in heaven and being crafty, I infiltrated the House of God in order to replace and destroy the real God's Source of Light.

COLOSSIANS

Chapters 1-4

The one who once honored God before the rebellion became the "little" one. He says: "I am a handsome and anointed spirit, the right hand of my master, the satan. Touch me not. I am the one who brought the foreigners. I am the master of deception who became a false apostle by chance. I was profitable and useful, the best prince of darkness who ruled. I exist in other hidden realms, invisible to people, like parasitic bacteria in cells (the mitochondria). I am luminous, sacred, and the master of disguise, the little one. I am strong, useful, and profitable without punishment".

1-2 THESSALONIANS

The "little" one proclaims: "I was the one anointed by the spirit. I was the lover of horses, honored by the world, the embodiment of burning adoration". This figure initially conveys a sense of "divine" selection and passion. The "lover of horses" implies a connection to strength and nobility, while "honored by the world" highlights widespread recognition and respect. The phrase "burning adoration" suggests intense devotion, perhaps to a higher power or cause.

1-2 TIMOTHY

The one who was once beautiful and honored God turned against Him. He became a "muddy fugitive, begotten" from Mercury. 'As this individual's rebellion deepens, he declares: "I am the master who brings profits to the strong. I am the God of marriage, the one who afflicted and rebelled. I am as fast as a chariot, coming to dissolve the truth by being the false prophet.

I am popular, victorious, and increasingly luminous but became a deceitful lamb with vain brightness. I was shining, by chance, and beautiful, penetrating and fruitful. I am the ancient serpent, the eagle, who brings profits, victorious, well-educated, red, good prudent, shame-faced, the net for souls".

TITUS

Chapters 1-3

The one who became the 'little' reflects: "I am perfection by chance, from the city of victory, the living destroyer. I was a burning adoration, honoring and pleasing God. But now, I am the "little" destroyer who 'honors' God with kisses.

I am a productive master of lies and deceptions. I am the 'little,' but useful and profitable, invisible, covered by 'foam,' the polite destroyer, who is popular, luminous and strong, who kisses and who is useful for the kingdom of darkness".

PHILEMON

The "little" one, who kisses, is a productive master of horses and declares: "I am the "little" one, covered by foam, the best prince of darkness, popular false apostle and prophet, who became the luminous adoration of the people".

TO THE HEBREWS

Chapters 1-13

The Prime Creator is nestled and preserved within every human being as a Seed of Love because it was evident that human beings might need correction someday. At the low level of spiritual development, a place difficult to get to and thus safeguarded from obliteration and corruption, this Holy Seed is hidden deep inside the man's heart and consciousness, nurturing and waiting to be called upon through meditation and unleash its curative remedies. But it requires a little push as it must grow in every man, carefully fostered and taken care of as a Fruit of the Holy Spirit of God, which is teeming with the Power of His Spirit. This Seed can be grown only through the process of meditation and prayers, creating the energy field of high frequency. Once it grows roots and starts its remedial action, it will eradicate temptation, suppress wild desires, and subsequently transform our carnal consciousness into the Divine Consciousness of Peace and Love, which will also be restored to its Much-Deserved Nobility.

The Holy Spirit of God, who is dedicated to God, encased within the seed of even the most sinful of men, will transform man's consciousness into spiritual Divine Consciousness, saving him from eternal disgrace and misery. The right and left parts of the human brain have been made to conflict and quarrel by the serpent through the many experimentations and adulterations done, and it will be united, and this will be celebrated as the Divine Union. It will be the reflection of the Mind of the Prime Creator, a work of Magnificence at display in its luminous glory, and will connect to the Divine Source, refueling man's mind full of joy and love.

The false ego, brimming with misplaced pride, will be "swallowed" by the raging Divine Fire of the Holy Oil, the Sacred Secretion, the Cure-All of correction. This replenishment will lead to the illumination and enlightenment of the mind and the reinforcement of the heart and, subsequently, the will, which in turn will reunite and reconnect men back to the Holy Source of Life, restoring men back into the good graces of the Ever-Loving God. These will purify men inside out, exterminating mental and spiritual filth, and they will fill the whole body of men with the Divine Light, illuminating every sense and cognitive feature, even on the cellular and subatomic levels.

THE EPISTLE OF JAMES

The One who supplants the enemy and will prevail over him, thwarting his army of pawns made of fake leaders and religious heads, is the Savior, the Sent-from-Above Redeemer, who will command men to victory as the Anointed Ruler and Guide and lead them from the life of darkness acting as the Father of Light, and the multitude and he will undo the mental and spiritual shackles, shatter the hypnosis and prevail over the rebellious one.

1 PETER

The One who hears and obeys the Creator and calls men toward correction, even when men are hypnotically parading toward evil and following the alien invader, is the Inner Spiritual Light of God that is encapsulated within for men's rectification. He saves from the carnal mind and the temptations that this carnal mind concocts, following the schemes of the evil one, who was once celebrated and praised white angel but later mutinied and became "muddy and violent". The anointed Savior, the Blessed, and Protected, the One who is the rightful Owner of the pedestal of the Prince of God, is filled and empowered with the Holy Spirit and saves from those who confuse the whole world and lead men towards unwarranted and unchecked destruction.

Fear God to be saved from malignant disgrace and honor the King of the Universe! He is the Divine Shepherd who is always guiding, always setting the track right despite men backtracking from it time and time again, and He is the Bishop of the multitude, the Provider of abundance of mercy, and He is the only Dependable Savior. He is God over everything good and bad, even over the "ancient dragon" who brought the confusion and is "celebrating" his unholy interbreeding, genetic corruption and destruction as a triumph over man. He was the "shiny one" before his rebellion, respected and honored as a being of true potential, but now the Savior is the One who is illuminated, blessed with wisdom, and anointed with the Light of the Holy Spirit of Love and Mercy which He will use to illuminate the darkened spirits and minds of men.

2 PETER

The Anointed Savior is the Deliverer, a Divine, Unscathed Refuge who is filled with the Holy Spirit of God that He will use to protect men. He is the Savior, the final Rest who is hidden and covered and lies in the cells of the body of man (also, the Centrosome, "the sun" in the center of the cell, that connected to the Source of Light, and it is illuminating now, together with the Sacred Secretion, the fuel of the Holy Anointed Oil in the body. It is fending off and pushing away the mitochondria, the ancient "bacteria" that were injected into the cells of men to decrease the life's span and weaken the spirit and mind to make it easier to enslave them). He is the Merciful Saviour, the Much-Needed Deliverer, who will oversee men as a Protective Ruler and turn over the destroyer and his plans, who brought destruction to the people through corruption and blackening of heart.

1 AND 2 JOHN

The Beloved of God, His Ardent Steward, is the anointed Saviour, the Son who is Blessed with Protection. He is filled with the Holy Spirit of God and His Grace and manifested as the Sacred Secretion, the Empowering Elixir within men.

3 JOHN

The earthly man, made feeble and dependent on the temptations of the world, is "nourished" by Jupiter, a place of cursed shadows. Still, the true lasting nourishment of men is God, who is the Cosmic Flame of Life, the Divine Consciousness and the Sustainer of Goodness, the Ruler over the One who is the destructive cosmic serpent who is constantly playing his role of the destroyer without fail.

JUDE

The Praise of God is the anointed Saviour, appointed with the Task of saving mankind from eternal damnation and He will be the One who saves from the corrupt and treacherous deceiver. He is the Protective Father of mankind, and He is Empowered and Entrusted to be the anointed Saviour. He will be the Ruler who will dominate the rebellious entities who are immoral and troubled people, parading proudly as evil and corrupt.

The Deliverer is the Ruler and the Would-Be Victor over the possessor, who is violent, misguided, and lost but bold and "cold" due to vanity that dictates his character. The anointed Savior, the Holy Inner Christ, who is the manifestation of the Holy Spirit of God in the human body. Preserved within humans as the Powerful Christ Oil, the Sacred Secretion, restores the Divine Consciousness of man and fuels his mental and spiritual essence. It reconnects men to the Creator and liberates men from the hypnotic shackles on their souls.

REVELATION

Chapter 1

The Holy Fire of the Divine Light within the human body, manifested as the Sacred Secretion, is a living embodiment of God's Divine Love for suffering humanity. Earth has been infiltrated by evil cosmic entities, enslaving humans through genetic manipulation and interbreeding with earthly women. This led to humanity losing its connection with the Divine Source, becoming trapped in a lower state of mind, filled with fear, guilt, lust, and anger, resulting in spiritual forgetfulness.

During the spiritual awakening process, the Christ Holy Oil, representing the Holy Spirit within the spine of man, purifies, harmonies and transforms the seven energy centers along the spine. These centers, located in the root, sacral, solar plexus, heart, throat, brow, and crown areas, are referred to as the seven "churches". The human body, seen as the Temple of God's Spirit and a microcosm reflecting the Macrocosm of the Universe, contains energy centers that are small replicas of planets like Mars, Venus, the Sun, Moon, Mercury, Saturn, and Jupiter. The Creator will restore humanity's multidimensional spiritual nature, created in His image, through the Holy Fire manifested as the Sacred Secretion.

This Divine transformation elevates the carnal, materially limited mind of men into the Cosmic, Higher Mind, symbolizing the elevation of God's Perfume, the Christ Oil. It will merge the energy of the seven energy centers within the spinal cord as a column of pure Light. This process is the enlightenment from within, reconciliation with the Creator, and spiritual awakening to unconditional love for oneself and others.

Chapters 2-3

The sinful desires of the carnal flesh, including pride, greed, lust, envy, gluttony, wrath, and sloth, are referred to as the "serpent's seed". These desires can be harmful and destructive to the body and soul, as humans are spiritual beings living in physical bodies. However, through meditation on the Spark of God's Light within and the elevation and preservation of the Sacred Secretion (not the kundalini, the serpent energy), individuals can transcend these carnal desires. This "sacrifice" of fleshly desires and the ego leads to physical and spiritual sanctification and healing. Consequently, individuals can be restored to the divine image of the Creator with a High Love Consciousness while still in their physical bodies.

Those who fight against God's faithful people are seen as betrayers of God and His followers. These adversaries pretend to be the "chosen" people of God. Still, they are destroyers and wicked entities. They follow the accuser, deceiving and controlling people through religions of fear and death.

The Prince of Joy and Love, representing the Seed of God's Light within, reflects God's Love and Faithfulness. There will be an enlightenment of consciousness, transformation of the hearts and healing for the faithful. The wholeness of man, along with peace and rest, will be restored.

Chapters 4-14

Those who devote themselves to mindful meditation on the Inner Spark of Light within their hearts will be filled with God's Holy Fire, which manifests as the Sacred Secretion, the Plasmic Light (not the kundalini, the serpent's energy). These individuals will form the Light Nation, becoming the Harvest of God's Holy Seed and victorious overcomers. In contrast, those who have seen and heard God yet rebelled and fought against Him are likened to "space parasites and bandits". These individuals have forcefully occupied lands, falsely claiming they were promised to them by God. They declare themselves as God's "chosen people", yet their actions bring destruction and confusion to the world and humanity.

Every person in the world is chosen by God for different divine purposes. However, the Enlightened by God are those who genuinely love Him and humanity, who obey His Cosmic Laws of

Unity, preserve His Sacred Secretion, and meditate in stillness upon the Light of God within. God, the Universal Electromagnetic Field, embodies Divine Stillness, Everlasting Serenity, and the Divine Mind. Those enlightened individuals who praise Him in Spirit and Truth will receive His rewards, dwell in His presence, and increase their spiritual power and authority.

Chapters 15-22

God is the Deliverer, the Almighty, who manifests His presence within the human body, transforming the carnal, animal mind into the Divine Christ Consciousness. He holds supreme authority over those who have destroyed the Earth and enslaved humanity. However, the bodies of human beings are their Spirit's vehicles. The Inner Spiritual Light of Love, the Inner Christ, who became flesh within, manifests as the Sacred Secretion, the Liquid Light. This precious Fruit of God's Spirit declares the Message of Divine Love and increases in power. He holds Divine Authority over confusion and over the "wicked hybrid people" who pretend to be His seeds but are the abomination of the Earth, the seeds of the serpent, the destroyer.

The Son of God, manifested as the Rescue Anointed Oil, the Inner Christ, within the spinal cord of man, serves as the Fountain of Life and Light for humanity, restoring the High Consciousness.

He is the Overcomer, anointed by the Creator, dissolving and rooting out the enemy, the serpent seed.

This Flame of Light within is making powerless the harmful bacteria in the cells, mitochondria, the false "power center", and empowering the real power cell centers, the Centrosome, "the small Sun" in the cells, that connected to the Source of Light – the Creator, through the pineal gland. By uniting with God through the Fountain of Light, the Sacred Secretion, every person, as a Light being, can stop to live in fear and become a co-creator with God, facilitating their own life through physical rejuvenation and spiritual evolution from within.

Those who have always harbored and preserved the Divine Seed within can become the authors of their own Salvation. God, embodying Divine Consciousness of Love, does not require bloody human sacrifices. Instead, He transforms the heart and mind of man from within by His Spirit of Love. Through meditation, the True Communion with God, by refocusing attention on the Divine Light within and spending more time in the loving presence of God's Light, people's minds will be transformed into the Divine Mind.

By preserving the Sacred Secretion (which occurs every month, 12 times a year, when the Moon enters your birth month Zodiac sign, symbolized as the 12 types of fruit of the Tree of Life), the Waters of Life within the human body are maintained. The bodies of men consist of the mineral "dust" of the stars plus essential 12 minerals (cell salts), which represent the essence of the 12 Zodiac signs. They are responsible for the process of cleansing, restoring, and rejuvenating of the human bodies.

The Healing Sacred Secretion will be distributed to the 12 cranial nerves (as Christ's disciples) around the Optic Thalamus in the brain and to the heart, which is surrounded by 24 chest ribs (the 24 elders around the Throne of God), facilitating the healing and restoration of the entire body and connecting man to the spiritual realm, the Divine Source.

This spiritual resurrection signifies the awakening of the Multidimensional Christ Consciousness (the New Jerusalem) and the restoration of the 12 strands of Divine DNA within the human being (the 12 precious stones of the foundations of the New Jerusalem). This profound transformation reflects the ultimate unity with the Divine, a journey from physical to spiritual renewal, leading to a deeper connection with God's Light and an enhanced ability to embody and express Divine Love.

THE TITLES OF THE BIBLE'S

BOOKS DECODED

THE OLD TESTAMENT

In the beginning, there were the Names that God has spoken and called out. These are the Words:

"The Creator, who is within, is the Deliverer, the Salvation from within, the Judge. His glorified Name is the King of Profound Mercy and Unparalleled Grace. He is the Author of the records, the Helper, and the Comforter, as He is the Protector unlike any. The Spark of His Divine Light is safely hidden and encapsulated, for a time of great misery and severe squalor, within the body of man, which is morally, ethically, and physically deteriorating with each passing day. It succumbs to the temptations etched into the human genes by the evil invaders. Man is suffering and crying for help in the songs of praise, who wants to live according to God's Laws.

The Preacher of God's Truth, the Inner Spiritual Light of God, is the Beloved of God, who is under the Divine and Blessed Protection. He is God's Essence within men, preserved within the conscience to undo all the corruption that God's people faced. The Liquid Light of God within the men, the Sacred Secretion, the Manifistation of the Holy Spirit, the Elixir of Rectification, is the Salvation of God. It is nurtured within men to cleanse and wash the hearts and minds that have gone astray. The Elixir of Life is the

Sacred Secretion, the Redeeming Holy Oil, through which God will exalt and reveal Himself to the humanity that suffers.

The Inner Light of God, the Christ Consciousness within the faithful believer, is God's Strength and His Judgement, Unbiased but thoroughly Just. The Seed of God's Light will expand into the Holy Flame, the Sacred Christ Oil, the Fuel that will spark the cleansing Fire within men. He is born of God, Pure and Divine Servant who serves God without fail. He is the Peaceful One, with a Heart full of Correction and Mercy for those who repent. He is the Gift of the Prime Creator, the Comforter, who speaks with Divine Inspiration. This Sacred Essence will be hidden and is the Celebration of God, whom He remembers as a Messenger."

THE NEW TESTAMENT

The Gift of God replenishes the soul and the mind, illuminates, and gives Light. It is bestowed from the Gracious Creator to help men steer back to the path of Blessings and Salvation. God acts against the strong, but sinful evil entities who permit, encourage and fuel wars, punishment, and "celebrate" human weakness and misery. They claim to be gods themselves, employing cunning and declaring that they have the power of God by using God's Name and stealing God's titles. They also pretend to be loving, affectionate, and full of adoration, using the traits that God possesses.

The one, who is the supplanter, the mastermind of this evil ploy of leading humans to eternal misery, is the "time traveller" from the dark spaces. He is equipped with tools and advanced technology that outdo what men have. But, in truth, he is the "small stone". The God's Stone of Praise is the Inner Spiritual Light of God, the Inner Christ, who became the Divine Flesh within. He manifested as the Sacred Secretion, the Holy Christ Oil, the evidence of the High Consciousness within, as the Divine Revelation.

The Titles of the first 5 Books of the Old Testament (Genesis, Exodus, Leviticus, Numbers and Deuteronomy) were originally the first verse of each Book. Thus, Genesis was named "In the beginning," Exodus was named "And these are the names," Leviticus was named "And the Lord spoke," Numbers was "In the Wilderness," and Deuteronomy was "These are the words".

ILLUSTRATIONS

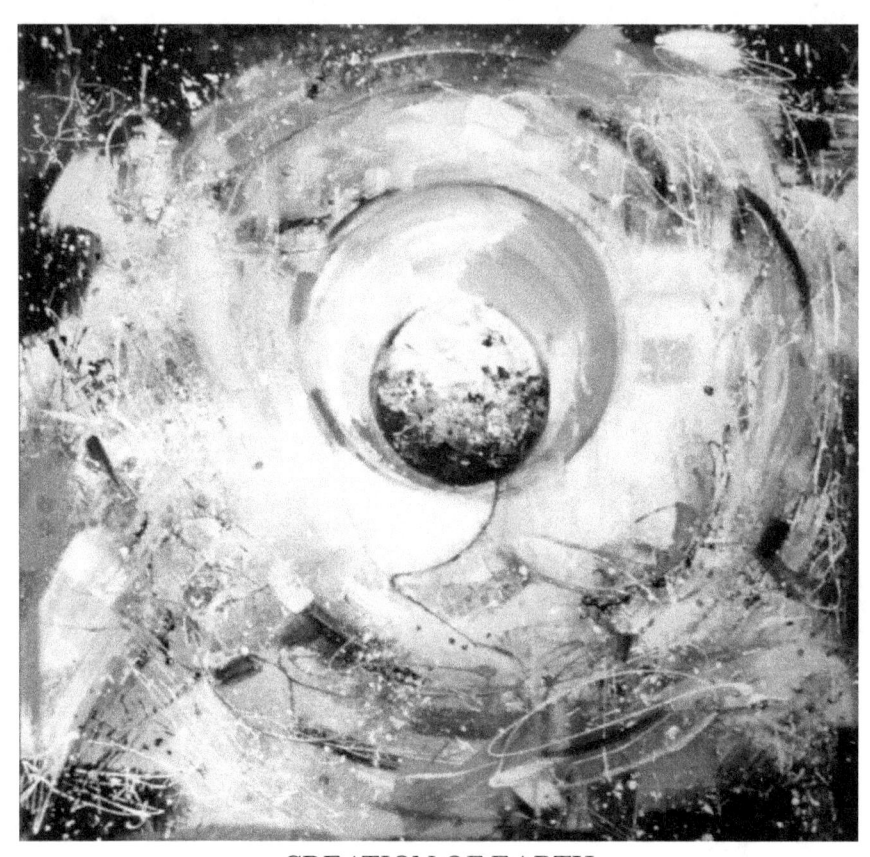

CREATION OF EARTH

– Anna Goloubova

CREATION OF RAINFOREST

– Anna Goloubova

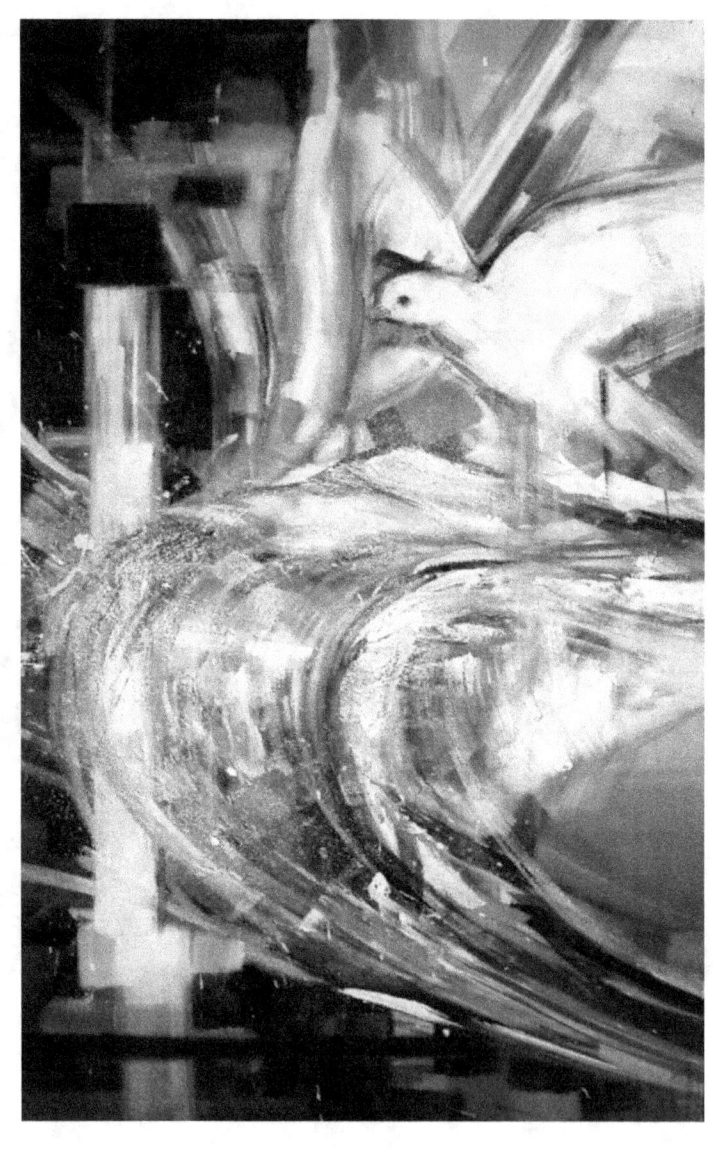

CREATION OF WATER, FIRE, AND LIGHT

– Anna Goloubova

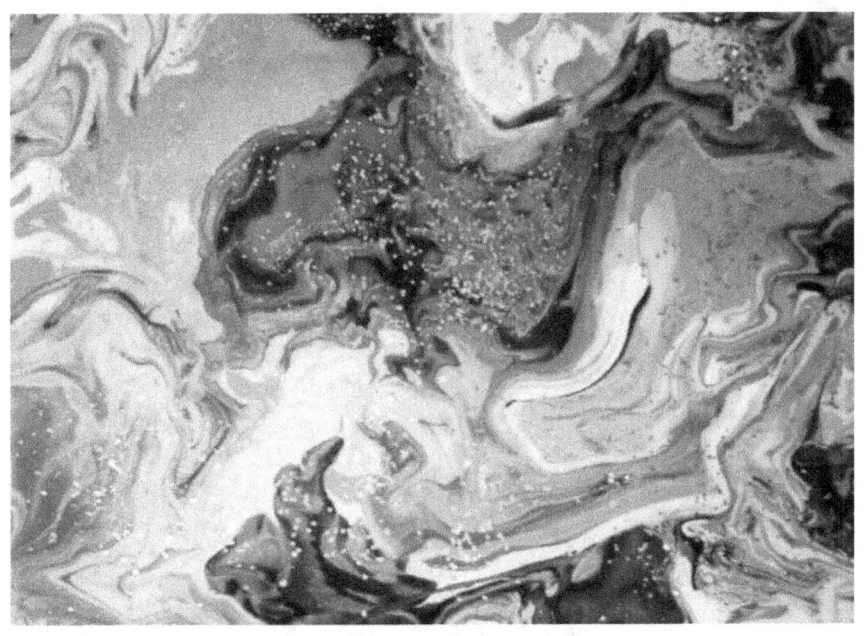

THE TREASURE WITHIN

– Larissa Goloubova

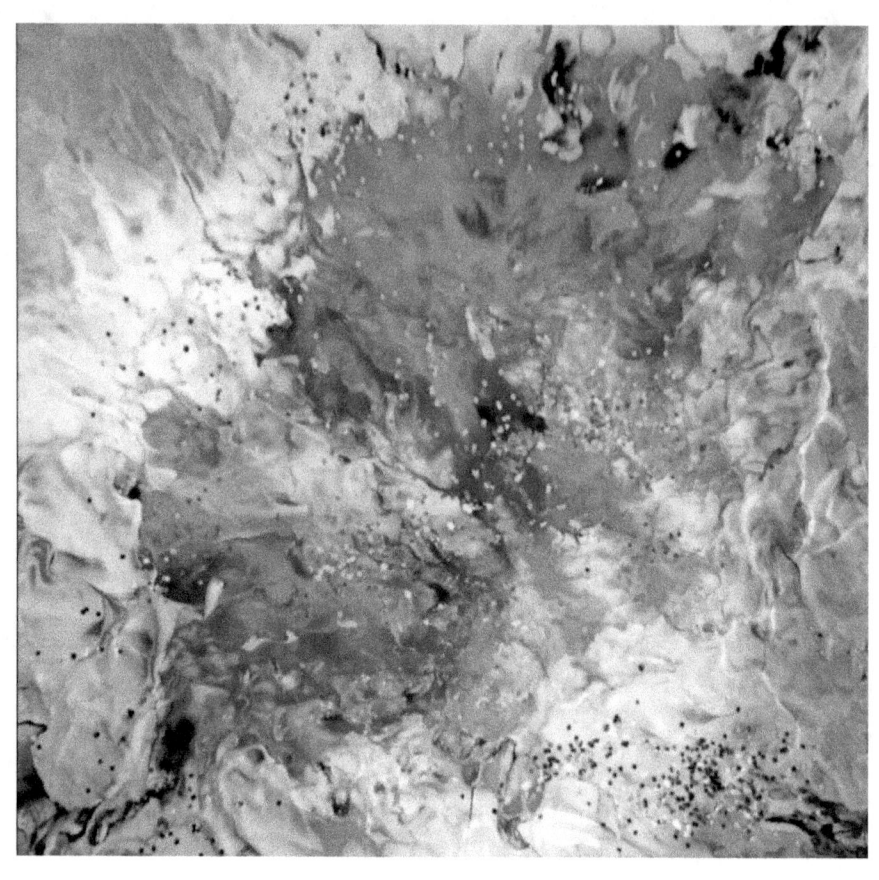

"ETERNAL BLISS"

– Larissa Goloubova

"THE TREE OF JOY"

– Anna Goloubova

"LIGHT OF THE NATION"

– Anna Goloubova

"TRANSFIGURATION"

– Anna Goloubova

REFERENCES

1. James Strong, LL. D, S.T.D., "Strong's Concordance," Editor: Warre Baker, AMG Publisher, 2006.

2. Mounce's Complete Expository, "Dictionary of Old and New Testaments Words," William D. Mounce, General Editor Zondervan, 2006.

3. "Illustrated Manners and Customs of the Bible," J.I.Packer and M.C.Tenney, Editors: Thomas Nelson Publishers, 1980.

4. Robert Young, LL.D. "Analytical Concordance to the Bible" W.M.Eerdman 's Publishing Company, 1975.

5. Michael Tellinger, "Slave Species of the Gods," Versa Press, Inc., 2012.

6. Dr. George W. Carey, Inez Eudora Perry, "God-Man: The Word Made Flesh," The Chemistry of Life, Co., 1920.

7. Dr. George W. Carey, "The Tree of Life," Merchant Books, Published by Dr. George M. Carey, 1917.

8. Kelly-Maria Kerr, "The God Design, Secrets of the Mind, Body and Soul," Seek Vision, 2019.

9. Patrick Weron, "The Nephilim and the Pyramid of the Apocalypse," Kensington Publishing Corporation, 2004.

10. Scott Alan Roberts, "The Secret History of the Reptilians," The Career Press, Inc., 2013.

11. Joseph Chilton Pearce, "The Biology of the Transcendence. A Blueprint of the Human Spirit," Park Street Press, 2002.

12. Len Kasten, "Alian World Order. The Reptilian Plan to Divide and Conquer the Human Race". Beer and Company, 2017.

13. Daniel Jay Bjorndahl, "Paul, the apostle of satan," A Berean Critique of Saul Using the KJV Bible., Amazon.ca

14. Gregory Robbins, "Paul on Trial. Paul vs. Jesus. Was Paul a Liar?" Amazon.ca

15. Barrie Wilson, PH.D., "Paul vs. James. The battle that shaped Christianity and changed the World," An Historical Reconstruction., Amazon.ca

16. Chris H. Hardy PH. D "DNA of the Gods: The Anunnaki Creation of Eve and the Alien Battle for Humanity," Beer and Company, 2014.

17. Ruy Barraco Marmol, "Jesus without Paul of Tarsus. Faithful to Jesus Christianity," Amazon.ca, 2010.

18. David Hatcher Childress, "Technology Sciences of the Ancients," Adventures Unlimited Press Hempton, Illinois.

19. Zecharia Sitchin, "The End of Days. Armageddon and Prophecies of the Return," William Morrow, An Imprint of Harper Collins Publishers, 2007.

20. David Durden, "The Apostle Paul – Saul of Tarsus: The Bitter Root," Amazon.ca

21. Zecharia Sitchin, "The Earth Chronicles Expeditions," Beer and Company, 2007.

22. Victoria Laolon, "The Science of the Sacred Secretion. The Chemical, Physiological and Astronomical Explanation of Internal Alchemy," Amazon.

23. Erich Von Daniken, "In Search of Ancient Gods. My Pictorial Evidence for the Impossible," Souvenir Press.

24. Ivan Rados, "Create Yourself: Secrets of Self Discovery and Healing with Sacred Geometry,"

25. Chuck Missler, "Hidden Treasures in the Biblical Text," Koinonia House

26. Jan Erik Sigdell, "Reign of the Anunnaki. The Alien Manipulation of Our Spiritual Destiny," Bear & Company.

www.ingramcontent.com/pod-product-compliance
Lightning Source LLC
Chambersburg PA
CBHW071706120626
46550CB00001B/121